TAKING CARE OF OUTDOOR GEAR

TAKING CARE
OF
OUTDOOR GEAR

By the Editors of
Stackpole Books

STACKPOLE BOOKS

Printed in the U.S.A.

Library of Congress Cataloging in Publication Data
Main entry under title:

Taking care of outdoor gear.

1. Outdoor recreation—Equipment and supplies—
Maintenance and repair. I. Stackpole Books (Firm)
GV191.76.T34   1983   688.7'6028'8   83–533
ISBN 0–8117–0841–1
ISBN 0–8117–2148–5 (pbk.)

Contents

Preface

THE PAST DECADE has seen a tremendous explosion of interest in outdoor activities, sparked by the development of new fabrics, metals, adhesives, and coatings which have made outdoor equipment lighter, cheaper, and more comfortable. Space-age backwoods trekkers need no longer lug 50-pound packs; canoeists needn't fear rapids and rocks. Everybody's drier, warmer, and able to go farther faster with fewer hassles.

Of course, there's a price to pay: you can't afford not to know how to take care of your outdoor gear. It's almost universally true that lighter means less strong, and that more sophisticated means harder to clean, maintain, and repair. That's one reason for this book: We hope to keep you ahead of the wear and tear that will turn your high-tech gear into low-tech junk.

There's an information transfer process at work here. Manufacturers, dealers, outfitters, and repairpersons constantly find new ways to improve outdoor gear. Sometimes they pass their findings along by word of mouth. Sometimes they write it down in articles, pamphlets, or books. Sometimes the information stays underground for years. In this book, we've tried to dig it out and present it in a logical, comprehensive package with something for everyone, whatever their interests, skill, and experience. You may find some of the information familiar; you may disagree with some, based on personal experience. Some of it is "common sense"—that most uncommon wisdom. We hope it will prove useful and valuable.

The manufacturers' associations, outfitters, and repairpersons who provided help and information are listed in the Appendix. In addition, we'd like to thank the following for significant contributions of time, energy, and material:

Dennis Watts, Wildware Limited, Harrisburg, Pennsylvania
David Brown, Great Falls Canoe and Repair, Vienna, Virginia
John Rutkowski, Mountain Mend, Boulder, Colorado
Charles Kroll, Bear Archery, Gainesville, Florida
Robert Anderson, Forrest Mountaineering Ltd., Denver, Colorado

Finally, the editors would like to thank Ken Books and Ann Markowicz.

Air Mattresses

AIR MATTRESSES AND sleeping pads make rough camping smooth. In choosing an air mattress, look at the thickness of the plastic or rubber covering and the construction. Usually, mattresses with internal baffles are sturdier and will stand up to abuse better than those without baffles because they will still support weight if one or more tubes is punctured. Rubberized canvas or canvas-over-rubber outer covers are the most sturdy, although their weight may make them prohibitive for backpacking.

Sleeping pads of closed-cell material (such as Ensolite) and open-cell material (spongy "foam rubber") are rugged and suitable for backpacking because of their low weight. They cannot be punctured, and, though they are usually not as comfortable as inflatable mattresses, they are much warmer.

USE AND CARE

Air mattresses should never be spread where there is danger of something sharp puncturing their skin. All stones, roots, pine cones, etc., should be removed before spreading an air mattress, and most experienced campers spread a plastic ground cloth on the ground before laying down the mattress. This not only protects the mattress but helps keep dampness from siphoning off body warmth, one of the biggest complaints about inflatable mattresses.

In cold weather, inflating an air mattress by breathing into it can cause condensation and the formation of ice crystals inside the mattress. This will not necessarily harm the mattress, but when the water vapor or crystals

1

liquify, the water can pool around a valve and refreeze. Too, moisture inside can contribute to the growth of mildew, which will weaken and eventually destroy some plastics. If you're auto- or boat-camping, a treadle or hand pump is thus a better way to inflate a mattress.

Air mattresses should never be inflated to rock-hardness. Not only will the mattress be uncomfortable, it will be extremely vulnerable to damage from lumps, belt buckles, zippers, etc. If your mattress has a tube-type or push-pull valve, or a valve stem like a bicycle tube, inflate it fully, then slowly deflate the mattress while you're lying on it until you're comfortable. Otherwise, trial and error will teach you the proper inflation.

Air mattresses should never be deflated and packed while wet because mildew may grow in moist areas. If possible, stand the mattress against a tree or other support until it air-dries. If this isn't possible, wipe it off as best you can and pack it loosely until it can be reinflated and stood up or hung up to dry. To deflate an air mattress, open the valve and roll the mattress from the other end, taking care not to pinch or crease the fabric.

Do not fold an air mattress, as the creases will weaken and eventually spring leaks. Store an air mattress either lying flat or hanging, half-inflated. If this isn't possible, roll up the mattress loosely from the bottom and store it in a dry place, away from direct sunlight, which is particularly hard on plastic. Place a drip of oil on brass valves.

Inflatable mattresses should never be cleaned with harsh solvents, bleaches, or abrasives. Regular washing with bland soap and warm water will keep them clean. If you notice tell-tale dark spots of mildew forming, a mild vinegar-and-water solution will remove the spores. Never try to scrape off pine pitch or road tar with a sharp knife. Gentle rubbing with a cloth will often heat the tar or pitch enough to make it easy to pick off with a fingernail. Rubbing baking soda over tar or pitch spots will help remove them.

REPAIR

Repair kits for plastic air mattresses are inexpensive and should be carried whenever you pack a plastic mattress. Be sure to cut the patch large enough to cover the damage adequately and coat the entire area under the patch with cement. (If you have trouble pinpointing a leak, try washing the mattress with soapy water—the bubbles will show you where it is.)

Rubberized canvas air mattresses can be patched with a canvas patch and cement. The patch should be cut at least one inch larger than the tear or hole and should be coated with cement on both sides and allowed to dry, then cemented over the damaged area. Rubber mattresses can be patched with a regular automobile tire patch kit.

Splits or cracks at seams or between tubes are probably fatal wounds, but before you toss the mattress, try building up several layers of cement, then patching, then coating with several more layers of cement. This just might work. In a backwoods emergency, try gumming up pinhole leaks with pine pitch, then cover them with a piece of adhesive from a bandage.

Sleeping pads are nearly indestructible unless you spill stove fuel, kerosene, or gasoline on them, or leave them sitting in the sun. Both will cause deterioration, the first quickly, the latter over a period of time. Covering foam pads with colorful material will keep them clean and protect them from snags. Taping with wide cloth or plastic tape will keep the edges from splitting or crumbling from being rolled up and tied. (If you use flat nylon web straps to tie your pad, the edges will last much longer.)

Both closed-cell and open-cell pads can be washed with soap and water —no powerful detergents, bleaches, or fluids.

DOWN-FILLED MATTRESSES

A nice variation of the common air mattress is a down-filled air mattress made by Jack Stephenson, maker of Warmlite sleeping bag systems. This pad is made to fit into a compartment in Warmlite bags, but there's no reason you can't use one by itself or with another bag to get the comfort of air support with the warmth of down.

The Stephenson DAM (Down Air Mat) uses a baffle system to keep the down from escaping through the air valve. An ingenious pump system using the sleeping bag stuff sack with a nozzle attached as a pump eliminates the problem of blowing moisture into the mat with your breath. Blowing one of these mats up by mouth will rapidly saturate the down, making it useless as an insulator.

Stephenson offers several care tips for his DAMs, some of which also apply to standard air mattresses. Don't over inflate. About two-thirds to three-fourths full is all it takes for comfort and warmth. If the mattress supports you off the ground when sitting on it, it is too hard. Avoid the temptation to sit several people on it. And don't bounce on the mattress: one extra bounce and you may tear out a baffle, or start a tear that'll let go the rest of the way in the middle of the night!

When it is very cold, warm the valve under your jacket before attempting to inflate or deflate a mattress. Vinyl is tough and durable but gets too stiff to flex right when very cold. In severe arctic conditions, use a foam pad, or at least a backup pad of closed-cell polyethylene. Don't use Ensolite, which is vinyl and gets stiff and cracks.

The down will shift eventually, especially if you deflate it rapidly. You can minimize, or almost totally avoid, shifting between tubes with slow deflation. Shifting of down within a tube can be corrected by shaking and patting as required. Shift between tubes (generally from outside tubes toward middle ones) can be corrected by inflating about two-thirds, then shaking down toward the foot end. Stand on the head ends of tubes with excess down, hold the flapper valve open with a pen and rapidly push air out of over-filled tubes towards foot, thus blowing some down into adjacent tubes. Repeat as needed until down is evenly distributed. There should be no dark areas; the right amount of fill is very translucent.

You can protect mattresses somewhat from mildew damage by waxing them occasionally. Common floor wax is easiest to use, and is okay if it has vinyl or acrylics in it. Don't use any kind of wax with silicones in it: if you do and later damage it, it can't be repaired because nothing will stick to it. Wax can be removed by washing in hot water and detergent.

The pump sacks can be damaged by trying to yank the plug out of the valve without pulling on the plug itself, or by not warming it in cold water. Such damage can be fixed by hand-sewing the rim of the plug back to the sack with long radial stitches, then sealing it. A little silicone lube or water repellent on the nozzle part will make it easier to use.

Aluminum Canoes

ALUMINUM CANOES ARE easy to repair, durable, light, and fast. Their big drawbacks are their noisiness and vulnerability to serious damage from "pinning" against rocks in moving water. Aluminum gunwales and thwarts will kink, and hulls dent severely and not pop back as ABS hulls will.

The best aluminum canoes—often described as "whitewater models"—are tempered. This tempering adds a great deal of strength and rigidity to the hull, thwarts, and gunwales. You should never take an untempered "still water" aluminum canoe into serious rapids. Aluminum canoes get hot and cold, making them uncomfortable in extreme weather.

WAXING AND CLEANING

Maintenance requirements for aluminum canoes are minimal. The finish will oxidize and become dull, but unless you're a compulsive polisher you needn't be concerned with that. In fact, the aluminum is building a protective layer of oxidized metal, so it probably shouldn't be removed. You can slow the oxidizing process on a new aluminum canoe by washing and waxing it with automobile paste wax, if you desire, and can remove the oxidized layer by washing with soapy water to which trisodium phosphate (TSP) has been added. This chemical is available from industrial cleaning supply companies, and should be mixed and used according to the manufacturer's instructions. Rinse it off thoroughly. Wear gloves.

Abrasive cleaning compounds and steel wool soap pads will also remove oxidation and surface dirt, though they will mar the surface somewhat. If you use your aluminum canoe in salt water, rinse it thoroughly with fresh water after use.

Anglers sometimes lament the "shine" of an aluminum canoe, and often paint the bottom—or try to. Painting is not recommended for aluminum canoes, as it is time-consuming and requires special paint. Also, once scratched, painted aluminum requires extensive work to touch up. You have to remove as many layers as you've put on. That goes double for repairs; in order to make a strong, watertight patch, it's best to remove all the paint, and that can prove difficult.

Nevertheless, if you must paint, do it right. Check with the manufacturer or dealer first. Most will recommend a thorough cleaning and scrubbing with TSP or a product containing it, followed by several primer coats and the finish coat. Special anti-fouling marine paints require special primers, too, which can drive the cost of your camouflage job through the ceiling.

FIELD REPAIRS

One of the big advantages of aluminum canoes is ease of field repair. Repairable damage ranges from small dents and creases, to bent or broken gunwales, to leaky rivets. The temporary repairs described here will last long enough to get you home where more permanent repair can be done.

Small Dents, Creases, and Punctures. Small dents, where the metal hasn't creased, can be pounded out with your hand or the heel of a boot; if they're very small or above the waterline, there's no particular disadvantage in leaving them. Dents with creased edges or dimples should be pounded out with a rubber mallet. Hold a block of wood against the other side and work from the edges in, striking softly. Creases are potential weak spots, so if the dent is deep or below the waterline, plan on patching it for a permanent repair.

If the crease is sharp enough, call it a tear. Again, field repairs aren't very difficult, and the advantage is that anything you do in the field won't hinder a more permanent repair later. Carry a tube of epoxy putty and a roll of duct tape and you'll be ready. Make sure the epoxy putty is "aluminum proved"; it should state on the label that it is designed for use on metal. Clean the area as best you can, rough it up a bit with emery cloth (another toolbox item), let it set up per instructions, and slap a couple of pieces of duct tape over the area.

In a pinch, chewing gum can plug a small break. Chew it until soft, lay it on the break, and melt it into the crease with a match, lighter, or candle held on the opposite side of the metal. (If this is awkward, you can apply heat directly to the gum, but that can be messy.) Work the melted gum into the crack, let it cool, and finish it off with duct tape.

Pitch from pine cones also will do a good job of patching small breaks. Work it in with a knife blade or other metal tool.

Keep in mind when using epoxy that you're probably going to make a permanent repair later, and that means a patch. If you smear epoxy all over the place, you'll have a hard time getting a more permanent sealant to stick. You'll probably cut out a section of the hull to patch it, so limit the epoxy to the most severely damaged area, which you plan to remove later.

A better material for repairing cracks and small punctures is silicone rubber caulk sold in building supply stores for caulking around metal chimneys and similar places. It's ideal for aluminum canoes because it flexes and dries semi-hard and waterproof. For field repairs, it has two disadvantages: it takes a long time to set up, and it comes in large, somewhat unwieldy containers designed for caulking guns. If you're going to be on the move, then, epoxy is the material for temporary patching. As we'll discuss later, more permanent work is best accomplished with silicone rubber sealant.

For larger holes, you can make a "permanent-temporary" patch out of fiberglass cloth and resin. Although this kind of patch can be done in the field without a lot of equipment, it covers large holes well enough to stand up to rough treatment and will last for a summer. Fiberglass patches on canoes are rather unsightly, however, and may in time work loose around the edges, particularly if they're large, due to the craft's flexing. A fiberglass patch will also stop a tear from expanding or lengthening, something an aluminum patch won't do unless you are able to drill holes at the end of the tear.

Since this is a "field" patch, we'll assume you don't have power tools or heavy cutting tools available. Remove as much burred and damaged metal as you can with what you've got, and pound out dented areas to a rough approximation of the hull's contour. Take sandpaper, steel wool, emery cloth, or, for want of anything better, a piece of stone, and thoroughly rough up the entire area of the damage, extending out to one inch beyond the stressed area.

You'll have a rough, messy-looking area to work with, to be sure, but remember that you'll probably be cutting it away anyway to put on an aluminum patch. With that in mind, leave at least one inch between the area you're patching with fiberglass and any obstruction such as the keel or gunwale. That one inch is important because you'll be cutting away all of the fiberglass patch and must have firm metal to fasten the permanent aluminum patch to.

With the area roughed up and cleaned as thoroughly as possible, cut a fiberglass patch to fit—rounded corners are best. If you're fixing a big area, cut several patches.

If you're covering a large hole, you'll need something on the inside of the hull to help support the resin-soaked cloth patches while they set; cellophane is a good choice, as epoxy resin won't stick to it. Experiment with other kinds of plastics you have available by testing small pieces with the resin. You don't want the resin to bond to them. Cellophane tape will do in a pinch. Tape a piece of cellophane firmly to the hull, making it as stiff as possible.

Saturate the first cloth patch with epoxy resin, not polyester resin, which will not stick to aluminum. Position it over the area to be patched and smooth it out with a piece of wood, taking care not to push the cloth into the hole or against the cellophane backing. The epoxy will begin to set up fairly rapidly, so if you're going to layer several patches, put the second and third—well saturated with epoxy resin—on while the first is still tacky. Let the entire patch dry thoroughly—overnight is best, or at least several hours—in a warm, dry environment before removing the backing.

This quick patch will last until you care to replace it, and it should be watertight and flexible, at least at moderate temperatures. It will take a fairly stiff blow without puncturing but is vulnerable to abrasion damage. In time, the flexing of the hull and the different expansion and contraction rates of the two materials due to temperature changes will loosen the patch. As a one-season patch, however, it will suffice.

Dented Bottom. Large dents in the keel area often follow a whitewater mishap. Although they look awful, they can be field-repaired without great effort, provided the keel isn't kinked to the breaking point and no rivets have popped.

Beach the canoe and place two 4-inch diameter logs on level ground, parallel to the keel, about one foot apart. These logs should be free of branch stubs (trim them well with an ax), and should be at least three-fourths as long as the canoe. Position them so that the center of the dent is at their center, and make sure they won't roll out from under the canoe. (You may have to flatten one side to keep them from rolling.)

With the logs in position, and a helper available to steady the canoe, jump on the center of the dent with your feet together. The dent should pop out. Inspect the area carefully for popped rivets, cracked creases, etc., and patch as described above if necessary.

A tempered aluminum canoe will take this treatment in stride. A cheap aluminum canoe may not. If in doubt, you can soften the blow somewhat by placing the canoe on sand or dirt instead of the logs before jumping on the center of the dent.

Damaged Gunwales and Thwarts. Bent or kinked gunwales and thwarts are another matter. If the bend is not too severe, you can try to pound it out using two hatchets, one on either side. If the metal has kinked, however, your best bet is to splint the area with a paddle or piece of wood until you can make permanent repairs at home.

A broken thwart is a serious problem that should be fixed before

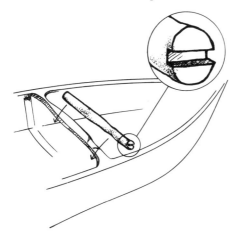

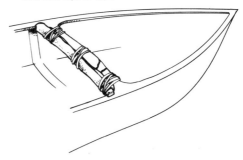

lash with rope or tape

Fixing a broken thwart. Notch both ends of a green sapling to the gunwales and lash it to the thwart with rope or duct tape.

subjecting the canoe to rough water; otherwise, the missing support will lead to popped rivets or overstrained gunwales, both potentially dangerous.

Cut a springy green sapling to fit beside the broken thwart. Notch both ends to fit the gunwales, and lash it to the thwart with rope or duct tape. You can sometimes push out a dented gunwale by cutting the sapling a little long and applying pressure downward to make it fit.

A broken gunwale is trickier, since you won't be able to lash around it. Also, the hull may be severely dented or even torn at the impact point, so you'll have to think about patching as well as reinforcing the area.

One way to splint a broken gunwale is to cut a green sapling and notch it to fit the thwarts (or seats) fore and aft of the damaged area. Lash it to each thwart to provide support and prevent further bending of the hull.

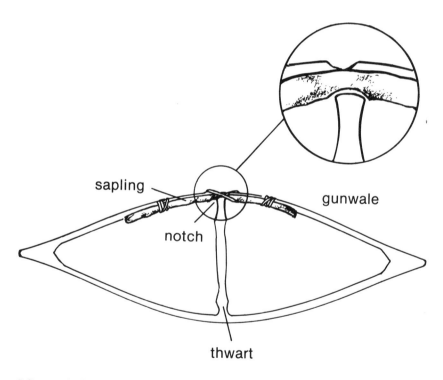

sapling

gunwale

notch

thwart

Splinting a broken gunwale. Cut a green sapling and notch it to fit the thwarts fore and aft of the damaged area.

Look for loosened rivets on the gunwale and remove them if possible to allow a nylon line to pass through. Lash the splint to the side of the canoe and patch the hull if necessary. A second gunwale splint on the side opposite the damage can help prevent further bending and provide structural stiffness.

Loose Rivets. You can recognize loosened, leaking rivets by the tell-tale ring of oxidized aluminum around the rivet head, caused by slight movement of the rivet. You can tighten a loose rivet in the field by holding the butt end of an axe against the head and striking the tail with another axe, hatchet, hammer, or heavy pliers. A dab of epoxy and a strip of duct tape will seal the rivet until it can be replaced.

PERMANENT REPAIRS

Aluminum replacement parts—thwarts, keels, gunwales, seats, deck plates, etc.—are available from most manufacturers, although you may have to order through a dealer (and pay his markup) to get the right part. It's worth it, though: you can make professional-quality repairs on aluminum canoes and boats easily, and with a minimum of practice. Also, original equipment replacements are shaped correctly, so if you've really bent your canoe out of shape, you have at least one piece shaped correctly to start with. (Reshaping a gunwale made of tempered aluminum is not an easy task.)

If you just want to get by at minimal cost, you can do a reasonable job of straightening keels, reshaping gunwales, and removing large dents with little more than an hydraulic jack, some sledge hammers, a few lengths of chain, and a solid wall to brace against. In fact, you'll be ahead of the game by trying to repair major damage before ordering replacement parts, since you can always replace the parts if you aren't satisfied.

If your canoe is badly damaged—keel and gunwales kinked, thwarts bent—a trip to an automobile or truck frame straightening shop can save you a lot of needless and frustrating pounding, jacking, prying, etc. You may have to talk the guy into taking on the task, but his equipment is designed for straightening stiff frame members, and it can do a great job on aluminum.

The second professional you want to visit is an aircraft mechanic. Most small airports, where the weekend fliers congregate, have at least one guy who can straighten, weld, and patch tempered aluminum. Haul your canoe to him, buy him a cup of coffee, and pick his brain. He has seen most kinds of damage and can offer valuable tips on how to make a truly strong patch or repair.

While we're talking about pros, locate a canoe repairman who specializes in aluminum work. (Local canoe clubs are a good place to find such resource people.) Besides lending moral support and offering good advice, he can supply rivets, tools, and, most important, aluminum stock of the right thickness and temper. This is important because you don't want to patch with metal weaker, softer, or more flexible than the rest of the canoe, for obvious reasons. If he has a scrapyard, you're in business and can scavenge the needed parts. For low-cost repairs, you can't beat used material.

Aluminum can be welded, as you probably know, but it isn't advisable to weld patches on the hull or, for that matter, to weld structural members. The reason is simple: the heat necessary to bond two pieces of aluminum is sufficient to remove the temper. That makes a weak spot just where you don't want it, around a previously damaged area. An aircraft mechanic can weld aluminum pieces (if there is no other alternative) without taking any more of the temper out than necessary, but don't trust the job to anyone other than a full-time professional who's used to working on planes or boats.

Flexibility is important in whitewater craft, and welding a patch of metal onto a hull can destroy the smooth flexing action necessary for proper performance in the water. Even worse, the weld itself can crack from the stress of flexing, leaving you in worse shape than you were before. Spot welded stembands (the protective strips at the bow and stern), cleats, eyes, tie-down rings, etc., should never be trusted to withstand hard use. You'll find them only on the cheapest canoes or those that have been "improved" by the owner.

With these preliminaries in mind, you're ready to tackle serious repairs. For the sake of this discussion, let's assume you've pinned your aluminum canoe against a rock while negotiating Class 4 or better rapids —it's pretty beat up, in other words. You've bent the boat into a banana shape. The keel is kinked in two places; the gunwale on the downstream side is, too. The other gunwale is bent the other way: convexly. The center thwart is bent downward. There are more rivets loose than you care to count, and the downstream side is torn open. (The question comes to mind: can this canoe be saved? Yes, it can. It's going to take a lot of work, though.)

Straightening Bent Gunwales and Thwarts. Step one in repairing a badly damaged aluminum canoe is getting it approximately straight. This, as noted above, can be accomplished fairly well by a cooperative frame straightening shop. Or, you can jury-rig a straightening system from a three-to-five-ton hydraulic jack, several two-by-fours, ten feet or more of tow chain, and a handy cinder block wall. You'll need a friend, too.

Rig the jack nearly horizontally in the center of the damaged area. For the concave gunwale, for instance, center the jack on the damaged area and brace it against a length of two-by-four held against the other gunwale. Put the other two-by-four on the damaged side and slowly turn the jack until it is wedged securely enough to stay there by itself. This will take four hands to accomplish: you need to hold two boards and the jack at the same time.

Once the jack is tightly in place, move the canoe against the wall, centered. Standing inside the canoe, slowly apply pressure by turning the jack handle. You'll feel the strain throughout the canoe and probably be tempted to try to jump on the dented bottom to remove that big dent. Don't do it—you'll pop the jack loose if you do.

If you have a second jack-and-block available, however, you can work both ways at one time. Rig the second jack beneath the bent thwart, with blocks to spread the force on the hull and on the thwart. (If the bottom dent isn't centered beneath a thwart—either an intact one or a bent one—leave it for later and concentrate on the gunwales first.) Work both jacks slowly. If you still have help, work them both at once; otherwise turn one a few turns, then the other. The bent thwart will "fight" against your gunwale-straightening efforts, so your upward pressure will make the outward force more effective.

If you don't have two jacks, or if the bottom is so torn up that you don't feel confident in jacking against the thwart, or if the thwart itself is badly kinked, you should consider removing the thwart entirely and replacing it with a new one. If so, saw it off at each end, close to the gunwales, with a hacksaw, and cut a piece of two-by-four the exact length of a new thwart. (You're going to replace the thwart, but not until you've done the heavy work on the gunwales, so don't try to use a new thwart for bracing purposes.)

Continue jacking until the hull is approximately back to normal shape. If you visit a canoe repair shop before beginning, as we suggest, be sure to take along a large piece of cardboard and scissors to cut a template. Getting the hull and gunwale back to the original curve is tough without one. If you've bought a new gunwale, use that. If the "upstream" gunwale isn't too badly out of shape, use it. But use something.

When the hull is back to near normal, insert the board cut to replace the thwart. Even if you've left the thwart in, brace the canoe with a board.

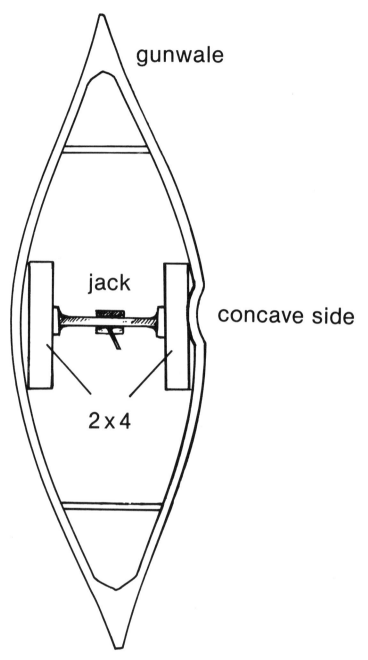

Straightening a concave gunwale with a hydraulic jack and 2 × 4s.

Remove the jack-and-board rig. At this point, you'll still have a kinked gunwale. Use two sledge hammers to unkink the gunwale. Hold one on the outside and strike the inside smartly, moving the backing hammer as needed.

If you're going to replace the gunwale completely, you'll have to drill and punch out a lot of rivets at this point. Note that you should straighten the gunwale and side of the hull before removing the damaged gunwale. The reason for this is that you need the strength of the gunwales to straighten the hull—otherwise you'll just push a new dent into the hull.

If you're just interested in patching the gunwale, however, all you need to do now is remove those rivets that are sprung. Use a power chisel to knock the heads off. Or drill through the head and work out the rivet with a punch. The best patching material for gunwales is ¾-inch aluminum channel stock, available at most hardware stores. It should be nontempered so you can drill it and punch it easily. Cut a piece long enough to extend four to five inches past the damaged area. Since our "sample" canoe has two kinks in the gunwale, you'll need quite a long piece of stock.

Wedge the stock against the inside of the hull, beneath the gunwale, with the "open" side toward the inside of the boat. Use several vise grips or large C-clamps to hold it in place, and mark the rivet holes from the outside. Remove the stock and drill holes for the rivets, then replace it and rivet it into place with a pop rivet tool.

You can also use stainless steel bolts here, but don't use brass, zinc-coated, or uncoated bolts, as they will rust or corrode the aluminum and loosen.

Before setting the rivets, coat them with silicone rubber sealant. If you use bolts, use large flat washers on each side, and coat them liberally with silicone before tightening them down.

Straightening the convex side is a little more difficult. You need to place a two-by-four against the side of the gunwale and rig a jack horizontally between the canoe and the wall, and to accomplish this you must have a way to counter the force of the jack. That's where the tow chain comes in.

Take a two-by-four block about a foot long and gouge out a channel deep enough to hold the tow chain on one side. Place that side, with the center of the chain in the channel, against the wall, and place the jack on the other side. Hook the ends of the chain to the canoe in whatever way you can—best is to hook the ends at a point where a thwart or seat frame meets the inside of the gunwale. You can also attach the chain to cleats, eye bolts, etc., at the bow and stern. If your chain is long, you'll need a piece

wall

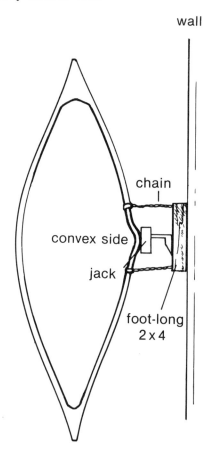

chain

convex side

jack

foot-long
2 x 4

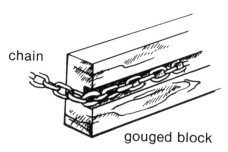

chain

gouged block

To straighten a convex gunwale, you need to place a 2 × 4 against the side of the gunwale and rig a jack horizontally between the canoe and the cinder block wall.

of two-by-four to fit between the jack and the two-by-four you'll hold against the side of the canoe.

The procedure should now be clear: you're going to jack against the side of the canoe while the chain holds the ends against the jack's force. Work slowly and carefully, use your template to get as near true as possible. If the gunwale is kinked, replace or splint it as described earlier.

Repairing Damaged Bottoms and Keels. Use your hydraulic jack to push a large dent out of the keel area by rigging it vertically with a two-by-four against the metal and another to brace against a solid overhead structure such as a rafter. If this is impractical, turn the canoe on its side and rig a chain-and-jack setup similar to the gunwale-straightening apparatus described above.

A better way to push out a dented bottom is to rig a steel bar underneath the gunwales and use that to jack against. This can only be accomplished if the gunwales are intact (or after they've been repaired). Place a two-by-four beneath the jack to spread the force.

A kinked or cracked keel piece can be replaced with a section of keel cut from a scrapped canoe, or with a keel repair kit supplied by the manufacturer. Grumman, the leading aluminum canoe maker, has keel stock available with detailed instructions. You'd be wise to check into its cost and availability; the keel section is so critical that you don't want to take a chance on messing up a homemade repair.

When you rivet any part of a canoe that will be below water, use the new "waterproof", or holeless, pop rivets. They're just like regular pop rivets except they have no hole through the center, so they're a little tougher to set. You need a heavy-duty rivet gun.

Patching. Small tears, hairline cracks, gouges, and punctures can be patched adequately with silicone rubber sealant. It comes in several colors including metallic silver, and makes an entirely waterproof, flexible repair. Rough up the area around the damage with a coarse grinder to help it hold.

Larger damaged areas call for a permanent patch. There are two ways to patch aluminum hulls: with fiberglass and with riveted aluminum. Neither is very pretty, but either can do an adequate job of keeping your feet dry. An aluminum patch is preferred because, if properly done, it will preserve the strength and flexibility of the hull. (The procedure for making a patch from fiberglass cloth and resin is described in the section on field repairs.)

Before making any attempt at patching, inspect the damaged area carefully. You want to remove all the metal that's been bent, buckled, or gouged. Pound out any dents with a rubber mallet, and draw a line around the area you want to cut out with a marking or grease pencil. Don't be stingy. There's no economy in making a patch too small, and if you try to secure a patch to weakened metal, you'll have a weak patch, period.

If the damage is a crack or tear, drill a ⅛-inch hole at each end of the tear to stop further tearing. If the hull is not dented in, merely punctured or torn, you don't need to remove much metal. If, however, it has been pushed and stretched, cut it out.

Drill a ⅜-inch hole through the metal inside the line you marked, insert tin snips and cut away the damaged area. You can also use a power chisel, which does a good job on tempered aluminum. Remove the metal and push out any bend you put in the edge of the cut by holding a wood block against the inside and striking the outside with a rubber mallet.

Cut a piece of tempered aluminum stock one inch larger in all directions than the hole and, using the mallet, form it to fit the hull's curve. (Here, the advantage of cutting a patch out of a scrapped canoe is obvious: it's already curved to fit.) Round the corners of the patch and file the edges to remove any burrs. Position it over the hole and trace around the edges with your marker.

If the hole is larger than three or four inches in diameter, you'll need to double patch.* Use your first patch as a template to cut a second. Round and deburr it, then mark the hull on the inside.

Using a center punch, make starter holes at the four corners of the outside patch. Leave a ½-inch margin.

Next, cut two pieces of neoprene rubber about ¼-inch larger than the patch. Neoprene rubber, the kind used in scuba divers' wetsuits, will "give" and push back under pressure to make a tight seal to a flexing hull. Smear silicone sealant on one side of the rubber and press it onto the inside of the outside patch. Spread a thin layer of silicone sealant on the hull, using the mark you made on the hull as a guide. Carefully place the patch (with the rubber attached) onto the hull. When the silicone has set up enough to keep the patch in place, drill through the patch and hull in each corner, using the punched marks as guides. Use the right size for the rivets you've bought —³⁄₁₆- or ⁵⁄₃₂-inch rivets are adequate.

---

*If the hole is smaller than three or four inches in diameter, or in a spot not subject to much stress (just under the gunwale, for instance), a single patch on the outside of the hull is sufficient. Follow the directions given for making the outside patch and inserting rivets.

When drilling through the hull, place a wood block on the inside and push against the drill's pressure to avoid denting the area, which will cause a gap between the patch and the hull. This will also prevent burring of the hole.

Using the holes through the hull as a guide, repeat the neoprene-and-silicone procedure with the inside patch, taking care to align the patch as closely as possible with the outside patch.

Holding your wood block firmly against the inside patch, drill through the inside patch from the outside, inserting the drill bit through the hole you previously drilled. Using stainless steel bolts, nuts, and flat washers, bolt through the two patches and the hull, drawing down the nuts firmly on the inside. These are temporary fasteners which will be replaced with rivets.

Your patches are now held firmly in place, so you can mark and drill holes at one-inch intervals around the edges. Always use the center punch to keep the drill bit from walking around on the patch surface, and always use a wood block inside the hull to back up the patch. Maintain the ½-inch margin between the edge of the patch and the center of the holes.

Coat the rivets with silicone sealant before inserting them, then set with the rivet tool. You can also set rivets with a ballpeen hammer and backing block of steel, or with an air hammer and backing block. Practice on scrap if you're inexperienced. After the final rivet has been set, trim the excess neoprene around the edges of the patches with a razorblade knife. Smear a little silicone sealant around the edge. Your canoe is permanently patched.

Replacing Rivets. Replacing a rivet is considered a "permanent repair" because it requires drilling. The discussion about leaking rivets under field repairs assumes that the rivet is merely loose, not broken, and that the hole hasn't been damaged. If the rivet or hole is badly damaged, the temporary repair will be very temporary, and you should plan on replacing the rivet at the earliest opportunity.

To minimize damage to rivet holes, remove rivets by drilling through the head. First, center punch the rivet head lightly; you can use a nail or ice pick, the important thing is to give the drill bit a bite so it doesn't wander off center. Using a bit slightly smaller than the diameter of the rivet shaft, drill through the head, stopping when you judge that the bit has entered the shaft. Then, with a punch, dull chisel, or screwdriver blade, knock the rivet head off by holding the punch parallel to the hull (at a right angle to the shaft of the rivet) against the head and striking it smartly with a hammer. The head should pop off with one moderate blow. If not, don't hammer on it. Take the next size larger drill bit and repeat the drilling procedure, taking care not to go too deeply into the rivet shaft, and knock off the head. You want to be careful not to bend the hole out of shape by hitting too hard.

With the head off, drive the shaft and tail of the rivet out of the hole with a punch and hammer. Hold a hammer head, the butt of an axe, or another substantial piece of steel against the other side as a bucking board to prevent the hull from denting from the force of your blow. Hold the bucking board *beside* the rivet tail, not on it.

Select the correct replacement rivet. (Manufacturers and dealers/-repairmen can tell you what size is right.) Coat the rivet shaft with silicone sealant if you have it, and insert the rivet into the hole. With a bucking bar held firmly against the head of the rivet, hammer the tail with a ballpeen hammer until it seats tightly. You can also use a hammer attachment for a power chisel, common in automobile body shops. A power hammer makes setting a lot of rivets at one time quite easy and quick.

If you have a pop rivet tool, hold the bucking board against the tail side of the rivet but take care not to push hard enough on it to push the rivet back through the hull. Practice on scrap until you have it down, particularly if you're using the holeless waterproof rivets, which require a heavy-duty rivet tool to set.

If you break a rivet on a seat, thwart, or deck plate in the field, remove the rivets and replace with sheet metal screws or stainless steel bolts and nuts, where possible. Otherwise the working of the boat will enlarge the rivet hole and by the time you get around to replacing the rivet, it may require a larger size. As we stated earlier, avoid the use of steel (galvanized or not), copper, and brass bolts and nuts on aluminum for any but the briefest temporary holding action. Prolonged contact with these metals will erode aluminum. If you must use steel fasteners, use stainless steel, or, in a pinch, use a thin plastic or rubber gasket between, say, a steel washer and the hull.

Replacing a broken rib or an aluminum keel is not particularly difficult, but it can be time-consuming since you will have many rivets to remove. On this critical area, be especially careful not to enlarge the holes. Drill *only* through the rivet head, and be sure to use a drill bit smaller than the shaft, unless you're removing "flush" rivets, which are countersunk into the rib. For those, use a drill bit the *same* size as the shaft, and, after center-punching lightly as described above, merely touch the spinning drill bit to the center-punched area. The bit should grab the head and snap it off cleanly without damaging the hole or twisting the rivet shaft. Again, practice makes perfect. Try your luck on a scrap canoe first, if possible.

With the broken rib removed, pound out any dents in the hull and inspect for hairline cracks around rivet holes. Replacement ribs are available from manufacturers (again, you may have to order through a dealer), or you can try scavenging from scrap canoes. Position the new rib inside the hull, and make sure the rivet holes line up.

Remove the rib and smear a thin layer of silicone sealant on the hull, covering the entire area under the rib. This is especially effective at stopping leakage around rivet holes that have become enlarged slightly through damage or removal of the rivets.

Bolt the new rib in place at each end and in the middle, then rivet it in place, beginning at the center bolt and working toward each end, alternating sides with each rivet. Take your time and make sure each rivet seats well; coat them with silicone sealant before inserting. Remove the bolts and replace with rivets.

Ammunition

EXPERIENCED SHOOTERS KNOW, and most people will be heartened to discover, that ammunition by itself isn't very dangerous or hard to handle safely. Without the support provided by a firearm's chamber or other close confinement, a cartridge or shotgun shell will discharge inefficiently—that is, it will not "fire" the slug or pellets at high velocity.

Ammunition subject to fire or extreme heat, for example, is not as dangerous as many people fear. When a shell is heated to the point of ignition, the heavy slug or pellets will hardly move at all, while the shell or cartridge case will travel somewhat farther. Small fragments of metal or plastic from the casing, primer cups, or unburned powder may be hurled short distances with sufficient velocity to cause injury, however, so it is wise to keep ammunition well away from heat and flame, and to stay clear of ammunition caught in a fire.

Ammunition isn't very sensitive to shocks, either. Strict standards applied to ammunition manufacture insure that shells and cartridges will not explode from rough handling or falls, especially when they are stored or shipped in their original containers or packages. All shell and cartridge types are tested thoroughly before marketing for shock resistance.

Commercial ammunition will not "mass explode"—that is, an accidental discharge of one cartridge or shell in a carton or case will not result in simultaneous or subsequent discharge of others. Thus, any number of shells may be stored together without increasing the risk of dangerous explosions. The "Fire in the Ammo Factory" scare stories, which show up in "action" movies and comic books, are largely fictional. According to the Sporting Arms and Ammunition Manufacturers' Institute, Inc., a trade association of manufacturers of guns and ammo, there are no verified instances of injuries caused by ammunition caught in a fire. Tests conducted by SAAMI members have shown that the "pops" heard during such incidents are caused by exploding primers; propellent powder burns inefficiently and makes little noise. Whizzing sounds are not from slugs or pellets but from flying primers and caps—not very dangerous.

This information notwithstanding, proper precautions should be taken when handling, storing, and disposing of ammunition. Handloading, a fast-growing hobby among shooters, is beyond the scope of this book, but it, too, has its safety rules and precautions. Anyone attempting to reload shells or cartridges should receive expert advice and study the procedure thoroughly before handling a shell.

If ammunition outside a gun is benign, ammunition inside a gun is extremely dangerous, especially if that ammunition has been mishandled in such a way as to dent, bend, puncture, crease, or otherwise distort the cartridge or shell. A crooked casing means misalignment inside the chamber, which can cause a sliver of lead to shear off the slug inside the barrel or chamber itself. This can cause the action to jam or, in extreme cases, can cause a barrel to explode. Any shell or cartridge that is difficult to chamber should be carefully inspected and the firearm should not be discharged until the reason for the difficulty is discovered and remedied.

Preventing physical damage to new cartridges and shot shells is as easy as keeping them in their original packages, away from bumps and jolts. Ammunition should be carried in loops or belts to prevent it being accidentally crushed.

Ammunition should not be immersed in water or exposed to solvents, paint thinners, petroleum products, ammonia, or similar materials. Such chemicals may penetrate and affect the primer or propellent charge, causing misfires or "squib" shots, with resulting obstruction of the chamber or barrel.

Blank cartridges, by the way, should be treated with the same caution as other ammo. A blank detonated by fire will sound considerably louder than a regular cartridge, but is no more dangerous. Ammunition subjected to physical damage or exposed to chemicals or extreme heat should be disposed of safely. It should never be buried, burned, or dumped in a waterway. Local authorities have established procedures for dealing with unserviceable ammunition, and a simple phone call to the nearest police station may be all that's needed to get rid of suspect ammo. Ammunition manufacturers, too, will dispose of ammunition. Written permission from the company should be obtained before shipping such ammo.

Arrows

FOR MANY YEARS the most common material used for arrow shafts was Port Orford cedar, a straight-grained wood found only in the state of Oregon. This is still a very popular arrow material, although not used as extensively as it once was due to the emergence of newer shaft materials.

One of these is fiberglass cloth that is saturated with resin, then wound on steel mandrils and baked to form tough tubing. After baking, it is removed from the mandrils and finished. Another, and perhaps the most popular, present-day arrow material is aluminum alloy tubing. This is produced in many sizes and *spines,* a term referring to relative stiffness.

Cedar arrows are the least expensive, so are a natural choice for the beginning archer. Fiberglass arrows are the choice for many bowhunters because of their toughness, while aluminum arrows are used by practically all tournament or target archers, simply because they can be more closely matched in spine and weight than the other materials.

SELECTING ARROWS

In order to match arrows to your bow, you must consider their weight, spine, and length. Arrow weight will vary with the bow and type of arrow used. Field or hunting arrows are ordinarily heavier than target arrows.

To determine the right arrow length, hold a yardstick against your breastbone and reach out on it with both arms extended straight in front of you. Where your fingertips touch the yardstick is the correct draw length. Now match your draw length to your bow's marked draw weight. For each inch of draw over or under eighteen inches, add or subtract two pounds to the listed draw weight. When you place an order for matched arrows, include the weight of the bow they will be used with, your draw length, and the type of arrow point desired (target, field, or hunting). Stores selling archery tackle generally have this information plainly marked on arrow boxes.

Due to the compound bow's release weight, a variety of arrow sizes can be used. For hunting, use the bow's peak draw weight as the figure with which to match your arrow weight. This arrow will provide greater energy upon delivery than a lighter-spined arrow. Use your compound's peak weight as a good starting point for target or field shooting, but experiment to find the best spine for your bow, your release, and your shooting style.

CARE AND STORAGE

Arrows should be inspected periodically for possible damage. If you are shooting wooden arrows and you find one that is splintered, discard it. A splintered arrow can cause serious injury to the shooter. A roughened or nicked shaft, however, often can be smoothed with sandpaper and then polished with oil or furniture wax. Although aluminum arrows are quite tough, they easily bend from hitting a solid object such as a rock or a wall. A bent arrow should never be shot, as it can stray way off the intended line of flight. Never attempt to shoot an aluminum arrow that's been bent back into shape.

When withdrawing arrows from a target, hold one hand against the target face, grasp the arrow shaft at the target with your other hand, and draw it out in a straight line. If your arrows have feather fletching, make sure the feathers do not come loose from the shaft.

Crushed feathers, or those matted down by rain or snow, can be restored by twirling them in steam from a teakettle. Most arrows now have plastic fletching, which does not require such care.

When not in use, arrows should be kept at moderate temperatures. Many archers keep them in a specially made box with a frame that keeps the shafts straight and the fletching separated.

Replacing arrowheads is easy. For field and target points, any good glue will hold the point securely. When the glue has dried, set the point with a center punch, nail or wire cutter, putting a small dent in the metal to hold the point to the wood.

Most serious bowhunters spend considerable time resharpening factory broadhead points to a finer edge. This can be done at home with a vise, file, and whetstone, or in the field with a small arrowhead sharpener or file. It is usually best to touch up the edges on a hunting arrowhead just before you nock the arrow, especially if you've not protected the points during transport, because arrowheads rapidly lose their razor edge from contact with quivers, packs, or other arrowheads. When sharpening arrowheads, pay strict attention to how much metal you remove and be sure the head remains balanced.

Axes

AXES REQUIRE LITTLE maintenance besides sharpening, but proper sharpening is a must. A dull ax won't cut, but neither will one that's sharpened wrong. An ax that's sharpened wrong will chip, develop a burred "rolled over" edge, crack, or, more serious, bounce off a log instead of cutting into it.

CHOOSING AN AX

As with most outdoor equipment, you get what you pay for when selecting an ax. Cheap "drugstore" axes and hatchets are often made from inferior, untempered steel and have softwood handles. You won't be able to sharpen them, the heads will crack and dent, and the handles will split the first time you mis-strike. Pay the price and buy a good one.

Look for "tempered" and a brand name stamped on the head; avoid stainless steel or crudely painted heads. (Some makers carefully paint the heads with plastic paint. That's okay.) An oiled, hardwood handle with a straight grain is best, and it should be firmly anchored to the head. Avoid knots, cracks, and streaks of light-colored wood, which indicate weak spots. Some manufacturers fill the eye—the opening in the head where the handle fits—with epoxy. This seals the opening and prevents moisture from seeping in to deteriorate the wood, but makes removing broken handles difficult. On axes with painted handles, you can spot cracks or loosening handles by looking for cracked or chipped paint.

To determine if the handle is shaped correctly, rest the ax on the bit and the knob (the "short side" of the fawn foot). If the bit touches at about its midpoint, the ax is said to be "hung" correctly: it is balanced, and will strike true. Hold the handle at the foot and let your arm relax. If the head just clears the ground or floor, the handle is the right length for you. Similarly, you can use a plumbline to determine if an ax handle is straight. Rest the ax on its head and sight with a plumbline from the blade edge to the center of the foot. They should line up, or nearly so. If not, you'll have quite a bit of trouble striking true, and so would be better off replacing the handle or choosing another ax.

There are many head shapes to choose from in both full-size and belt axes and hatchets. It is beyond the scope of this book to discuss the merits of each, and you'll find woodsmen willing to put their bet on any of them. For most general camping and backpacking, a hatchet or belt ax will do fine; you can use the butt to drive in tent stakes or poles. For heavier work, a full-size single- or double-bitted ax is necessary. The double-bitted models give you an added degree of versatility: you can sharpen one blade to a rounded, heavy-shouldered edge for log splitting and brush cutting, and keep the other razor sharp for serious logging—or filleting fish, for that matter! If you have a double-bitted ax so sharpened, paint one blade a different color so you can spot it immediately. A bright yellow is easy to spot in the dark. While you're painting, paint a spot on the handle for the same reason.

SHARPENING

Probably more good axes are retired on disability pensions because they were improperly sharpened than for any other reason. You can ruin the best ax by ruining its shape: a rounded, convex profile is what you're after. A convex, "needle-nose" shape will crack and rollover or wedge itself into whatever you're chopping. If you have a sticky ax, check it's blade: you may find it's been improperly honed to a wedge shape. A rounded bevel is not only stronger, it is easier to work with, since chips will be shed cleanly and not stick to the log.

Never sharpen an ax on an electric grinding wheel. The intense heat generated by the rapidly spinning wheel can burn the blade and cause it to lose its temper. You've no doubt gotten away with sharpening tools on an electric wheel by constantly dipping the blade in water to cool it off. With small tools, you can get away with it because the thin blades dissipate heat rapidly. The massive ax head isn't so easy to cool, and you can ruin the temper before you realize it. A hand- or pedal-powered grindstone is safer, but it's best to get used to using a file and whetstone.

Use a clean, medium-toothed 10- or 12-inch flat file. You'll be filing from the eye to the cutting edge, so wedge the ax firmly in a vise or between two logs in a position that will allow you to comfortably stroke the blade. File on the "away" stroke only; if you're rehabilitating a badly dulled blade or correcting a convex edge, start two or three inches back and work toward the edge, taking off enough metal to create a new, round edge. Lift the file at the end of each stroke.

The blade should be filed into a fan shape, with slightly more metal at the corners, the "heel" and "toe" of the blade. Count your strokes, and turn the blade often, making sure you give each side the same number. Keep the file clean and turn it from time to time if both surfaces are of equal coarseness.

Inspect the profile often to make sure you're not taking too much metal off near the cutting edge; remember, concave is the shape you're after. Don't be concerned with a fine burr which will appear at the edge of the blade. You'll be removing that with a whetstone.

When the blade is correctly shaped, and evenly sharpened, sight along the edge. You should see a smooth, even border of newly filed metal, tapering toward the ends, no bright spots, no file cut marks, and an even burr. Keep filing until you have that, then take a fine whetstone and remove the burr, moving the stone in a circular motion along the edge from heel to toe across each face of the blade.

Test the blade by carefully rubbing your fingernail lightly along the edge: it should be sharp enough to cut into the nail, with no pulling or grabbing, which indicate burrs or dull spots. Again sight along the blade. There should be no unevenness in color; light spots indicate dull spots.

After whetting the blade, give it a fine coat of light oil or WD-40 and rub it in with fine steel wool to prevent rust. No other maintenance is necessary, and the edge should last through a sizable cutting session with no more than an occasional touch-up with the whetstone. Before you use your ax in frigid weather, warm it over a stove or near a fire. Cold metal is brittle and will crack.

AX HANDLES

Ax and hatchet handles are most often made of hardwood and wedged into the head with metal or wooden wedges. Never store an ax by leaning it against a wall. Don't let it lie in the sun or near a source of heat. Hang it up or lay it flat to avoid drying out or warping the handle, and sheath it. Don't sink it in a convenient stump, where it can pose a safety hazard.

Fixing a Loose Handle. If the handle becomes loose, you can tighten it temporarily by soaking the head in water, which will cause the wood to swell and make the head tight. This, of course, is only a temporary measure and is not recommended for any but emergency or short-term situations. The wood will dry out and the ax head will still be loose. Any ax left in the sun, in fact, will soon have a loose handle.

It's easy to cut wooden wedges with a knife. Before you pound one in, though, take a look at the eye and handle end to determine why the handle worked loose. Did it crack? Did a wedge fall out or shift? Is the neck of the handle split? Or the head itself? Did someone drive a wedge in crooked? You can save yourself some time and effort by finding out what caused the handle to loosen and taking remedial steps first.

Remove any wedges that are undersized, placed crookedly, or cracked by grasping them with a pliers and pulling. Wood-gripping metal wedges may be hard to remove, and if you can't get the old one out, you'll need to work carefully with a narrow chisel or dull knife to loosen it. It's better to remove a small wedge completely than to try to add another one beside it. For one thing, you stand a good chance of cracking the handle by accidentally driving the old wedge farther into the handle with the new one. For another, you may find that the new wedge, especially a wooden one, will crack when driven against the metal one. Also, it's quite likely you'll not get the new wedge in tightly, and end up with two loose wedges instead of one—and still have a loose handle! So try to remove the old wedge, if at all possible. Naturally, if someone tried to fix a loose handle by driving in a couple of nails, you'll want to get them out.

Once you've removed all that hardware, you're ready to put in a new wedge. Make it to last: use a thick chip of hardwood, cut with the grain, long enough and thick enough to keep the head tight. How long is long enough? Measure the depth of the split in the handle and subtract ¼ inch. You don't want the wedge to "bounce" off the bottom of the slit when you drive it home, nor do you want it to stick out of the slit. How thick? Here, you've got to measure the eye and the two halves of the slit handle. The wedge and the two halves together should be as wide as the eye *plus* ⅛ inch. You'll want the wedge to compress slightly and to compress the handle slightly when you drive it in. If you're working in a warm room, ³⁄₁₆ over isn't too much, as the wood will shrink when exposed to outside tempera-

view from top

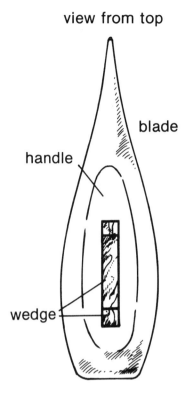

blade

handle

wedge

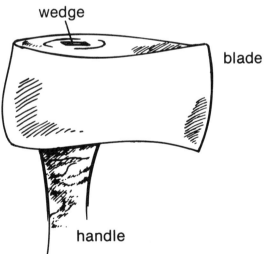

wedge

blade

handle

When you are replacing the wedge of an ax handle, make it last by choosing a thick chip of hardwood cut with the grain and long and thick enough to keep the head tight.

tures. Here, you must measure carefully, making sure that you're measuring the handle halves at the right place. If you have removed the head, replace it and tap the handle on a hard surface to settle the head firmly on the handle. (Many woodsmen cut off the "fawn foot" so that the foot is parallel to the ax head. This makes it much easier to tap the handle firmly into the head without striking a glancing blow or cracking the handle.)

With the head settled on the handle and straight, check to see if the end protrudes. If so, mark it ⅛ inch above the top of the head and cut it there. Then measure the thickness, as described above, and cut a slightly tempered wedge as long as the eye. Before placing the head on the handle permanently, check the condition of the eye and remove any burrs or dents with a coarse file. Also look at the part of the handle that's inside the head. If it's split or cracked you're probably going to have a loose head before long, no matter how carefully you place the wedge.

Now replace the head on the handle, tap the foot to settle it, and turn the ax over, placing it head down on two blocks set so that the protruding handle will emerge between them. Tap the handle firmly into the head, making sure you hold the ax straight up and down, with a hammer. Don't hit it hard enough to make it bounce around. Then turn it foot down, place it on the floor or ground, and drive the wedge in with short, even taps. It should sink to the level of the head or slightly below, and the handle should be wedged firmly on each side against the inside of the eye. Once you're sure that everything is firmly in place, take a coping saw and cut off any of the wedge or handle that protrudes—there should be a little sticking out.

Care of Handle Shaft. The shaft of an ax handle should be lightly worked over with sandpaper from time to time to remove splinters. Don't use steel wool for this purpose, as it will leave tiny wires imbedded in the handle, which can easily become imbedded in your hand. After sanding, rub in a little linseed oil.

A trick some ax wielders use is to carefully drill a hole a couple of inches into the foot, stuff it with cotton, wet the cotton with oil, and plug it with a piece of dowel or handcut plug. The oil-soaked cotton will keep the end of the handle waterproof.

The handles of axes and mauls used for splitting wood often shatter just below the head, especially when an inexperienced woodsman misses his mark. There's no way to repair a handle broken at that point, but you can protect the handle by "whipping" it with wire.

If you've ever whipped the end of a rope to keep it from fraying, you know the procedure: wrap wire around the handle in a series of tight loops, after first having laid a loop along the handle. When you've wrapped six inches or so, tuck the running end through the loop, and pull the bitter end toward the head, so that the running end is pulled snugly under the coils of wire. Cut the bitter end with a pair of wire nippers. Nearly any flexible wire will do the job, but it should be thick enough to provide protection. Speaker wire or electrical cord will do.

The beauty of this method of protecting the handle is that you don't have to drill or nail into the handle, which weakens it. Eventually, of course, the wire will wear out and become loose, but it's easy to replace, and you can carry a couple of feet of wire in your pack for field repairs. Sure beats duct tape.

AX SHEATHS

Keeping your ax in a sheath will prevent accidents, but it can cause rust to form on the head. If you have a leather sheath, keep the inside clean and free of condensation by wiping it out before sheathing the ax. Remove the ax from time to time check for discoloration. If the ax head is discolored, buff it lightly with fine steel wool, oil it, and replace it in the sheath.

Leather sheaths are usually put together with rivets. If your sheath isn't, set a couple of rivets in the seam to prevent the blade from cutting through the thread. Or you can insert a strip of copper sheeting into the sheath, pushing it into the seam with the ax head. Copper will form itself to the shape of the blade and will not damage the blade at all. (For that reason, you should also use copper rivets rather than steel.)

Leather sheaths can be protected with a coating of wax shoe polish. Too heavy applications of oil-based dressings will make the sheath too soft to withstand repeated insertions and removals of the blade.

A temporary blade guard can be made from a length of rubber or plastic hose. Simply cut a piece of hose as long as the blade and split it. The blade will slide right in. A flattened tin can with the ends removed will also protect a blade during transport.

A similar, more permanent guard can be made from a block of wood. Cut a piece of soft wood as long as the blade and a couple of inches thick. Cut a groove deep enough to accommodate the entire blade edge. You can make this guard more secure by attaching a rubber band or loop cut from an inner tube to hold the head firmly in the groove.

Backpacks

MOST BACKPACKS ARE made of woven nylon, usually heavyweight Cordura, coated with urethane. This fabric is strong and water resistant, though not completely waterproof, and can be cleaned according to the instructions given in the *Nylon* entry.

It is not advisable to try to seal the seams on nylon backpacks. You're unlikely to get the pack completely waterproof anyway, due to the large number of seams, pockets, zippers, straps, etc., and seam sealing, complicates repair of backpacks because a sealed seam can't be ripped out all at once but must be pulled apart stitch by stitch. A raincover made to fit the pack will keep your gear as dry as sealed seams, if not dryer.

For some reason, many people don't think about keeping backpacks clean, but they should. Dirt not only fosters mildew growth in nylon, it is the greatest cause of zipper failure—and replacing zippers is expensive and difficult.

Clean backpacks thoroughly before you store them. Before laundering, vacuum out all crumbs, dirt, and debris from pockets and the main cargo space. Clean all zippers as described below. See *Nylon* entry for tips on removing stains. Store bags hanging up, away from sunlight.

CARE AND REPAIR OF ZIPPERS

Only metal zippers should be lubricated, and then only if they are cleaned regularly to prevent the lubricant from trapping dirt, which will abrade the teeth and especially the slider. Clean metal zippers with alcohol or a lighter fluid and a stiff brush. Solvents won't hurt the urethane coating, but don't soak the pack. Use a bit on an old toothbrush and brush the teeth like you do your own. Blow dust and dirt out with air pressure.

Lubricate metal zippers with beeswax, which will help prevent corrosion by forming a thin coating on the teeth and slider, or silicone lubricant, which will make a worn zipper extra slippery, or graphite from a "lead" pencil.

Nylon zippers shouldn't be lubricated at all, as oil, wax, or grease will attract dirt and hold it against the teeth and slider. Nylon is slippery enough without oil, if you keep it clean. Clean nylon zippers with soap and water and a brush. Washing the backpack itself regularly will keep the zippers clean and healthy.

The first thing people do when a zipper doesn't work is stitch across it to keep it closed. The second thing they do is rip out the zipper, thinking to save money by replacing the entire zipper. The third thing they do is send the pack to a repair shop, where the zipper is indeed replaced—needlessly. Zippers can be repaired, both temporarily and permanently, at home. Replacing a zipper is tough.

A gaping zipper, where the teeth open up behind the slider as it is pulled across the track, is the result of dirt which has abraded the interior of the slider to the point where it won't channel the teeth together. As an emergency measure, all you need to do is squeeze the sides of the slider together with a pair of pliers at the "Y" end. You're likely to fracture the slider, but it will stay together long enough to give you a few zips.

To replace the slider you must unstitch and resew part of the seam at the foot of the zipper, but that is much easier than trying to sew in a whole new zipper. The only problem is finding a new slider to match your zipper. Frostline, the company that makes outwear kits, may have sliders to fit; luggage repair shops probably do, too, although getting them to sell you *one* slider may be tough. You need the stop at the end of the track, too, as you'll fracture the old one getting it off. If you find a zipper that matches yours—they come in a few standard sizes—buy it and remove the stop and the slider.

With the seam unsewn and the stop removed, remove the broken slider. Fit the teeth together completely along the entire length of the track. Split the zipper at the foot end about one inch, then feed each side into the wide end of the new slider and even the ends of the tape and gradually work the slider to the end of the track, pushing the teeth together as needed. With the slider the whole way to the end, and the teeth all completely together, install the new stop with a pair of pliers. Resew the tape and seam at the bottom end of the zipper.

REINFORCING STRAPS AND SEAMS

Most straps on quality packs are bar-tacked with a line of closely-spaced stitches across the end of the strap to secure it to the body of the pack. If a strap begins to pull loose, or if your pack doesn't have bar-tacked straps, you can sew it at home. It's tough, perhaps too tough for your home sewing machine, but it can be done. Practice on a scrap piece of webbing and nylon first before you tackle your pack.

The secret is to use the largest needle that fits into your machine—a size 20 commercial sewing needle is ideal. Use number 33 spun polyester thread, and set the machine for eight stitches per inch. Use seam sealer to keep the threads from causing leaks.

The points of maximum stress on a backpack are the bottom seams, with pocket seams a close second. Ideally, these seams will be flat lap seams with the edges of the fabric fused to prevent fraying. Unfortunately, many manufacturers don't fuse edges, leaving loose threads at the seams that will, in time, fray and cause the seam to open.

You can prevent this by applying a flame or, better yet, the tip of a soldering iron or woodburning tool to the seam to melt the loose threads together. This is definetely worth the time and hassle, because when a pocket seam or main seam lets go, it usually does it all at once—invariably, just when you're fording a stream!

MODIFYING PACKS

Modern pack designers have thought of nearly everything, it seems, but they still haven't come up with an easy way to change the size and shape of the cargo space inside the pack. One way you can do this is to make pockets of nylon fabric and secure them to the main pack body with snaps or Velcro strips. Nylon fabric, Velcro, and snaps are available at fabric shops; the nylon needn't be coated to go inside the pack. The pockets can be as simple as a piece of fabric folded over and sewn along the sides or as elaborate as a double-gusseted, reinforced-bottom, flapped pouch. Probably the simpler the better, but there's no limit on size. Remember to seal any seams you put through the exterior wall of the bag, and fuse all edges with flame or heat to prevent fraying.

Adding grommets to backpacks is easy with a grommet tool. Again, remember to fuse any edges you create to forestall fraying. It's usually a good idea to first patch an area where you want to place a grommet, especially if it will take any great amount of stress.

BACKPACK FRAMES

Pack frames are usually made from sturdy, trouble-free aluminum tubing, which requires no maintenance. The frame will oxidize and begin to look grey soon after purchase unless it is anodized, but that's of no consequence. You can clean and polish it if you wish with any commercial metal polish, but there is no practical value in doing so and the frame will begin to oxidize almost immediately anyway.

It's unlikely that you'll bend or break a pack frame in normal use, but if you do it can be straightened. The manufacturers of pack frames can't seem to decide whether a stiff or somewhat flexible frame is best, so you're likely to run into either kind. The stiff frames are rather brittle and likely to kink if you try to rebend them into shape.

One method that will minimize the likelihood of kinking is to cut a piece of dowel, slightly smaller in diameter than the tubing, about six inches longer than the distance from the bend to the open end of the frame. Cut one end at a 45-degree angle. As you bend the frame member back into shape, drive the pointed end of the dowel into the tube, with the long side of the pointed end against the convex side of the bend. This will give you a strong lever to push on and will keep the tubing from kinking at the point of the bend.

Of course, anytime you bend a tube, you'll have some kinking. If you can't minimize it—perhaps the aluminum is too stiff to bend back—patch it by pop-riveting a sleeve of copper or aluminum tubing around the frame at the point of the kink. Copper water pipe is available in several thicknesses and corresponding stiffnesses. You want the medium thick, medium stiff grade.

For a typical kink, cut a piece of tubing three to four inches long, file off any burrs at the ends from your cutting, and split it lengthwise. This can most easily be done with a hacksaw, with the tubing secured in a vise. Spread the split tubing slightly and work it over the frame tubing until the kink is at its center. Put the split side of the tubing on the side away from the kink (on the side that was convex when the frame was bent) and secure it with two screw-type hose clamps. These clamps can be tightened down

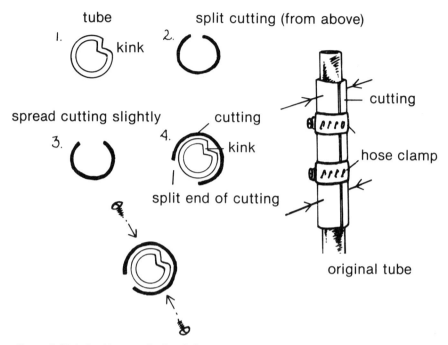

To repair kinked tubing on a backpack frame, cut a piece of tubing three to four inches long and split it lengthwise. Work the new section of tubing over the frame tubing until it covers the kink. Secure with two screw-type hose clamps and install pop rivets.

to compress the tubing as much as possible and will hold the tubing in place so you can drill through the tubing and frame. Drill 90 degrees from the split in the tubing, and install pop rivets through the tubing and frame. It's not all that pretty, but it will work.

Batteries
(Automotive and Boat)

AUTO AND BOAT batteries (6 or 12 volts) are simple machines that will work efficiently and reliably for a long time if properly maintained and handled. Unfortunately, many people neglect even the most simple maintenance and inspection and thus shorten their batteries' lives.

Wet-cell batteries produce electricity by means of plates of two different metals surrounded by an acid solution. As the chemical reaction that produces the charge takes place, acid is consumed. Thus, the batteries' condition and lifespan can be determined by a simple test of the electrolyte's acidity, which any garage attendant can perform in a minute. Eventually, the electrolyte will wear out, as will the metal plates inside, and the battery will then be fit only for recycling. Modern batteries can be expected to last three to four years under normal conditions and with regular inspections and maintenance.

PREVENTING BATTERY FAILURE

Batteries fail for four main reasons: overcharging, undercharging, vibration or shock, and neglect.

In an automobile system, overcharging is usually the result of a malfunctioning voltage regulator, alternator, or both. The most reliable indicator of overcharging of the electrical system is excessive water use. Under normal conditions, a battery's liquid level should be nearly stable, with only occasional topping off needed. Constant need for water calls for a thorough electrical system checkup. An overcharged battery will overheat and its plates can warp, disturbing the flow of electrons and causing failure of the cell.

Undercharging is also caused by a malfunctioning electrical system and, while less easy to detect, can quietly rob your battery of productive life. When a battery is not receiving enough charge, its plates harden—it grows old faster. The surest sign of an undercharging system is a shiny coating on the "Negative" terminal resembling varnish.

Vibration and shock can cause internal and external damage to wet-cell batteries, the most common being broken plates, straps, separators, or terminals. Of these types of damage, only a broken or loose terminal is readily apparent. Evidence of such structural damage is a battery's inability to "hold" a charge indicated by rapid or overnight loss of power. Once broken, a battery is fit only for recycling, so it should be handled with care and never dropped, crushed, or subjected to constant vibration. Always store a battery in such a way as to prevent its being knocked over or off a shelf. (Leaving a battery set on concrete or bare ground, by the way, will cause a slow discharge. Never assume that a battery so stored is dead—it may merely need a charge.) Never set a battery on its side.

Neglect takes many forms, but by far the most common is failure to regularly check the liquid level in the battery. A healthy battery will use some water, and if the level is allowed to drop far enough, permanent damage can occur. If a plate—or a portion of a plate—dries out, it will not reactivate; that is, once allowed to dry, it will not produce electricity even when immersed in potent electrolyte. It is, in fact, dead. Simply adding water can prevent such premature loss of generating power.

Any water that is safe to drink, except mineral water, is safe to use in a battery. However, water of high mineral content ("hard" water), water that contains metal impurities, petroleum products, alcohol, nitric acid, hydrochloric acid, or acetic acid, and salt water will seriously impair performance. High concentrations of these impurities can cause battery failure. Water that has stood in a metal container (except lead or lead-lined containers) should not be used in batteries. The best water is distilled water, with rainwater a close second.

CLEANING TERMINALS

Battery terminals should be cleaned regularly. A white residue on the terminals is a sign of an overcharged or over-discharging battery and is cause for inspection of the electrical system for shorts and other malfunctions. However, some buildup is normal over time, and this residue can be removed easily by removing the cable terminal from the post and washing the post and battery top with a medium-strong solution of baking soda and water. These white deposits should never be touched or allowed to contact bare skin or any valuable fabric, as they are highly acidic. Swab the top of the battery and the posts with a brush and the soda solution, taking care not to let the solution enter the battery itself. If the deposits are hardened and brittle, carefully scrape them off with a knife or terminal-cleaning tool.

Applying lubricant to the terminal post is not necessary, although this has become a common practice to facilitate removal and reconnection of the cable terminal. If the terminal doesn't fit, replace it. Never pry up on it with a screwdriver or other tool; never hammer it down onto the post. Most terminals are made of soft metal and can easily be opened or closed.

Batteries
(Flashlight and Lantern)

FLASHLIGHT AND LANTERN batteries come in four varieties, each with advantages and disadvantages.

Carbon-zinc cells—"standard" flashlight batteries—are inexpensive, and that is their main virtue. They discharge quickly, especially with prolonged continual use, and are extremely sensitive to temperature. As the temperature decreases, their output decreases. This makes them extremely inconvenient for use during winter, but it has a benefit, too. You can keep carbon-zinc cells in the freezer almost indefinitely with no loss of potential power. All that's needed is to let them warm up before use.

A weak carbon-zinc cell can be heated in an enclosed, sunny spot or beside a campfire to increase its output. In fact, many "dead" batteries can be rejuvenated simply by heating as the chemical reaction that produces the charge will increase up to about 150° F. Take care not to heat the battery beyond that temperature, and avoid heating a battery too quickly, otherwise the casing may split and the chemicals leak.

Alkaline batteries can also be heated to improve their performance. These superior batteries produce more power longer and at lower temperatures than do carbon-zinc cells. For these reasons they are better for winter camping. Alkaline batteries are said to have a longer shelf life than carbon-zinc cells, but storage in a cool or cold location is good idea for any battery, and they are not excepted.

Nickel-cadmium cells are rechargeable. That is their main virtue and is the only justification for their greater cost. They lost power quicker than alkaline cells (and about as rapidly as carbon-zinc cells), but cannot be rejuvenated by heating. Cold storage is again indicated.

Lithium batteries are new to the marketplace but have proven themselves superior in all respects. Lighter than other cells, they produce nearly twice as much power as alkaline cells, and do so over a much wider temperature range. Lithium cells operate efficiently at extremely low temperatures, making them a natural for winter camping under severe conditions. Under normal conditions, they're expected to last five times as long as alkaline cells, and can be stored up to ten years with no loss of power. No special storage conditions are needed, as lithium batteries are not as heat-sensitive as their predecessors. Cost is the only drawback to lithium cells, but it is justified by their performance.

Batteries shouldn't be left in flashlights, lanterns, radios, etc., for long periods of time, as there is often a slight discharge of power due to corrosion on contact points or faulty connections. Contact points can be cleaned with a mild baking soda solution; a light buffing with steel wool will remove hardened corrosion. A thin film of oil on contact points will help prevent corrosion buildup. Rub corrosion with an ink (typewriter) eraser to remove. Keep batteries dry at all times, as moisture will penetrate the seams and cause rust and corrosion to form. In humid climates, batteries can be stored in closed containers with a dehydrating agent, such as silica gel packets.

Bows

WHEN YOU THINK of a bow, it is natural to think of wood. But today's composite or laminated construction has practically superseded the all-wood bow. Fiberglass impregnated with resins has become standard backing and facing for bow limbs, and often is used without wood core laminations for this purpose. Various bow limb components are joined together under heat and pressure, generally using an epoxy as the bonding agent. Alloys of magnesium and aluminum are often used for bow handles and for the eccentric wheels or cams employed in compound bows.

TYPES OF BOWS

Straight bows, also called longbows, can be made from a single stave of wood or be composed of laminations of wood and other materials such as silk, sinew, rawhide, or fiberglass. As its name implies, the limb ends of a straight bow are not reflexed or bent. A longbow is generally as long, or longer, than the archer is tall, and is used for hunting large or small game and target shooting.

Recurved bow design makes bowstring leverage longer as the bow approaches full draw by forming a reflexive bend in the bow limb ends. This also adds "cast," the velocity imparted to an arrow from the energy stored in a drawn bow. Recurved bows are stressed higher than straight bows and shoot an arrow somewhat faster than straight bows having the same draw weight.

The draw weight of a bow is the force (measured in pounds) needed to draw the arrow fully back to the user's anchor point. The draw weight of target bows is generally between 30 and 45 pounds; hunting bows have draw weights from 45 pounds to 70 pounds.

Adult bows of both types range from 4½ to 6 feet in length. Shorter models are useful for hunting in brushy country or from elevated stands; longer ones are used for tournament or recreational target shooting.

The compound bow is the latest innovation in the sport. A typical compound is a rather short, flat-limbed bow with fiberglass limbs fitted into a handle of metal alloy or wood. Compound bows are equipped with a clever system of eccentric wheels (pulleys) which store energy. At the beginning of the draw, there is a fast buildup of draw weight, which then tapers off quickly to a lesser weight at full draw. This makes a compound bow much easier to hold and aim than a straight or recurved bow and helps compounds discharge arrows with more velocity than longbows or recurved bows. Light steel cable connects the bowstring to the eccentric wheels. Most compound bows have a "takeup" device for adjusting the draw length to correspond to the arrows being used. This adjustment also synchronizes the rotation of the eccentric wheels through a cable feedback pulley system, adding stability not possible with conventional bows. The latest type of compound bows now uses cams in place of eccentric wheels. Cams are able to store even more energy and inpart greater arrow velocity.

Compound bows are never solidly welded together in one piece as are most conventional bows. Pairs of short limbs, formed and finished separately, are fitted into slots or grooves in handle risers and held in place by the stress of the bow being in a permanently braced position. Compounds are strung by the manufacturer and are rarely unstrung except for replacement of a bow string or cable.

STRINGING AND UNSTRINGING

Stringing and unstringing a bow is an important and potentially dangerous operation: dangerous to the bow, not usually to the archer. The danger, particularly with recurved bows, is limb twisting. A slightly twisted bow shaft is a weakened bow shaft. A strung bow should be inspected for twist by holding it face down with one tip on the ground and the other at waist level. Look down the length of the bowstring, and if the bow is properly strung, the string will align perfectly with the bow's centerline. Even a slight deviation indicates improper stringing, which should be corrected before shooting.

There are three standard methods of stringing a bow. A modern cord bowstringer is easiest and safest. The traditional step-through and push-pull methods require a bit of practice to perfect. Since compound bows are left strung, stringing and unstringing are necessary only when replacing a worn or damaged string or other part. Because compound bows differ in their configurations of wheels and cams, the manufacturer's recommendations should be followed when unstringing a compound.

Standard bowstrings should be broken in before use. String them by any of the methods described below, pull them to near full draw, and slowly let them return. Do not release the tension abruptly. Do this several times, gradually increasing the pull to full draw. It's good practice to break in several bowstrings and keep them handy for field shooting, target practice, or hunting.

Inspect bowstrings periodically for wear. If the serving—the string wrapping where the arrow is nocked—becomes worn, you can reverse the string, which will place the worn spot below your nocking point. Never shoot with a string that shows fraying of loose strands. Keep the string well waxed.

Before stringing the bow, the archer should secure the lower bowstring loop in the grooves of the lower bow tip. This can be done with a rubber band placed only a short space from the end of the loop, so that it won't interfere with the movement of the string. It's much better to use a rubber bow-tip protector. This is a tightfitting rubber sleeve that holds the bowstring loop and also protects the bow's lower tip.

In the step-through method of stringing a bow the string's upper loop is detached from the bow and held in the archer's left hand. The right hand is placed on the bow's upper limb in such a way that the palm of the hand is against the back, or concave, surface of the recurve. The curve of the bow's lower limb goes over the outside of the archer's left ankle. The archer then puts his right leg between the bow and the string, with the bow's center section against the outside of his right thigh, or hip. The left heel is raised, keeping the lower bow tip away from the ground or the floor. The right hand presses the upper tip inward or to the left, while the left hand moves the upper bowstring loop toward the upper tip. When the tip moves close enough, the archer slips the loop over the bow tip and into the string grooves. When he's sure the loop is properly seated in the grooves, he relaxes the pressure on his right arm and the bow is braced.

To prevent limb twisting when using the step-through method, the string must be held in alignment with the bow and the bow's center should be placed against the archer's thigh so that equal pressure is applied to the bending of the bow limbs. Only the ball of the left foot should be on the ground. The raised heel, pointed outward, helps to keep the string in alignment with the bow.

To unstring a bow, the same procedure is followed in reverse. Most right-handed archers follow the sequence described when using the step-through method but some find it more natural to use the opposite hands. When the bow is unstrung by this method, the upper string loop can be held by slipping it under a rubber band wrapped around the bow's upper limb near the tip. There also are commercially-made string keepers that serve the same purpose.

A string keeper is not needed with the push-pull method of stringing, because the upper bowstring loop encircles the bow loosely instead of being free when the bow is unstrung. The archer grasps the bow at the handle with his right hand and pulls, while pushing away with the left hand. The bow's lower tip, with the lower string loop securely in position, is held against the inside of the instep of the right foot. The archer should be careful not to let the bow tip touch the ground or the floor but should place the tip in the hollow of the inside instep just above the sole of the shoe. As the left hand pushes, it also slides up the limb until the upper loop can be slipped into its grooves.

The push-pull method is safe for the bow but can be hazardous for the bowman, since the upper limb may slip from his hand and whip back to crack him on the skull. This can happen also if the upper bowstring loop is not securely seated in the bow-tip notches. Anotehr objection is that this procedure may be difficult for a person with short arms and a heavy bow. The step-through method, while safer and easier for the archer, may result in a twisted bow limb if the maneuver is not performed properly.

Using a bowstringer is practically foolproof from the safety angle, both for the archer and for the bow. An inexpensive bowstringer can be carried in the pocket. One model is simply a foot strap with a little leather pocket for the bow's lower tip. Another consists of two elements that fit on the bow's tips and a length of braided nylon cord. First, the string is attached to the lower bow tip, with the upper loop around the bow's upper limb. After slipping the bow's tips into the two ends of the stringer, the archer simply places his foot on the cord and flexes the bow. The tips bend as the archer pulls his bow upward, sliding his upper bowstring loop into position.

CARE AND STORAGE

Modern bows are delicately balanced instruments, particularly when strung and under tension. Never use your bow as a walking stick and take care not to strike objects that nick or scratch it. Scratches can turn into splinters and eventually result in limb failure. After being exposed to rain or other moisture, the bow should be wiped dry and should be transported, unstrung, in a soft or padded bowcase. Compound bows are never unstrung and so are transported in that fashion. When transporting a bow in a vehicle keep it encased and make sure it is not exposed to excessive heat or direct sunlight because too much heat can badly warp bow limbs.

Never draw a bow farther than your normal draw length. This can result in a broken bow as well as injury. When using a conventional bow in cold weather it is a good idea to flex it several times to "warm it up" before shooting.

When storing a bow, either a conventional or compound type, do not stand it on end in a corner. Support it horizontally across pegs or flat on a shelf. A cool, dry spot such as a closet next to an outside wall is generally a good storage place. The attic or furnace room is not.

Even with careful use and frequent cleaning, a bow will occasionally show cracks and checks in the finish. A good paste wax can help preserve and protect the bow, or you can use a cleaner-and-polish combination especially made for use on bows.

Wrapped leather handles on older bows sometimes work loose or wear through. They can be replaced with rawhide thongs wound around the handle. Before putting a new handle on the bow, remove the old leather and all the adhesive. You may need to use a solvent such as alcohol or carbon tetrachloride to remove the old adhesive. Coat the bow and the thong with household cement, wind the rawhide tightly, and hold it in place until dry.

Moving parts on a compound bow occasionally should be lubricated with a light oil. Make sure sand or dirt does not get into the wheels, cams, or other moving parts. Most compound bows are sold with an instruction manual telling the owner how to adjust or "tune" the bow to best fit his draw length and shooting style. However, only a minimum amount of adjustment should be attempted by the bow owner. Any overadjustment resulting in damage to the bow will void the manufacturer's guarantee. If other than basic tuning is required, the bow should be taken to a service outlet having experience in this line, or should be returned to the manufacturer for the necessary work.

REPAIRING SPLIT LAMINATION

Laminated fiberglass or fiberglass-and-wood bows can, with age, begin to separate. This usually occurs near the tip of either arm, and can be caused by poor stringing practices or by using the bow improperly. If you notice one layer beginning to pull away from the others, do not use the bow at all;

it will be considerably weakened and, even worse, unbalanced. You can easily break it beyond repair.

A split in the lamination isn't necessarily cause for replacing the bow, however. Depending on the severity of the split, the kind of material used in the bow, and the availability of the proper adhesives for that material, you can with little difficulty repair a split bow. Before beginning, consult a local archery shop or experienced bowyer. Remember, you can't determine a bow's strength from its appearance, and you don't want to string, much less attempt to shoot, a bow that's not properly repaired.

With this in mind, and with the proper adhesive for the job, you're ready to begin. First, clean the bow and get all dirt, dust, and debris out of the crack. If the split is on the face near the end of a limb, place the bow in a vise, face up, with the handle protected with newspaper. This will allow you to flex the broken limb to open the split as much as possible.

If a split develops near the handle, put the bow in the vise in such a way as to allow you to insert a thin blade into the split and gently pry it further open, without moving the bow. If you must put the unwrapped shaft into the vise, protect it with newspaper or a piece of leather otherwise the steel jaws of the vise will chew on the shaft. Clean the exposed surfaces.

Follow all directions on the adhesive container to the letter. Usually, you'll need to mix two liquids, although newer single-step adhesives are also being used. With the bow in the vise, spread the split with a knife blade and liberally coat both surfaces with adhesive. Press the split together and wrap with waxed paper. This is important, as the adhesive will be forced from the split and will stick to whatever it can.

Next, place two strips of lath or other wood strips wider than the bow face on either side of the bow and clamp with C-clamps. This is a temporary measure to prevent the lamination from separating and developing bubbles. You next wrap the bow and wood strips with rubber bands cut from an inner tube. Wrap them as tightly as you can, stretching the rubber to its maximum. Once wrapped, remove the clamps and follow directions for curing the adhesive—some require heat, some don't.

When cured, remove the bands and file and sand off any excess adhesive. Finish with progressively finer grits of wet or dry sandpaper. Clean out the string grooves with a small round file.

You'll need to check for twisting after such a repair job. You can use the round file to remove material from the string grooves and thus center a string that's off center.

Calls

BIRD AND GAME calls are delicate instruments that are subjected to extreme weaether conditions, and that is the reason many fail. Simple preventive measures can keep your call in service for years, however.

Most calls fail because of dirt or moisture gumming up the reed. Calls should never be carried loose in a coat pocket or pack, since they are bound to pick up bits of lint, tobacco, or other debris. Keep them in their case. A zip-lock sandwich bag is also a good carrying pouch. A carrying lanyard is a good investment that will keep the call handy, yet free your hands for other work. It will also keep the call away from dirt and, most importantly, away from moisture.

If you get a bit of debris inside the call, don't tear it apart trying to clean it. Instead, insert a clean nail, straightened paper clip, or other long thin instrument into the call and raise the reed slightly. Be very gentle, as you don't want to change the reed's alignment or break it. With the reed slightly raised, blow backward into the call. This should dislodge any particles in the reed area. Tapping, shaking, and applying high pressure from an air compressor are not recommended. Of course, you should never blow a call after eating or chewing tobacco or chewing gum.

Besides dirt, moisture is a call's prime enemy. Blowing warm moist breath into a call on a frosty day will cause condensation, which may freeze inside the barrel or on the reed. Wooden parts can also swell, changing the pitch of the call drastically. A good way to reduce condensation is to keep the call on a lanyard inside your shirt or jacket; this lessens the difference in temperatures between your breath and the inside of the call, and thus minimizes condensation. Many experienced hunters carry several similar or identical calls in the field. That way, when one becomes wet, it can be retired with no loss of calling time.

Never try to dry a wooden call by applying heat. The wood will warp or crack and the call can be ruined. Hard rubber calls, though, can be taken apart and dried with hot air or left in the sun to dry without risk, since they won't absorb moisture. Wooden calls should never be jammed together tightly when dry, as they will absorb moisture from the atmosphere or your breath and swell, possibly cracking from the expansion.

Wooden calls can be modified, although most manufacturers tell you to do so at your own risk. Modifications of tone and blowing effort can be made by loosening the reed and moving it on the reed base. You can also file or sand the contoured end of the reed base, or thin the end of the reed itself, to make a call raspier, shriller, or easier to blow. Take care, though because you can easily ruin an expensive, carefully crafted tool by careless removal of wood.

If the finish on a wooden call is worn, you can restore its beauty and help it repel moisture by rubbing boiled linseed oil into the finish with your hand. Don't use varnishes or lacquers on a wooden call.

Cameras

LIKE BINOCULARS, MONOCULARS, and scopes, cameras require special care to stand up to the rigors of outdoor use. With the advent of fully automatic, lightweight cameras in the 1970s, outdoor photography came into its own: it is no longer just a rich man's sport; no longer requires a plethora of heavy gear. Unfortunately, many of the new 35mm lightweight cameras are not as durable as earlier models, and special care and modifications are needed to help them withstand the rigors of backcountry use.

PROTECTING YOUR CAMERA
To keep the cost of their high-tech cameras within reasonable limits, manufacturers often stint on quality in cases, straps, attachment rings, lens caps, and other protective devices. There is little you can do to strengthen such items, so they must be replaced with sturdier gear.

The typical leather camera case is a worthless piece of impedimenta, useful only for protecting the camera body against dents and bumps. It will not absorb shocks well enough to protect internal optical mechanisms, which themselves have been, in many cases, cheapened and made more fragile. With their generally impractical design and stiff snaps, camera cases also add a "fumble factor." The solution is simple: discard the case or leave it at home.

If you plan on traversing rough terrain and don't need your camera at your fingertips at all times, wrap it in a towel or spare sweater and stuff it deep in your pack or use a belt-type camera case available from outfitters. If you want to keep it handy, on the other hand, you should do all you can to strengthen its carrying system and protect the camera body against physical damage. You can't really have it both ways: if you want the camera ready for instant use, you can't keep it totally out of harm's way. But there are protective measures you can take.

Start with the strap. Throw it away if it's a typical skinny leather strap with light metal attachment rings and replace with a wide, adjustable fabric strap with heavy-duty rings and quick-release spring snaps. Not only will this rig be more secure, it will be more comfortable.

On the camera body itself, the posts—the eyelets where the strap attaches—are vulnerable to wear. If your camera has removable posts, a camera repair shop can easily replace them. If the posts are cast as part of the body, you've got more of a problem. Try inserting a section of plastic or metal tubing. Held in place with glue, an insert can absorb most of the friction from the attachment ring. (A small grommet, such as an eyelet for use on leather garments, will work.) A thin strip of plastic electrician's tape or duct tape will also help strengthen this weak spot.

The edges of the body take a lot of abuse, and, while this doesn't impair performance, it can reduce the camera's resale value significantly. One solution is covering the bottom of the camera with several layers of duct tape, overlapping the edges. When you want to remove the tape, the adhesive residue can be removed with alcohol or lens cleaner. Other possible solutions are coating the camera body with clear varnish or lacquer, or applying a self-adhesive plastic coating available in hobby stores. Both these materials give a somewhat neater appearance (if you're careful in applying them), but are hard to remove neatly and give minimal protection.

Lens caps are a nuisance, although they do protect well. The "fumble factor," is great: anytime you have to remove a lens cap to shoot, you run the risk of dropping it or of smudging the lens.

A good alternative is a clear filter of good optical quality. Fixed to the lens, it provides all the protection of a lens cap and needn't be removed. Of course, it will take a beating, but is much easier and cheaper to replace than a lens. A lens shade can also protect your lens, as well as improving the quality of outdoor photographs by cutting down ambient light which may fool a built-in meter. Similarly, a rubber eyecup will cut down ambient light entering the meter and will also protect the rear of the camera.

FIXING LOOSE SCREWS

Screws loosen readily because of vibration, so check your camera after transporting it by plane, boat, rec vehicle, or auto. A small sewing-machine or eyeglass repair screwdriver should be a part of every outdoor photographer's kit. Repeated loosening and retightening can wear away delicate threads, however, so you may want to seal the tightened screws with Loctite, an automotive sealer and waterproofer. A tiny drop will not only prevent the screw from loosening, it will seal out moisture, preventing deterioration of the threads from corrosion. A dab of clear fingernail polish can also do the job.

If a screw has been loosened and tightened too often, or if corrosion has eaten away some of the threads, you may not be able to keep the screw tight. To get an extra "bite," tighten the screw as far as you can, then tap the screwdriver with a tack hammer and draw it down another quarter turn. This is at best a temporary solution to a serious problem, but if you coat the screw with Loc-tite first and daub a bit on the screw head after tightening, it may stay in place for years. A camera repairman with ingenuity and experience may be able to re-tap the hole and supply a slightly oversized screw. Unless you're particularly skilled with tools, this is a repair you should not try at home.

Plastic screws are particularly vulnerable to stripping from hurried or careless removal or tightening. The batter cap is usually the first to go, and there's not much you can do to protect this vulnerable area except take care. If the slot becomes worn, cut another at right angles to it with a small file or hacksaw blade.

COLD-WEATHER PRECAUTIONS

Severe weather complicates photography. Other than keeping your camera as dry as possible, and giving it every opportunity to dry thoroughly with the back open, there is little you can do about highly humid conditions. A silica gel dehydration packet inside the carrying case can help reduce internal condensation.

Cold stiffens mechanical parts, slows shutter speeds, reduces battery output while increasing recovery time, and makes film brittle. If you plan a photographic expedition in frigid weather, have your camera cleaned and lubricated beforehand; lubricants stiffen in extreme cold, but a lot is better than a little. Special winter lubricants are available, but expensive.

Batteries are troublesome in cold weather—the AA cells used to power flash units on some compact 35s and film winders are notorious for failing at low temperatures—so carry extras inside your parka or shirt. (You might eschew the power winder because of its appetite for AA cells and because it can tear sprocket holes out of cold, brittle film.) At present, lithium cells aren't available in AA size but probably will be in the future, and their cold-resistance will make them worth the cost. (See *Batteries* entry.) Silver oxide cells now used in some automatic cameras are much better in the cold than their predecessors, mercury batteries.

There isn't much you can do about shutters slowed by cold except bracket your exposures.

Cold complicates problems of condensation, too. If you're in the habit of breathing on a lens or filter to clean it, get out of the habit fast: your breath will freeze on the lens and stay there until the camera warms up. Every time you enter a warm place—even a tent that's only a few degrees warmer (albeit more humid) than outside—your camera will fog. Wiping the external lens or filter is no problem, but internal condensation is another matter. Putting the camera in a plastic bag before bringing it indoors can help by bringing in a supply of cold air with the camera which will buffer it against the rapid temperature change that causes condensation. If you want to shoot right after coming inside, the only solution is to unload the camera and carefully wipe the lens from the inside, then reload and use a spare lens that's been kept indoors for your shot. Even this won't work under conditions of extreme temperature contrast, or when the indoor air is especially humid, so you may be frustrated anyway. As long as the camera body stays cold, wiping is not effective, as moisture will condense on it promptly. There's really no good way around this problem other than using two cameras, one for outdoors, one for in. Another precaution, don't load cold film into a warm camera since moisture will condense on it as rapidly as it will on a lens or filter.

DRYING AND CLEANING

A camera repeatedly subjected to temperature changes that produce internal condensation will show signs of corrosion on its metal parts in time. The best way to dry it is to set it aside in a warm location, preferably with moving air, with the back open. Never set it in the sun or try to dry it with heat.

If you drop your camera in snow or water, immediately brush and wipe off all external water, unload the camera, remove all batteries, and swab out as much water as you can with lens tissue. Wrap tissue around a thin screwdriver or knife blade to reach as far into the camera as you can. This emergency field first aid will not protect your camera totally, but it will help.

As soon as possible after returning to camp, open the camera and remove as much water as possible with tissue. Some photographers have in their kits a small bulb syringe for blowing dust off internal parts. This tool also can be used to suck up water from hard to reach places. Caution: don't try to remove any internal mechanisms, and never force mirrors, gears, or other parts in order to reach tight spots. Your camera will need professional help anyway, and you may as well resign yourself to the fact that you can't use it again until it has been completely dismantled and dried, but there's no point in adding a repair bill to the cleaning bill. Set the camera aside to dry with the back open, but frequently manipulate all moving parts such as shutters, lens releases, winders, etc., to prevent them from freezing up after their lubrication has been washed away. Before closing the camera to take it to the shop, put a packet of silica gel dehydrator inside—every little bit helps!

Cleaning a camera is a professional's job, too, but there are things you can do in camp or at home. Dust and grit play havoc with moving parts and lenses, and so should be removed as soon as possible. A bulb syringe is invaluable for gently blowing these away. Lens tissue moistened with lens cleaner and wrapped around the end of a small paintbrush or knitting needle can remove lint, dirt, and smudges from the internal glass surfaces. The paintbrush itself, if kept clean, can be used to remove dust or lint from hard to reach surfaces. Don't tear down the camera completely and keep your hands off the mirrors, gears and shutter release mechanisms inside.

While you have the camera open, note any place where the black finish has been scratched or worn off a metal surface and touch it up with flat black paint. A shiny spot inside a camera, believe it or not, can reflect light onto film, causing mysterious spots and streaks. Pay close attention to the film sprockets and rollers. Foreign material here can scratch or tear film, particularly if the film is cold and brittle.

Canoes

THE PAST DECADE has seen an explosion in outdoor recreation in general and in canoeing in particular. Much of the interest in canoe and kayak sports has been sparked by the development of new materials, chiefly thermoplastics, that make whitewater canoeing economically feasible and safer and flatwater canoeing cheaper and less maintenance-intensive.

Fiberglass, ABS (acrylonitrile/butadiene/styrene), and polyethylene have joined aluminum and canvas-covered wood as commonly used materials for kayaks and canoes, and have nearly eliminated the canvas/wood combination as a serious contender in the marketplace.

Despite their great advantage over aluminum and canvas/wood in strength, cheapness, and freedom from maintenance, space-age canoes and kayaks have their problems, too, and need special care and repair techniques. In fact, though minor repairs can be made in the field, plastic and fiberglass canoes need more intensive care with more exotic materials than their older counterparts. It's a trade-off: you can patch aluminum and canvas/wood canoes easily in the field, but you'll find yourself doing it more often; your plastic or fiberglass canoe, on the other hand, will take the small knocks better, but when it's due for a trip to the shop, it's a serious undertaking.

Since repair and maintenance techniques differ for each type of canoe and kayak, this information is presented in separate entries.* Several topics

---

*The repair and maintenance information in the individual canoe entries apply to modern kayaks made of the same material. Traditional folding kayaks rate their own entry, as do inflatable boats and wooden boats. The information on repairing aluminum and fiberglass canoes is applicable to aluminum and fiberglass boats as well.

—adding flotation, portaging, and storage—applicable to various canoe types are discussed here.

ADDING FLOTATION

Wood/canvas canoes float by themselves, as do ABS laminate canoes. Aluminum, polyethylene, and fiberglass canoes must have foam flotation built in in order to stay off the bottom when capsized.

All canoes used in white water need additional flotation, even naturally buoyant ones. The reason for this is simple: when empty, an ABS canoe may weigh less than 70 pounds on dry land or riding high in the water; *fill* it with water, however, and you've got a 2,000-pound load! Turn that load sideways in a rushing stream, and you've got a projectile that will destroy anything in its path except rocks, which will destroy *it*. For flat-water paddling, the factory-installed flotation is good enough—if you flip the canoe, stay with it, and guide it to shore. In white water, though, additional flotation is a great safety feature, provided you install it properly.

Flotation bags are commercially available for whitewater craft, but they are fairly expensive. Make sure you install them and secure them both underneath the thwarts and to the bottom of the craft, otherwise water coming in over the sides will lift the flotation bag out of the canoe and take its place, and you'll be in the same fix you'd be in without any additional flotation.

A handy way to attach anything to the inside of a polyester, ABS, or fiberglass boat is with rubber "pancakes" with D-rings attached. These can be glued to the inside of a canoe wherever you wish to put them and will stay put. Kits with full instructions are available at many canoe shops. Lash gear or flotation material to them with woven nylon cord.

You can use a truck inner tube as flotation, and an advantage of doing so is that you can pump it up with a hand pump designed for bicycle tires. They're easy to repair, too.

Secure an inner tube—or any flotation material, for that matter—to an aluminum canoe by drilling a series of holes along the gunwales, between the thwarts, and lacing across the boat with nylon cord. Make the holes in pairs one-half inch apart, six inches between pairs, along both sides. Smooth out the holes with a round file to remove burrs, and lace the cord "shoelace" fashion in criss-crossing pattern from side to side. This will hold the inner tube firmly in place.

Another idea for flotation is to use a twin-size waterbed, lashed in with parachute cord as described above, and pumped up with a vacuum cleaner with the flow reversed. This isn't as tough as it sounds, and is actually a very effective flotation system. "Blemished" waterbeds are often available at reduced prices, and they are sturdy and easy to repair. The biggest advantage is that they are wide enough to fit tightly from gunwale to gunwale, and thus act as a barrier to water coming in over the sides.

PORTAGE AND STORAGE

A lot of canoes get beat up on the ground, either during portages or while stored. A few commonsense rules for dry-land activity can help prevent an expensive accident.

It's not wise to beach a canoe, even one that's lightly loaded. The problem is that when you push a canoe onto dry land and then walk up the middle of it to disembark, you place unusual stress on the keel area. Do it often enough and you'll have cracks or worse.

For the same reason, don't get into a beached canoe or load it while it's aground.

Carrying a canoe is an acquired skill that can be easily learned. But don't play hero. If you can't carry the load, don't try. Remember that you can always make another trip.

A carrying yoke is a worthwhile investment, or you can improvise one in the field by lashing two paddles between the center and forward thwart in an inverted "V"—narrow end forward—to allow you to carry the canoe on your shoulders. Carry it as near the center as you can.

Canoes can be carried safely atop cars if you have a secure carrier and follow directions for its use. Remember, a canoe makes a perfect airfoil when carried upside down and will lift, or try to, working its way loose if not properly tied. A canoe flying off your car at highway speeds is no laughing matter. Always tie two ropes from each end of the canoe to your car, improvising a secure attachment point on the bumpers or grill. Check the rig frequently while underway. A few safety lines thrown over the top don't hurt, either.

Winter storage of your canoe requires little but common sense. Keep the canoe out of the way of potential hazards like tree limbs and chimneys. Store it upside down, on two sawhorses, with both ends secured with ropes. Remember, a canoe is an airfoil, and will flip, flop, and fly in the face of a stiff wind.

Overhead storage is good for canoes, too. Rig up eyebolts at each end and hoist the canoe out of harm's way. Any preservative work on wooden parts should be done before storage. Moisture is wood's big enemy, and you want to prevent rot by keeping the wood protected with varnish or oil.

Plastic canoes get brittle when cold. Indeed, extremely cold temperatures make ABS and poly canoes as fragile as glass. Don't handle or transport a plastic canoe when the temperature is below zero.

Canoe Paddles

LIKE CANOES, PADDLES need care. The best way to minimize damage and consequent repairs is to prevent it, and that includes buying the right size paddle. Held vertically, the front paddle should reach from the floor to the paddler's chin; the rear should reach to the paddler's eye level.

A too short or too long paddle not only tires the paddler, it gets knocked against the canoe, rocks, and gunwales a lot more than necessary —and that breaks paddles.

There are many blade shapes available, and materials for paddles include ABS plastic, aluminum (shafts), and polyethylene as well as wood. Solid wood paddles are cheaper than laminated wood paddles, but not as strong and much more prone to warping. Inspect any wooden paddle for splitting edges, visible knots or cracks and opened grain before using.

The handles of wooden paddles should not be varnished, but should be sanded smooth and treated with boiled linseed oil. Renew the treatment from time to time. A broken handle can be repaired for temporary use with a splint of PVC water pipe, split and bolted to the handle or fastened with small wood screws. You should drill the pipe before putting it on the shaft.

Shafts can also be wrapped with twine or wet rawhide to repair a crack or split. In an emergency, splinting will also get you back home.

A lot of canoeists thin the blades of stock wooden paddles to make them enter the water more cleanly. This also makes them vulnerable to splitting. Repair splits with epoxy glue, cyanoacrylic "super" glue, or similar high-tech adhesive. A thin copper edge piece is easy to make and fasten at home, and it will help prevent splits.

A split blade can also be repaired by drilling a series of small holes on each side of the split and lacing wire in a criss-cross fashion over the split. And, of course, duct tape and strapping tape will keep a paddle together, too.

Warped wooden paddles can be straightened by either burying them in moist ground or wrapping them in cotton batting kept moist and placed inside plastic wrapping. Believe it or not, a paddle will straighten itself if kept moist like that.

Never lean a paddle to store it. Hang it up. And keep it away from salt-loving porcupines who will quickly gnaw it to splinters for the salt from your sweaty hand.

Plastic-bladed paddles can be patched, mended, and ground to shape. Refer to the section on patching in the *Plastic Canoes* entry.

Canteens

AN ALUMINUM CANTEEN needs little maintenance beyond an occasional thorough cleaning with soap and water. Be sure to rinse it thoroughly to remove soap film. (The cautionary notes about acid and alkaline substances given in the Cookware section apply to aluminum canteens also.) Because of their design, canteens are hard to clean thoroughly, so it's best not to carry anything but water in your canteen. If you do carry sugary drinks, rinse the canteen very carefully immediately after emptying it.

After rinsing, store the canteen upside down with the cap off to facilitate drying. Rinse out once again before refilling.

Aluminum canteens will develop tiny seep holes, often impossible to locate exactly for patching, from abrasion and banging against hard objects. Keep the canteen's canvas or cloth cover patched—air mattress patches or duct tape will suffice—and protect the canteen from hard knocks. If severely dented or punctured, silicone rubber caulking compound will seal it.

The cork-lined plastic caps on canteens are often the first spot to show wear. Worn threads contribute to leakage and loss of liquid through evaporation. Seal them with plastic electrician's tape. (A piece of string wound around the threads will also seal, but will become unsanitary in time and should be replaced promptly with tape.)

In time, the cork liner will crumble, spoiling the seal and abetting evaporation. A rubber gasket—simply a circle of rubber larger than the diameter of the canteen's mouth—will solve this problem.

As an alternative to traditional canteens, some backpackers use plastic baby bottles to carry liquids. These have several advantages: they will stand up to abuse, can be cleaned easily and thoroughly, and will fit into the side pockets on most packs. Their only disadvantage seems to be the cap. Using a blank insert in place of a nipple gives you a two-piece cap, with the small insert sure to get dirty or lost if handled carelessly. Gluing an insert into the cap can help.

Plastic water bags have recently appeared on the backpacking scene and by all reports serve satisfactorily. Their advantages are lightness and ease of cleaning. Negative features are vulnerability to puncturing and melting if handled carelessly. When empty, water bags should be hung upside down and allowed to drain completely. In cold weather, when the danger of freezing exists, keep the water bag half full rather than completely full; it can then freeze without bursting. The bag shouldn't be completely emptied in freezing weather either because the sides can freeze together. Apply grease or oil—cooking oil is fine—to the spigot in winter to keep it from freezing solid.

Canvas

"CANVAS," AS A generic term, properly means heavy, woven cotton duck fabric. The term has come to mean, however, any of a number of natural and synthetic blends to which any of a number of sealers, water-proofers, and mildew-preventers have been applied.

"Canvas" today may mean 100 percent woven cotton, woven acrylic, woven nylon, woven polyester, vinyl-coated cotton or polyester, vinyl-laminated polyester, or vinyl-coated cotton/poly blends. Naturally, if you don't know what you've got, you won't be able to clean, repair, or store it properly, so the first step is to find out the composition of the fabric, its weave pattern, its coatings (if any), and any special care instructions the manufacturer may suggest.

The following information on care and storage is broken down into the most common categories of blends and coatings, but does not take into account the many applications of those fabrics. For example, a fabric that may be washed with detergent and dried at low heat may be sewn into a garment, cover, or tent also containing fabric or material that may not be washed or dried with heat. Since it is impossible to cover all such situations here, the final word on care of such outdoor gear rests with the manufacturer.

Any attempt to cover all the generic and brand names of outdoor fabrics would soon be dated, as new blends and brand names appear, disappear, and are changed constantly. The following chart, prepared by the Industrial Fabrics Association International, includes the most common fabrics and the chief manufacturers. If you don't know who made the fabric in your gear, write to the manufacturer or ask the vendor who sold it to you. If you're still not sure, try writing the IFAI, 350 Endicott Bldg., St. Paul, MN 55101, for more information.

TREATING AND PREVENTING MILDEW DAMAGE

Mildew is canvas's worst enemy. It will literally devour cotton fabric in a few weeks, and the acids it produces while feeding on organic material (such as leaf particles, food residue) imbedded in synthetic fabrics can destroy them nearly as fast.

"Mildew" can refer to a number of microorganisms. Most are tiny plants—algae, fungi, or molds—but bacteria can also destroy or stain fabrics, and yeasts can, in some cases, grow on fabrics. Whatever the specific type of microorganism involved, prevention depends primarily on proper cleaning and storage of gear, and secondarily on applying the correct chemical agent to the fabric.

Chemicals used for mildew prevention are often extremely volatile, and the amateur is well advised to proceed with caution. Once again, due to the wide variety of fabrics on the market, and the equally wide variety of antimicrobial agents produced and marketed to treat them, it is impossible to provide a thumbnail application guide.

In most cases, the manufacturer of outdoor or marine fabrics has already done the necessary research and testing and has treated the gear during manufacture. If, due to improper cleaning, handling, or storage, the chemical has been removed from the fabric, it is advisable to return the gear to the manufacturer for treatment. The chemicals used to inhibit the growth of microorganisms can also weaken fabric, make it more susceptible to degradation from exposure to sunlight, lower its water repellency, or discolor it, so the amateur can do more harm than good as often as not.

One treatment that is relatively safe and effective against many fungi is to mix a fungicide designed for use in wall paint with a silicone sealant for waterproofing cotton canvas. Such fungicides are available from paint and hardware stores, and should be used in the proportion specified by the maker.

"Clean and dry" are the watchwords for mildew prevention, whatever the chemical treatment used. Since fungi and yeasts need moisture and darkness to grow, keeping your gear dry is essential. Of course, it's not always possible to dry canvas thoroughly before packing, and that's why mildew inhibitors were devised. If you must pack damp gear, try to unpack and dry it as soon as possible—even a few additional minutes of drying time can help.

If a tent, tarp, or awning gets wet, it should be wiped off even if it's not going to be packed. Removing most of the surface moisture will aid in

CARE OF FABRICS USED IN OUTDOOR GEAR

Materials/Components	Brush	Water	Soap	Detergent	Bleach	Vinyl Cleaners	Clean on Frame	Clean off Frame	Rolled for Storage	Folded for Storage
Acrylics—Woven										
Boatcrylic Astrup Company Cleveland, OH	x	x	x	no	no	no	x	x	x	x
Sunbrella Glen Raven Mills, Inc. Glen Raven, NC	x	x	x	no	x	no	x	x	x	x
100% Cottons										
(Army, number & marine treated ducks)										
Boatex A Astrup Company Cleveland, OH	x	no	no	no	no	no	no	x	x	x
Boatex Boat Shrunk Astrup Company Cleveland, OH	x	no	no	no	no	no	no	x	x	x
Fashion Fabrics John Boyle Company N.Y., NY	x	x	no	no	no	no	x	x	x	x

Materials/Components	Brush	Water	Soap	Detergent	Bleach	Vinyl Cleaners	Clean on Frame	Clean off Frame	Rolled for Storage	Folded for Storage
100% Cottons										
Indantone John Boyle Co. N.Y., NY	x	x	no	no	no	no	x	x	x	x
Otis Permasol Glen Raven Mills, Inc. Glen Raven, NC	no	x	x	no	no	no	x	x	x	x
Vivatex Astrup Co. Cleveland, OH M.F. & H. Textiles Columbus, GA	x	no	no	no	no	no	no	x	x	x
Weathermate John Boyle Company N.Y., NY	x	x	no	no	no	no	x	x	x	x
Nylons—Woven										
Cordura Nylon Astrup Company Cleveland, OH	no	x	no	no	no	no	x	x	x	x

Materials/Components	Brush	Water	Soap	Detergent	Bleach	Vinyl Cleaners	Clean on Frame	Clean off Frame	Rolled for Storage	Folded for Storage
Nylons—Woven										
Enduro Nylon John Boyle Company N.Y., NY	no	x	no	no	no	no	x	x	x	x
Nylon Sailcloth Astrup Cleveland, OH	no	x	no	no	no	no	no	x	x	no
Polyesters—Woven										
Dacron Sailcloth Astrup Co. Cleveland, OH	no	x	no	no	no	no	no	x	x	no
Destiny 2 + 2 American Waterproofing St. Louis, MO	x	x	x	no	no	no	x	x	x	x
Vinyl-coated Cottons										
Viking II Astrup Co. Cleveland, OH	x	x	x	no	no	x	x	x	x	no

Materials/Components	Brush	Water	Soap	Detergent	Bleach	Vinyl Cleaners	Clean on Frame	Clean off Frame	Rolled for Storage	Folded for Storage
Vinyl-coated Polyesters										
Mariner III Astrup Co. Cleveland, OH	x	x	x	no	no	x	x	x	x	no
Merrimac Astrup Co. Cleveland, OH	x	x	x	no	no	x	x	x	x	no
Surf Mate John Boyle Co. N.Y., NY	x	x	x	x	no	x	x	x	x	x
Vinyl-coated Poly/Cottons										
Boat Topping Bruin Plastic Allendale, RI	x	x	x	no	no	x	x	x	x	no
Navatex Astrup Co. Cleveland, OH	x	x	x	no	no	x	x	x	x	no

Materials/Components	Brush	Water	Soap	Detergent	Bleach	Vinyl Cleaners	Clean on Frame	Clean off Frame	Rolled for Storage	Folded for Storage
Vinyl-coated Poly/Cottons										
Super Top Astrup Cleveland, OH	x	x	x	no	no	x	x	x	x	no
Vinyl-laminated Polyesters										
Aqua-Tex Herculite Protective Fabrics Corp. N.Y., NY	x	x	x	no		x	x	x	x	no
Brun-Tuff Boat Top Bruin Plastics Glendale, RI	x	x	x	x	no	x	x	x	x	no
Dura-Marine Duracote Corp. Ravenna, OH	x	x	x	x(mild)	no	x*	x	x	x	x
Marine Topping Sun Chemical Paterson, NJ	x	x	x	no	no	x	x	x	x	x

Vinyl-laminated Polyesters

Materials/Components	Brush	Water	Soap	Detergent	Bleach	Vinyl Cleaners	Clean on Frame	Clean off Frame	Rolled for Storage	Folded for Storage
ProTec John Boyle Company N.Y., NY	x	x	x	x	no	x	x	x	x	x
Weblon Weblon, Inc. Elmsford, NY	x	x	x	no**	X	no	x	x	x	x

Miscellaneous

Materials/Components	Brush	Water	Soap	Detergent	Bleach	Vinyl Cleaners	Clean on Frame	Clean off Frame	Rolled for Storage	Folded for Storage
Polypropylene Netting Chicopee Mfg. Co. Cornelia, GA	x	x	x							
Scotch-Mate Fasteners 3M St. Paul, MN	no	x	x	no	no					cool iron
Vinyl Netting Chicopee Mfg. Co. Cornelia, GA	x	x	x							

X—may be used   no—against manufacturers suggestions

* Kelite solution recommended for vinyls.

** Fantastic/Mr. Clean type cleaner recommended. Abrasives of any type strongly discouraged.

the evaporation of water from the tiny spaces between the filaments. Wipe gently with a chamois or sponge, but do not brush or scrub vigorously because the abrasion can break down coatings and introduce moisture into previously protected fabric.

Cotton and cotton/poly blends can be dried in the sunlight, but some coatings used on them are ultraviolet sensitive. Again, the manufacturer will warn if this is the case. In general, keep synthetic fabrics from prolonged exposure to direct sunlight while drying. Dry canvas by hanging it in a cool, dry environment. Store it in a similar place, taking care that it is not exposed to excessive humidity.

The chart on fabric care should help you keep your gear clean, which is nearly as important as keeping it dry. Dust, grease, food particles, and animal and bird wastes can all provide an excellent medium for growth of microorganisms, or introduce the microorganisms themselves. Some outdoorsfolks think keeping clean is somehow against the spirit of the backwoods, or perhaps they're harboring secret soap-and-water phobias from childhood. Either way, they're not doing themselves or their gear a favor. To give them the benefit of the doubt, perhaps the plethora of new fabrics and coatings has intimidated them into paralysis, but the bottom line is that most deterioration of outdoors fabrics is due to simple lack of proper cleaning discipline.

Even in the outback, it should be a minor chore to rinse off dust and grime from a standing tent, tarp, or backpack. So simple a preventive measure will pay dividends in longevity, provided, of course, that the fabric is dried thoroughly.

Although brushing can harm waterproofing, gentle vacuuming won't. If your tent or tarp has become dirty in the field, pack it loosely and as soon as possible vacuum it, then rinse it off.

Fabrics that show mildew growth can be treated, but by the time you notice the characteristic black or grey patches (fungi that grow on vinyl produce a permanent pink stain), the damage has been done and you will never remove the visible evidence. You can, of course, prevent further damage.

A dilute solution of vinegar—about 1 cup to 1 gallon of water—will remove many kinds of mildew microorganisms from nylon fabrics. (Mildew doesn't feed on nylon itself, but it does grow on the dirt particles imbedded in the fabric, producing acids that eat away the fibers.) This solution must be rinsed out thoroughly, however, since it, too, is acidic and will degrade nylon. A weak alkaline solution of lime (garden-variety "hydrated" is best) in water is also effective in stopping many fungi. Mix no more than ½ cup to 1 gallon of water; rinse thoroughly.

These preparations are effective on cotton as well, as is a dilute solution of oxygen—not chlorine—bleach. A word of caution: never bleach treated cotton. If you have a piece of untreated heavy cotton duck that has become mildewed, it can be washed and bleached, rinsed thoroughly, then treated.

PATCHING AND SEWING

Patching canvas is no more difficult than patching a pair of denim bluejeans, except that you need to consider the use to which the canvas will be put. If it will be stretched or subjected to continuous stress from pulling, or if it must be waterproof, a casually sewn patch will do more harm than good.

Iron-on patches, by the way, don't work very well. For one thing, they tend to roll up at the corners unless stitched down; for another, the adhesives they contain are nearly impossible to remove from woven cotton. If you're contemplating using an iron-on patch as a temporary patch, therefore, don't do it. Too, the heat needed to bond an iron-on patch to the fabric can weaken threads and destroy waterproofing.

If you need to make an emergency repair to a piece of canvas, a piece of duct or electrician's tape is better than an iron-on patch.

Give some thought to the area you intend to patch. If the damage is near a seam, cut a patch large enough to extend to the seam. You'll be able to stitch through the same holes, making waterproofing and seam sealing easier and more effective. If the seam is a flat or lapped seam, you may want to rip it out and incorporate the patch and fabric in one resewn seam, further increasing the strength of the patch.

If you're patching a "triangle" tear—a common type of injury to tarps and tents—tack the ends of each leg of the tear with several stitches at right angles to the direction of the tear before sewing on the patch. If possible, tack the point, too. This will make it much easier to sew through the fabric and patch once the patch has been stitched in place.

If you're patching a worn-through spot, trim the hole into a square or rectangular shape, making sure you remove all frayed material. This will make sewing the fabric to the patch easier, as it is much more difficult to sew around a circle than around a square.

A heavy cotton/poly or linen thread will do a good job on canvas, particularly so if it is waxed with paraffin or beeswax to facilitate stitching and repel water. Nylon monofilament fishing line can also be used and will do a fair job on nylon, but it tends to be difficult to sew due to its springiness and propensity for kinking and twisting. It will deteriorate with exposure to ultraviolet light, too.

The key to good sewing is to have a needle long and strong enough to penetrate the layers of fabric easily. An upholstery needle is ideal, as is a leather-working "glover's" needle with a three-sided tip. The squared edges of such a needle will open up the fabric, making sewing through several layers much easier. A slotted "key" from a sardine or coffee can can be made into a heavy-duty needle. Straighten the key and sharpen the end opposite the slot.

Backstitching—also called loopstitching—is the preferred method of sewing canvas, particularly when sewing patches onto a flat surface. The reason for this is simple: when sewing any stiff fabric, straight stitching tends to wrinkle the fabric, leaving gaps where water may infiltrate (or dirt accumulate, making an ideal place for mildew to grow).

Some canvas repair guides advise you to double-stitch, with two needles, as is often done on heavy leather. This method involves making two lines of straight stitching, one beginning from one side of the fabric, one from the other, with each stitch filling the space left by the opposite stitch. This is quick and effective and may be used for secure but temporary patching, where you intend to remove the seam in the near future, perhaps for more permanent repair. Straight stitching is easy to remove by cutting and pulling the thread through the material.

Backstitching's big advantage is that each stitch is locked into place, so that you can't lose a whole seam by cutting one stitch. Each stitch is independent of its neighbors. The only disadvantage of backstitching is that you tend to open up larger holes in the fabric, making waterproofing more difficult. This is a minor problem, however, when weighed against the advantages of strength and security backstitching provides.

To backstitch, mark the seam you intend to sew and, if you're an inexperienced tailor, mark gradations along the line about ⅛-inch apart. Knot the thread and pass the needle through mark number one from the top to the bottom fabric, pulling the entire length of thread through so the knot stops it. Then pass the needle through the second mark from below, again drawing the entire length of thread through. Complete the first stitch by pushing the needle down through hole number one again, *taking care not to cut through the thread already in place.* Pull the thread through the hole and go on to hole number three, again sewing through it from below and returning to pass through hole number two from above.

This is the sequence you'll follow until the seam is completed. At corners, double-stitch by reversing the sequence to change direction; that

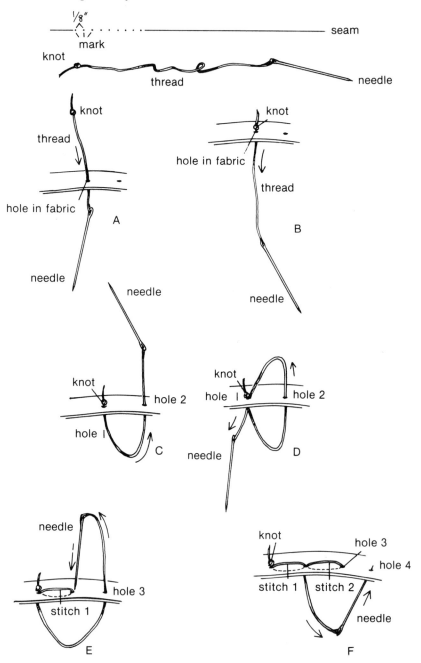

Protect against torn seams by backstitching.

is, instead of stitching across the corner from the next-to-last hole of one course to the first hole of the second, pass the needle through the corner hole from below a second time, then *down* through the first hole in the new direction, up through the corner hole, and down once more through the next hole. This technique will prevent a long cross-corner loop which can easily be snagged and pulled loose. It will also make a very strong corner.

End a row of backstitching the same way: repeat a stitch, then loop the thread underneath the last stitch and pull it tight. Clip the thread off close to the stitch and secure it with a dab of glue or silicone sealant if you prefer (especially if the seam is subject to stress), but this shouldn't be necessary if you've sewn carefully. The backstitching should last a long time.

REPAIRING GROMMETS

A torn-out or smashed grommet is a common problem. If you notice the fabric around a grommet beginning to fray or tear, you can make a temporary repair with household glue or tape to slow the damage, or you can tack across the tear with thread. These are at best delaying actions, however, and you'll eventually need to make a more permanent repair. The more damage you allow to happen, the more difficult it will be to repair it.

Grommet kits are available at hardware and marine supply stores. If you've never used one, practice on a piece of scrap canvas until you get the hang of it. Getting a grommet on wrong means you'll have to cut it out of the fabric, possibly making more drastic repairs necessary.

If possible, relocate the new grommet to stronger area. If not, patch the worn area as described above, then put the new grommet through both patch and fabric.

For nylon and other synthetic fabrics, see the nylon section.

PREVENTING DAMAGE

Although most repairs aren't difficult, prevention is still the best approach. Protect tents and tarps from contact with abrasive surfaces. Use wooden blocks underneath cot and stool legs. Pad sharp corners of items to be covered by tarps with rags or cardboard. Don't let canvas tarps or tents flap in the breeze. Never pin anything to a tarp or tent that's been waterproofed, and never touch the inside of a canvas tent that's wet on the outside. Allowing moisture to penetrate the fabric will weaken it and foster mildew growth.

Chambray and Corduroy

COTTON IS A perennial favorite. No matter what synthetic fabrics appear on the market, cotton clothing sells—and with good reason: cotton is comfortable, durable, attractive, and easy to clean. As an inner layer under wool or down, it wicks moisture away from your body; woven into mesh, it traps warmth against your body. Winter or summer, cotton is comfortable.

Two of the most popular weaves are chambray and corduroy: "work shirt and cords" is a good-looking, durable combination for work or play.

Chambray is a woven fabric having a colored "warp" and a white "woof," giving the characteristic faded appearance. Like canvas, which is a similar weave using heavier threads, chambray is extremely tear resistant and stretchable. It will give rather than tear, and maintain its structural integrity even when severely worn. Like denim, which is a bias-woven cloth, chambray holds patches well and resists fraying.

Corduroy, from the French *corde du roi,* "King's cord," is an even more durable fabric, which is why it's used for children's clothing.

Many modern chambrays and corduroys are blended with synthetics to decrease the need for ironing and resist stretching, sagging, etc. The most frequent blend is 65 percent cotton, 35 percent polyester or Dacron. Although rare, 100 percent cotton is worth looking for, as it can be bleached and washed in extremely hot—even boiling—water without damage.

Cottons and cotton blends are also treated with mildew- and stain-resistant chemicals, waterproofing, and a variety of dyes. Before washing any cotton article, find out its composition.

WASHING

Untreated 100 percent cotton clothing should be washed in hot water with heavy-duty laundry detergent. If the water is hard, a softener will aid cleaning, as will a small amount of baking soda added to the wash cycle. Most dyes used on cotton are able to withstand extremely high temperatures, and you should use water as hot as possible. If in doubt about the color-fastness, squeeze an inconspicuous corner of the article in a bowl of hot water for a few minutes. If the dye runs, use lukewarm or cool water for washing and cool water for rinsing.

You can use chlorine bleach on white cottons and oxygen bleaches on colors, but be careful about bleaching blends and finished cottons. Starching gives cotton clothing a neat appearance and helps "seal" the weave, making it more dirt-resistant. Starched cotton clothing is less absorbent, however.

Stains on cotton clothing should be treated before washing, and severely soiled garments should be soaked for 10 to 20 minutes in warm, soapy water. Work suds into the neckband and cuffs of severely soiled workshirts, or use one of the many pre-wash treatments on the market. Some of the most common stains and the preferred treatments for them are discussed below.

Corduroy that has been severely soiled should be soaked in lukewarm soapy water. Bad spots can be brushed with a soft brush, then rinsed before washing.

Chambray can be dried in open air or tumble-dried at high heat. Avoid over-drying. When the garment feels a bit damp, remove it from the dryer and let it hang to finish drying. Corduroy should be removed when still quite wet and hung to dry, otherwise it will wrinkle badly and, since it shouldn't be ironed, will be unsightly. Corduroy garments should be hung out when quite wet.

When completely dry, chambray should be ironed to improve its appearance and help seal the fabric against soil. Corduroy should never be ironed, but should be brushed with a soft brush in the direction of the wale when completely dry.

REMOVING STAINS

Common stains such as grass and foliage, blood, grease and oil, and rust are fairly easy to remove from cotton, but leather, tar, paint, glue, and resin stains are tricky. Always test stain removers on an inconspicuous section of the garment first.

Grass Stains. Grass and foliage stains will yield to alcohol. Use common rubbing alcohol with a cotton swab or pad, working from the center of the stain outward. Rinse and follow with regular washing. If the stain persists, repeat the alcohol treatment, then rinse and follow immediately with a strong detergent solution. Brush it in, let it soak, and rinse. Still tougher stains will yield to chlorine bleach used full strength, or hydrogen peroxide, though both these will probably affect the color. Always try the alcohol treatment first.

Bloodstains. Treat bloodstains when they are fresh if possible. Soak the garment in cold water, rubbing it gently together, until the stain is almost gone, then wash in warm, soapy water. A few drops of ammonia will help loosen old bloodstains; follow with a normal washing. If blood has stained thick corduroy and is still wet, apply an absorbent like cornstarch or corn meal to soak it up. Do not rub it. Absorbent materials should be sprinkled on and left to do their job, then brushed softly to remove most of the liquid. Follow with alcohol and washing.

Oil and Grease Stains. Petroleum stains call for a solvent if dried, but can be minimized by soaking up the goo with corn meal while wet. Grimy grease stains, such as you may get from working on an engine, are hard to remove unless you rub them first with lard or Vaseline. Waterless hand cleaners also will break down grimy stains. Road tar and asphalt are much tougher to remove. Scrape as much off as you can, and treat with a solvent, followed by washing. Turpentine can help. Follow all solvent treatments with washing in lukewarm water.

Animal and vegetable oils respond well to pre-soaks or direct application of laundry detergent. Wash in lukewarm water.

Rust stains. Lemon juice will remove rust stains. Moisten the stain with water, squeeze lemon juice directly onto it, and hold it in the steam above a boiling pot for a few minutes. Rinse with lukewarm water and repeat if necessary. Rust stains also can be treated with salt and lemon juice— sprinkle salt on the stain, squeeze lemon juice into it, and let it sit in the sun until dry. Rinse and wash as usual. Another rust stain treatment is to boil the stained garment in a cream of tartar solution. Use about a quarter cup of cream of tartar to each half gallon of water. Boil and rinse repeatedly.

Paint and Varnish Stains. If still wet, paint and varnish stains can be removed by washing with detergent in warm water. If the stain has dried, you must use a solvent: try turpentine on oil-based paints, thinner on varnish, acetone on lacquer, and alcohol on shellac. The difficulty in removing these stains is proportionate to the length of time the stain has had to dry. Well-set stains may need to be treated for an hour or more with a pad soaked in the solvent—use a plain cotton washcloth or towel. Wash afterward.

Glue and Resin Stains. The variety of glues and resins is so great that it is nearly impossible to generalize about their stains. Removing any chemical from fabric while still wet is recommended, either by scraping or using an absorbent material. Many commercially-available resins, such as those used on thermoplastics or fiberglass, will yield to solvents such as alcohol, turpentine, or cleaning fluid, but you should test first on scrap material or an inconspicuous part of the garment.

Coffee, Soot, and Leather Stains. Coffee stains can be removed from cotton by prompt sponging with cool water, followed by a half-hour soak in cool water, followed by washing in cold water. Or you can remove set coffee stains by stretching the material over a pan or bowl and pouring boiling water through the stain, then washing in lukewarm water. If cream has been added to the coffee, rub liquid detergent into the fresh stain and launder; if the cream-and-coffee stain has set, soak in warm, soapy water before laundering.

Soot stains yield to soaking in warm water with detergent added. If you've rubbed the stain in, apply liquid detergent directly, let it soak in warm water for a half-hour, then launder.

Stains caused by leather rubbing against cotton are tough. Try repeated scrubbings with detergent, followed by regular washing. Persistent spots will yield to hydrogen peroxide.

PATCHING

Cotton and chambray are easy to patch with needle and thread (see section on sewing and patching in *Canvas* entry). Iron-on patches stick to chambray better than to denim (but not at all to corduroy). Don't use masking, adhesive, or duct tape to close a tear, even temporarily. The adhesives are extremely hard to remove once they've set.

Chamois

ORIGINALLY "CHAMOIS" MEANT the skin of a small goatlike antelope that inhabited the mountains of central Europe and the Balkans. Overhunting made the chamois nearly extinct, and, since the beginning of this century, "chamois" has been used to mean a specially treated split sheepskin.

Genuine chamois—from the antelope—was prized for its unique qualities of water absorption and retention and its softness, which made it ideal for polishing precious metals and for sewing into garments. Modern chamois is equally as valuable for polishing and cleaning.

Sheepskin chamois can absorb and retain up to seven times its own weight in liquid, and so is valued for drying boats, vehicles, etc. It retains its water-holding qualities even when wet, and is completely lintless, making it ideal for this purpose. Chamois is particularly suited for use on guns, cameras, binoculars, etc., when used under humid conditions. Instrument cases can be lined with chamois, as can outerwear. It can also be used to filter water out of gasoline.

Before using a new chamois for drying or wiping wet surfaces, rinse it thoroughly in lukewarm water to remove excess tanning oils. A chamois used for drying and wiping wet surfaces should be washed after each use to restore its suppleness and preserve its absorbent qualities. Dry use requires less frequent washing, but if the chamois is soiled, it should be washed thoroughly.

Wash chamois in tepid (less than 95° F) water to which a mild soap has been added. Do not use detergents, saddle soap, leather cleaners, alcohol, lye, gasoline, or other solvents on chamois. Work suds through the leather by squeezing and swishing the leather through the sudsy water, then let soak for several minutes. Do not rinse the soapy water out of the leather. Rather, wring as much liquid out of the chamois as possible by twisting it by hand, then stretch and smooth it gently to remove the wrinkles and creases the wringing has caused. Hang the chamois to dry away from all sources of heat, including direct sunlight. When the chamois has dried thoroughly, fold it and rub it against itself to restore suppleness.

Chamois should never be left wet in a bucket, bag, or other closed container, and it should never be used with extremely hot water.

A chamois that has been left sitting in water or hasn't been dried properly will become stiff and nonabsorbent. You can soften it and restore its water-holding quality by adding a half cup of cooking oil to a quart of soapy water, working the mixture into the leather, and wringing it out without rinsing. Dry as described above. The chamois should soften and remain pliable.

Compasses

THERE ISN'T MUCH you can do to a compass, other than smashing it or subjecting it to an electromagnetic field, which will ruin its ability to indicate north. Keep compasses away from iron and steel objects, other compasses, magnets of any kind, electrical motors or generators, radios (transceivers as well), and television sets. Standard compasses, by the way, usually aren't waterproof, so take the same precautions with them as you would with any precision instrument in wet weather or when boating.

Cookstoves

COOKING IN THE outdoors can be as simple or as complicated as you want to make it. With ever-increasing numbers of backpackers, hunters, campers, and canoe voyageurs hitting the bush, firewood supplies are becoming severely depleted in some areas. Most responsible outdoorsfolks, therefore, make provisions for packing their wilderness kitchen—and that's when outdoor cooking becomes complicated.

Stoves for use in the outdoors range from 35-pound sheepherder's woodstoves, through bulky but efficient propane, butane, and gasoline campstoves, to featherweight backpacker's one-burners using several different kinds of fuel. As with all outdoor gear, each type of stove has its advantages and disadvantages, and you're advised to try out different models before buying, if you can.

Many people buy more technology than they need. If you're just going for a weekend in the park, you don't need a rock climber's mini-stove capable of cooking while hung from a rope sling in a howling blizzard. If you're carrying everything on your back, you don't need a two-burner propane campstove with oven. Remember, you always pay a penalty for lightness and portability in ease of operation, durability, and cost. Some would add safety to that list.

The plethora of lightweight stove systems has crowded one old favorite out of many people's consciousness. Sterno, which is a trademark rapidly becoming a generic term, is jellied alcohol. There are several stove systems made to use it, or you can easily rig your own. Alcohol has three big advantages over all other outdoor fuels: it is very easy to light, it can be put out with water, and it will not explode. Alcohol stoves have disadvantages, too; the biggest is lack of control. It's either burning or not; no adjustments possible. There are more sophisticated alcohol stoves available that are adjustable, however.

Considering the price of fossil fuels, their volatility and noxious odor, their poisonous by-products, and their ability to damage if not dissolve many fabrics used in modern outdoor gear, alcohol stoves rate a second glance.

Another ignored fuel is due for a come back. Charcoal, favorite of steak-searing suburbanities, has a place in the outdoors. Modern briquets, impregnated with chemicals that allow you to ignite them with a match, are a concentrated, hot, safe fuel in a convenient size and form. The advantages should be obvious: they're dry; they don't spill, vaporize, or destroy sealed containers; their dangerous by-products are few; and they are extremely versatile.

You can use self-starting briquets as fire starters, put them in any metal container and have a viable stove, or build a whole system around them with ovens, broilers, etc. You can light one to brew a cup of coffee or light a dozen to barbecue a steak. Best of all, when you burn them, that's it—no empty container to pack out, no refilling, no waste. Charcoal is a little slow, but who's in a hurry?

Look for sophisticated charcoal backpacking stoves on the market in the future, but meanwhile, if you've bought into a high-tech liquid or vapor fuel stove—or are about to—read on.

For the purposes of this section, we'll call gasoline and kerosene "liquid" fuel and propane and butane "vapor" fuel. Of course, both kinds are stored and carried as liquid, vaporizing just before ignition, but the difference in their storage systems and basic performance puts them in different categories.

Before getting into the various kinds of stoves and their use and care, heed this cautionary note: carbon monoxide kills, and all stoves produce it. Never operate a stove that is burning poorly; a yellow flame indicates incomplete combustion and consequent high levels of carbon monoxide. Never use a stove in a completely closed space, such as a tent. If your choice is cooking in a sealed tent or other shelter or going hungry, go hungry. Of course, the choice is seldom so limited. You can ventilate a tent while cooking and seal it later, and should. Carbon monoxide is extremely insidious: you can't smell it, see it, or recognize symptoms of poisoning until too late. If you feel suddenly drowsy, if your cigarette lighter won't work, of if you suddenly can't seem to perform simple tasks, you're possibly suffering from carbon monoxide poisoning or at least oxygen deprivation. Get air, fast.

GASOLINE AND KEROSENE STOVES

The principle of operation is the same for all liquid-fuel stoves. White gas or stove fuel is stored in a tank that is pressurized with a hand pump. The fuel is forced through a small tube to the burner, where it passes through a jet similar to those found in automobile carburetors. The fine spray of fuel mixes with air as it leaves the jet and vaporizes at the instant it's ignited, producing a very hot flame.

Large stoves usually have ported burners, which allow the air and fuel to mix in a protected space away from wind and contact with the cooking utensil. Smaller stoves may have plate burners, which mix the fuel and air in a relatively open space just below the platform (plate) where the utensil rests. Plate burners are superior for quick heating with a little fuel, which is one reason they're used so often on lightweight backpacking stoves. Ported burners are somewhat less efficient, but provide excellent simmer control. On larger stoves, ported burners make *cordon bleu* cooking possible; plate burners, on the other hand, are great for quick snow melting under adverse conditions.

Fuel Selection. Make sure you use the right fuel. Makers of sophisticated backpacking systems often provide two jets, one for gasoline, one for kerosene. There is a big difference between the two fuels in molecular structure, ignition temperature, and burning characteristics, and you must have the right jet for the fuel—or, put another way, you must buy the right fuel for your stove. Kerosene jets are smaller. You can use kerosene in a stove equipped with gasoline jets if you can cut down the pressure or supply of fuel to the burner. You can't use gas in a stove with kerosene jets; trying to will prove frustrating, as the weak, sputtering flame struggles to live.

Actually, "kerosene" and "gasoline" are rather vague terms. There are several different grades of kerosene, ranging from diesel fuel to odorless lamp fuel. Most stoves will do fine on the better grades of fuel—"white" kerosene, for instance—and there's no need to pay the premium price for odorless fuel. Diesel fuel and the cruder grades of yellow kerosene are more touchy. You should avoid diesel fuel at all costs. Your penalty for using cruder grades of kerosene is increased fouling and consequent more-frequent cleaning. There's no significant difference in heating capability among the various grades.

Gasoline is another generic term that bears a closer look. Time was, campstoves were designed to burn "white" (unleaded) gasoline, which was also available for model airplanes, lawn mowers, and the like. Nowadays, "unleaded" and "premium unleaded" fuels are standard for automotive use, and white gas is a thing of the past.

Stoves vary in their ability to use automotive unleaded gas. Some larger, less sensitive stoves can handle the anti-knock compounds and detergents in unleaded gas with little difficulty beyond increased cleaning requirements. Smaller, high-tech backpacking stoves usually won't do well on automotive gasoline, and the manufacturers recommend against it. Your chief problem, then, in choosing fuel is to match the gas to the stove, and here you must follow the manufacturer's recommendations or risk failure.

The Coleman company makes stove and lantern fuel specially blended with naphtha, which they claim is cleaner burning than white gas. You pay a premium price for it, if you can find it, and should weigh the benefits against the liabilities.

Starting and Operating. Whatever fuel you use in liquid-fuel stoves, avoid overfilling the tank. This is much more serious for the small stoves, since they need a precise amount of air in the tank to maintain pressure and properly vaporize the fuel. Stove manufacturers design filler tubes to make it difficult to overfill, but you can still do so by tilting the stove. Don't. You'll have a leaking stove, as the air pressure forces fuel through the cap seal, or else you'll have a stove that works for a few minutes, then quits as the air pressure drops. One outfitter of our acquaintance says 90 percent of the stove problems he has encountered resulted from overfilling.

Stoves with separate bottle-and-pump systems are less likely to be overfilled, but more likely to need replacement of the seals and gaskets because there are more of them. More on maintenance below.

Another reason to take care with fuel levels is priming. Most small stoves have small tanks that cannot hold enough air to produce sufficient vapor to ignite. Therefore, they have some sort of priming system—often an open cup which must be filled with fuel and lit, producing heat which warms the tube sufficiently to allow vaporization of the fuel coming from the tank. Priming is the most dangerous procedure you'll perform, and particularly so if your gas/air levels are wrong. Priming a cold stove takes practice, and you're wise to practice at home in an open area. Fumbling with numb fingers in a closed tent in semi-darkness invites trouble.

Using too much fuel in the priming cup will cause a flare-up and rapid burnout—dangerous and ineffective. Priming a stove that's hot, but not hot enough to vaporize its fuel, will also cause flare-ups. Let it cool down before restarting.

Increase the safety margin by using solid or paste fire starters instead of pouring liquid fuel into the cup.

Kerosene is notoriously hard to ignite—particularly the cruder grades —so many kerosene stove owners have learned to pack along a small amount of gas for priming.

Once burning, you need to monitor a liquid-fuel stove constantly, particularly the little ones. Either too hot or too cold is no good. A too hot stove is prone to flare-ups, which are dangerous. And these stoves get *hot:* temperatures *inside* the fuel tank can exceed 150°, playing havoc with vaporization, not to mention posing the threat of melting whatever you set the tank on.

Using a windscreen can increase temperatures and thus affect vaporization and combustion. If you find your stove running too hot, impossible to turn down or adjust, remove the windscreen. Find a sheltered place to set up without the screen.

Another thing about screens: If you're using them in snow, clear as much snow away as you can, or set up on a rock or platform. If you allow the screen to sink onto the snow, as it will, the air intake vents at the bottom will be covered, and the stove will starve for air as well as overheat, a dangerous combination that results in flare-ups, leaking, and possible disaster.

As you get to know your stove, you'll find that there's a delay in response between changing the valve setting and a change in the flame level. Adjust the valve carefully and wait for the stove to respond. You don't want to kill the flame under a half-cooked meal and then have to deal with a hot stove that must be re-lit. Nor do you want to open a stove too far and have a flame-thrower in your tent.

Some stoves are equipped with flint "sparker" lighting systems, and these have generally proven satisfactory in performance and safer than fumbling with matches. The only problem comes, again, in re-lighting a hot stove. The flint will not ignite the vapor, so you have two bad choices: use a match or refill the priming cup. If you plan ahead, practice at home, and learn how to cook, you can avoid this hazardous situation.

With some stoves you must warm the fuel tank between your hands before lighting. At extremely low temperatures, this can be a problem— both for your hands and the stove. Some dedicated liquid fuel users take their fuel bottles to bed with them. Never under any circumstances, apply a flame to a fuel tank, fittings, hoses, etc., in an attempt to vaporize cold fuel.

Cooking on a little backpacking stove is an exercise in balance. Manufacturers of "stove systems" often have designed the pots and pans to fit their stoves, and you're wise to stick with the factory equipment. Too large a pan placed on a plate-type burner will screw up the air/fuel mixture and result in incomplete combustion. Keep a lid on whatever you use to cook, and check for sputtering yellow flames which indicate smothering.

Care and Cleaning. Maintenance requirements are fairly high for liquid-fuel stoves, since the fuel tends to leave deposits on jets and will work on seal, tube, and gasket material. Cleaning metal parts—jets, primarily— is easy. You can poke a wire or jet-cleaning tool through to remove deposits, then heat the part with a match or candle flame and drop it into water to remove film and stubborn gunk.

At the other end of the system, inside the fuel tank, there is a pickup tube and some sort of filter-and-screen arrangement that will become clogged with fuel deposits. This can be cleaned by dropping it in hot water.

The air pump assembly usually has a leather plunger, tube, and one-way check valve to prevent pressurized fuel from entering the pump assembly. The leather plunger will dry out, resulting in air leakage and failure to pressurize. All that's needed is a drop or two of oil to soften the leather and make it fit the tube tightly.

The check valve often has a spring which can break. It isn't too difficult to replace this spring, but some stove manufacturers have made it difficult to remove the entire assembly. If you're not sure, don't try to remove the check valve assembly.

That goes double for rubber O-rings inside the tank. For some reason, manufactures make it difficult to remove and replace these tiny seals. O-rings at the fuel tube outlet, control valve, and filler opening are usually easier to replace. As always, consult and follow the manufacturers instructions.

Because of the "slipper" nature of liquid fuel, you must take care not to damage any metal fittings, including the filler neck. This is essential, particularly when you are replacing seals, filling the tank, etc. Before installing rings, seals, or other parts cover the threads with electrician's tape to protect them.

Large campstoves are less sensitive, but should be dismantled and cleaned at least once a year. Older stoves have cork filler cap gaskets, which must be replaced from time to time, and their leather pump seals will need re-oiling at least once a year. (You can, by the way, jury-rig a leather pump seal from a leather shoe tongue.) Stiff knobs on campstoves respond to a drop of oil, fat, or grease.

Storing liquid-fuel stoves requires removing all the fuel you can. Empty the tank and light the stove to burn off the remaining fuel. Storing fuel in the tank over the winter is bad business. The fuel will evaporate, leaving deposits in the fuel lines; and condensation can form, contaminating the fuel that's left. Never leave a tank pressurized for any length of time.

PROPANE AND BUTANE STOVES

Vapor fuels, butane and propane, have several positive and a few negative characteristics, insofar as outdoor use is concerned. On the positive side, they are very efficient, hot-burning fuels, which carry their own oxygen and thus do not deplete the environmental oxygen supply. Neither butane or propane is poisonous. They are, when packaged and handled properly, at least as safe as kerosene and probably safer than gasoline.

Their negative features include weight. These fuels are kept in liquid form in pressurized containers because they will vaporize at atmospheric pressure, hence the containers must be thick (and therefore heavy) enough to withstand high pressure. (Propane, by the way, must be kept under higher pressure than butane, hence propane tanks are heavier.)

Cost is another negative. Containers for small stoves cannot be refilled, so you waste a container (which you pay for) every time you empty one. You also have to pack it out, an annoyance. Refillable tanks used with large stoves make the cost factor negligible; in fact, vapor fuels are cheaper, BTU for BTU, than liquid fuels.

Starting and Operating. Vapor fuels are easy to start—no priming necessary—and they provide excellent variability, since the tank pressure is constant and all you do to adjust the flame is open or close one valve. There's no worry about overheating, flare-ups, repriming, etc., and there is no need to handle fuel, a significant safety consideration.

Of the two fuels, most stoves are set up for butane, which can be kept liquid at a lower pressure than propane and can therefore be stored and carried in a thinner, lighter tank. This is understandable for backpacking stoves, but brings about another problem: butane doesn't vaporize well below freezing (which is why propane is sold in the north for home heating and butane in the south). You can warm butane tanks between your hands to get them going.

A butane stove can be modified to accept propane—it's merely a matter of changing one fitting—but manufacturers seem ignorant of that fact and don't make quick-change fittings available. Since vapor-fuel systems are really simple—no more complicated than plumbing—a propane dealer with a talented service department can possibly help you change over your stove, or at least tell you why it can't be done.

We've been speaking of vapor fuel, but some stoves are set for liquid feed, which means the fuel remains liquid until it reaches the burner, rather than changing to vapor in the line. The difference is significant: pressure is higher in liquid lines, and hence more dangerous. On the plus side, you don't have to keep the fuel tank on a liquid-feed system upright. It can be laid down or turned upside down and still work. Many vapor-feed tanks must be upright to work; if you knock one over, a valve inside the tank cuts off the flow.

Leaks and Ruptures. A leak in a gasoline/kerosene stove is a mess, but not necessarily dangerous. A butane or propane leak, however, can pose a significant explosion risk. The reason is that these fuels are heavier than air and will sink and collect in pockets and corners where they can easily build up to explosive concentrations. For this reason, leak detection is a primary concern for vapor-fuel system users.

Fortunately, refineries long ago learned to add aromatic compounds to these fuels (which by themselves are odorless and colorless). The characteristic odor of these compounds has been likened to rotten skunk cabbage, although who was familiar enough with that odor to make the comparison we can't say. You'll be sure to recognize it, though, and should seek leaks in your system promptly.

Finding leaks is easy: mix up a batch of soapy water and brush some suds around fittings, hoses, tank connections, burners, etc. Bubbles will reveal the leak. If you're caught without soap, spittle will reveal leaks, too. Under no circumstances test for leaks with a match or other open flame. If you do, you'll have a flaming leak instead of just a leak. Dangerous.

On liquid-free systems, the check valve that controls the rate of feed may stick. If this occurs, remove it from the tank and immediately re-install it. It may seat. Never try to get a vapor fuel valve to open by rapping on it, as valves are usually made of brass which dents and cracks rather easily from such treatment. For the same reasons, don't overtighten flare nuts, valves, and other fittings.

Since butane and propane are kept in a liquid state under pressure—extreme pressure in the case of propane—they vaporize rapidly and "jet" when the pressure is released. If a valve or a line is broken, a plume of gas will escape rapidly. This is frightening, but not necessarily dangerous. As long as the fuel is not directed at a flame or allowed to concentrate, you don't have to worry about combustion. You have time to remove the cartridge from your tent or close the valve on the tank.

What *is* dangerous is trying to stem the flow at the point of rupture. When the liquid fuel hits the air, it vaporizes immediately, expanding and drawing heat from the air. The result is rapid cooling and condensation of water vapor; a leaking vapor fuel tank will resemble a leaking faucet in winter. The danger is very real: at the point of vaporization, these fuels can and will cause serious burns from *low* temperatures, very much like dry ice. The danger is greater with liquid-feed systems since the supply line is filled with liquid, not vapor.

If a tank valve lets go, therefore, don't react instinctively by trying to close it with your hand. In researching this section, we came across a story of a broken vapor fuel valve. The writer tried to stem the flow by holding his thumb over the valve, but failed and lost his fuel anyway. He complained that it took him hours to get feeling back in his thumb, but he's fortunate to have a thumb at all. Any doctor experienced with "cold burns" will tell you they're more dangerous than "hot" ones, if only because you can't relieve them with ice or cold water. Frostbite from vapor fuel is an occupational hazard in the bottled gas industry, but it needn't be a hazard for the outdoors cook. Hands off is the rule.

Don't worry if your tank shows frost during use. This is normal, not a sign of leak or malfunction. In fact, the frost line marks the fuel level and is as good an indicator of how much fuel remains in the tank as you'll get.

Cleaning and Other Maintenance. Vapor-fuel stoves are low-maintenance stoves. The fuel is extremely clean burning and doesn't have additives as gasoline does. The most that you'll be likely to need is an occasional blow-out of the tiny hole in the jet. You can do this with an air hose, or, if you have a large tank with a rubber hose, with that. Blow from the outlet side toward the inlet side to dislodge any debris or deposits from the aromatic compounds added to the fuel.

Don't use a wire, pipe cleaner, paper clip, etc., on vapor fuel fittings made of brass. The soft metal is easily scratched, which makes the orifice larger and the fuel feed harder to control. Blow it out. And carry a few spare fittings for field use.

This doesn't apply to clogged burners, though. You can poke grease or soap out of them with a toothpick, broomstraw, wire—whatever is handy —without harming the metal.

For some reason which baffles bottled gas servicemen, spiders love to build nests in gas lines that are not in use. It is routine procedure to blow tiny spider webs out of fuel lines that have been left to sit for a while. If your gas stove doesn't work, blow out the lines.

If you're using a campstove fed from a large tank with a pressure regulator and hose, and that tank has been refilled many times, there is quite likely to be a layer of smelly gook in the bottom of the tank. Never turn such a tank upside down, as the gook will clog the valve and whatever else it can get into. A malfunctioning pressure regulator cannot be fixed at home —take it to a service outlet.

You can change a valve in one of these large tanks, but it is a smelly job because of the aromatic compounds which have collected in the bottom of the tank. The job is a simple removal/replacement, but you must seal the threads on the new valve with "pipe dope." Before taking a valve out of a tank, make sure it is empty and unpressurized. If in doubt, don't mess with it.

If you own a large fuel tank—a wise investment if you're a regular user —keep the bottom free from rust. A good asphalt-based paint will protect this area from rust. Paint the outside of the tank white or silver to reflect heat.

Cookware

ALUMINUM, STAINLESS STEEL, cast iron, and nonstick cookware can all be used over open fires, charcoal, or liquid-fuel outdoor stoves. Glass cookware—even "ovenproof" cookware—must be used with care and should never be used directly on hot coals or over an open flame. Ceramic or glass cookware should not be placed directly over a heat source when cold, and should never be placed directly on a heating element, hot coals, or flame. To use a ceramic or glass casserole or saucepan, place it above the heat source on a grill.

ALUMINUM

Aluminum cookware has several advantages and several disadvantages for the outdoorsperson. On the plus side, aluminum is light, quick-heating, and easy to clean. It is, however, easily dented, prone to warping, and short-lived, especially when used over open fires. It is also easily discolored from minerals in water and food and from exposure to smoke, but this can be prevented by careful use.

Before using aluminum utensils, wash and dry them to remove any oily coating which otherwise may discolor with exposure to heat. New aluminum cookware should be wiped with cooking oil or shortening prior to first use, according to a leading manufacturer, to prevent staining.

To prevent the outside of cookware from becoming blackened by smoke and soot, coat it liberally before use with soap. The pot or pan will still blacken, but it will be much easier to clean without hard scrubbing. A lot of campers who cook over open fires don't bother to remove this coating, claiming that it helps transfer heat evenly to the interior of the cooking utensil, which prevents warping. A black exterior tends to absorb heat rather than reflect it, making a dirty pot much more efficient for use over a backpacking stove or small fire.

Separate blackened pots with paper towels when stacking them to prevent black marks inside utensils. Interior staining of aluminum cookware is hard to prevent, but can be minimized by using only wood, rubber, or plastic spatulas, spoons, and beaters in them. Scratches from metal implements give food a place to stick. Manufacturers caution against using any strong alkaline cleanser (caustic soda, baking soda) on uncoated aluminum. The aluminum will in time become pitted, although at first such cleansers give the interior a bright shine.

The best way to clean aluminum pans and pots is to let heat do most of the work: remove food from the utensil as soon as it's cooked and fill the pan or pot with warm water. Return it to the heat source and let the water boil, then swab out the inside with a plastic brush or, if in the backwoods, a clump of grass. This should remove most if not all stuck-on food. While the pan is still warm, wipe it with a rag or paper towel. If some stuck-on food remains, a plastic scrubber is preferable because it won't scratch the interior.

Stains and discoloration can be removed by boiling a solution of two or three tablespoons of cream of tartar, vinegar, or lemon juice in a quart of water in the pan for seven to ten minutes. Cooking acid foods such as tomatoes in an aluminum pot will remove stains. For severely stained pots, nothing will do but a thorough scrubbing with a steel wool pad, although this serves as a temporary solution only and will cause food to stick more easily in the future. Prevention by the above methods is better than hard scrubbing.

Nearly everyone has one "campfire" frying pan that has become too warped for use on a stove or grill. Warping and denting have given aluminum a bad name, but both can be prevented by careful use and proper care. Denting, of course, comes from careless handling and packing. Some dents can be pounded out—carefully, with a wood block held against the metal to absorb the jolt and prevent damage from the hammer—but again, prevention is better than repair.

Warping of aluminum pots and pans comes from overheating and too rapid cooling. Good-quality aluminum utensils can withstand extremely high temperatures, but they cannot handle rapid contrasts. Don't put an ice-cold pot on a bed of glowing coals; rather, warm it near the fire or on a heated rock before allowing it to contact the hot coals. Don't plunge an overheated pan into icy water. Let it cool first.

A lot of winter campers ruin aluminum pots by melting snow improperly. If you fill a pot with snow and plop it on a fire or over a flaming stove, the snow on the bottom will melt into water which, instead of acting as a buffer between the snow and heat, will "wick" up through the snow, leaving the bottom of the pot dry and prone to scorching or warping, or both.

To melt snow, make a small snowball and put it in the center of the pot, which is then heated slowly near the fire before being placed on it. When an inch or more of water is in the bottom, more snow may be added gradually, not all at once.

Non-stick coatings. Teflon, Teflon II, and Silverstone have become familiar names in the past decade or so, and their well-known attributes need not be enumerated here. Camping cookware using these modern materials has appeared on the market in recent years and from all reports has performed well. Its chief benefit is ease of cleaning, a definite plus for campers who aren't familiar with campfire cooking and who thus overheat and burn food.

Nonstick cookware will discolor over a period of time (the manufacturers of "third generation" nonstick material claim to have largely solved this problem), but this discoloration, though unappealing in appearance, is harmless. It can be removed by simmering a dilute solution of oxygen bleach (not chlorine bleach) and detergent in the pan for fifteen to twenty minutes. Use three tablespoons of powdered bleach and one teaspoon of liquid detergent in each cup of water. Automatic dishwasher detergent (three tablespoons per cup of water) and automatic coffee percolator cleaner (one-quarter cup per quart of water) can also be used.

Nonstick pots shouldn't be cleaned hot. Allow the pan to cool, then use warm, soapy water with a plastic brush or scrubber. Never use steel wool or copper scrubbers, or metal utensils, with nonstick coatings. (Of course, the outsides may be scoured.)

CAST IRON

Perhaps the oldest cooking material, cast iron is well suited to outdoor use. It retains heat well, distributes it evenly, and cleans easily provided it has been well and properly seasoned.

Seasoning a cast-iron pan, pot, or Dutch oven is a continual process because the coating will burn off, be scraped off, and dissolve in water as the pot is used. A seasoned pan should have a dull shine with no cloudy patches, rust, or rough areas. When the shine disappears, it's time to reseason.

To season a new cast-iron pan, first scrub off the factory-applied wax coating. This should be done with soap and water and a plastic or natural bristle brush, never a metal scouring pad. Dry thoroughly with a cloth, then place the pan in an oven set to low heat (175–200°).

When the pan has heated, coat it with cooking oil, fat, or shortening by rubbing the oil evenly over the entire inside. Pay special attention to the sides, and make sure the oil doesn't slop over the edge onto the outside of the pan.

Opinions vary as to the best oil or grease to use, with animal fat getting the nod from most experienced cooks. One method involves filling the entire pan or pot with grease, bringing it to a boil, and keeping it bubbling for six to eight hours. This seems a bit extreme: you can probably do as well by applying a thin, even coating of oil or suet, placing the pan back in the oven, resetting it to 275–300°, and reapplying oil or grease every fifteen minutes or so for an hour. Take care not to let the oil smoke or foam (again, animal suet seems better). Also, make sure the sides of the pot or pan stay covered with oil at all times. The oil will tend to run and pool in the bottom, so you must remove the pot regularly and spread the oil with a clean cloth. See that the pot sits level in the oven; otherwise, the coating will be uneven, and you'll have a half-seasoned pot.

After about an hour of regular reapplications of oil, let the pot remain in the hot oven for another hour, then remove it and wipe all liquified oil or grease from the sides and bottom. Return it to the oven,and turn the oven up to 400°. Let it heat for a half hour, then remove it and let it sit on the stove until cool. This completes the initial seasoning.

After the first seasoning, you can use the pan or pot, but take care not to scratch the coating. It's best not to use it to boil food; rather, fry a meal using plenty of grease or oil. Don't use metal utensils, ever; wood or plastic works best.

Probably the first time you use your pan, some food will stick to it. Clean it by adding warm water to the pan *while it is still warm* from cooking, and return it to the stove to heat. Just before the water boils, remove the pan and empty the water, then wipe out the pan with a dry cloth. If any food still sticks, repeat the process.

After cleaning the pan, reseason it by wiping it with oil and putting it back on the burner, heating it for ten minutes or so, then wiping out the oil. This should be done after each use ideally, but is especially important after the first dozen or so times you use the pot or pan. The object is to build up a layer of hardened oil that will not wash away or boil off.

The method for cleaning a newly seasoned pan described above can and should be used for all cast iron. Never scour or scrub a cast-iron pot with steel wool, or scrape it with a metal scraper—you'll destroy the seasoning and food will stick. Never use soap or detergent for the same reason. All you really need to clean a cast-iron pan or pot is water and heat and a rag or paper towel. If you can't get stuck food off with water and a wipe, the pan needs to be reseasoned. Some outdoors cooks like to toss a bit of wood ash in the cleaning water, claiming that the alkalinity helps remove food particles. This should be done with caution, however, since too-strong acid or alkaline solutions will remove the seasoning.

Warping should never be a problem with good-quality cast iron, provided you don't overheat and then cool it too quickly. Plunging a red hot pan into an icy creek will test even the best cast iron, and you'll probably have a cracked or warped pan. Actually, your pan should never get red hot, but if it does let it cool slowly. You can prevent overheating by putting the pan on a trivet or grill over coals, not flames, or by hanging the pot in such a way that it can be swung off the fire if necessary.

STAINLESS STEEL

Stainless steel is especially durable and easy to clean. Its hard, nonporous surface is resistant to wear and will not corrode permanently. In its various multi-ply and clad variations, stainless steel comes close to being the perfect cookware.

Stainless steel shouldn't be placed directly on a hot fire, as uneven heating can cause warping or the rainbow-hued discoloration called "heat tint." Use a trivet or grill, or suspend the pan or pot over a low fire. Letting salt or acid foods stand in a stainless steel pot can cause it to pit, but alkaline substances—like baking soda and wood ashes—can be used to clean stainless steel with good results. Starch foods like potatoes and rice may cause a stain on the inside of the pan. This can be removed easily with one of the many stainless steel cleaners on the market. Otherwise, all your stainless steel cookware needs is a thorough washing in warm water with soap or detergent, or an occasional light scrubbing with a nonabrasive cleaner or plastic scrubber.

Scorch marks on stainless steel pans and pots can be removed by leaving a strong solution of baking soda in the pan overnight. This will loosen burned on food, also. Never let baking soda sit in aluminum pans or pots, however.

Coolers

METAL AND PLASTIC ice chests are simple machines which need little beyond regular cleaning to last a lifetime. Some simple modifications and repairs can help keep them in service longer.

Their handy size and shape makes coolers attractive as seats or stepstools, two uses that can break the lid, weaken hinges and latches, and wear out or scratch the surface of the lid. The manufacturers usually caution against placing any great weight on the lid, but of course that warning is often disregarded. If you're going to use your cooler as a seat, strengthen the lid by glueing a piece of ¾-inch plywood to it. Cut the wood about one inch smaller all around than the lid, fasten it with silicone rubber for plastic lids or epoxy for metal ones. Finish the wood with nonskid marine paint, and the cooler will serve as a strong, if uncomfortable, seat for your boat.

GASKETS

In time, weighing down the lid will wear out the hinges and latch, making the lid impossible to seal tightly. You can check this by laying a dollar bill over the edge and closing the lid and latch. If you can pull the bill out of the lid, it's too loose. If your cooler has a gasket, replace it. Most do not, however, so you'll need to make one of your own.

The easiest way to make a gasket is to cut a bicycle inner tube lengthwise and fasten it with silicone rubber sealant or household glue. Wash the rubber throughly and let dry before attempting to fasten it to the lid, not the body of the cooler. Make sure you fill all spaces along the edge, including the corners, and take care not to stretch the rubber while gluing it, as it will shrink, leaving gaps. If you wish, cut and fit the entire gasket before beginning to glue it. Tape it into place to make sure of the fit, then glue.

Take care not to get oil, abrasives, solvents, or hot liquids on the gasket, whether it is homemade or original equipment. A light dusting with talcum powder will keep it flexible.

REPAIRING PUNCTURES

Plastic coolers are particularly vulnerable to puncture damage, both inside and out. For small holes, such as might be caused by an icepick, a drop of fingernail polish or a dab of silicone sealant is a quick remedy. For large holes, dents and gouges, and melted areas, more serious repair is needed. Unfortunately, the material most often used for plastic coolers is polyethylene, which has proven extremely difficult to repair—particularly if the patch must be watertight and if the damaged item is subject to twisting and flexing (as coolers are). No bonding agent presently available will bond permanently to polyethylene, a fact that has caused much dismay to the makers of polyethylene canoes.

There is a patching kit available for poly canoes, however, and it has been used successfully to mend small breaks on flat surfaces where flexing is not a serious problem. It is rather tricky to use, however, as it involves precise mixing of a two-part adhesive and requires the use of a propane or butane torch to pre-soften the plastic. Polyethylene can also be "welded" with a nitrogen torch or with an induction-welding system (see the description in *Plastic Canoes* entry), but anything that produces heat can damage the urethane insulation layer, so that's out.

The solution, for large breaks or punctures (on flat areas or corners) is a mechanical patch, which will strengthen the cooler as well as keep it watertight. Start by cutting a piece of ABS plastic larger than the area to be mended. If you're mending a corner, heat the plastic in an oven at about 350°F until it becomes flexible, then remove it and lay it over the corner to be mended (handle with protective gloves). It will form itself to fit the corner with ease. Of course, if you're fixing a flat side or lid, there is no need to heat the plastic.

Next, cut a piece of neoprene plastic the same size as the patch. Coat both sides with silicone rubber sealant and lay it over the break. Place the plastic patch on top, then drill $\frac{3}{16}$-inch holes along the edge of the patch, spacing them about a half inch apart. Fasten the patch to the cooler with stainless steel bolts, using a wide washer on both the inside and patch side.

Coat the bolts liberally with silicone sealant before inserting them. This patch won't be very pretty, but it will be strong and watertight. Until induction-welding shops are common, it is the only way to repair a broken corner with some chance of long-term success.

Steel-bodied coolers are less tough than plastic coolers, but easier to patch and repair. Steel can, of course, be welded or braised, but, again, the insulation layer precludes using heat. You can solder small punctures or cracks, taking care not to heat the steel surface too much. Automotive body filler compounds can be used for dents and larger punctures, and a plastic patch like the one described above can be used for large breaks.

STORAGE AND CLEANING

Both metal and plastic coolers should be stored with the lid propped open to prevent musty odors. Oil hinges regularly or spray with silicone lubricant to prevent rust and keep them operating smoothly.

The interior of your cooler should be cleaned with a nonabrasive cleanser. Many stains result from letting liquids stand in the cooler for long periods. Use refreezeable coolant packs instead of loose ice cubes or blocks, or freeze water in milk cartons to use in your cooler. These will store easier and, of course, contain the water as the ice melts. A similar solution can also provide fresh drinking or cooking water. Fill balloons with water and freeze them for use in the cooler. When the ice melts, you'll have pure water.

STYROFOAM COOLERS

Cheap polystyrene ice chests are at best one-season items, as reflected in their low cost. You can, however, stretch their useful lives by reinforcing the obvious stress points (corners and edges), and by covering the sides and lids.

Contact paper is an effective covering that also beautifies the cooler. Wrap duct tape around the edges and corners to protect against hard knocks. Inside, vinyl-coated contact paper can help keep liquids from staining the foam. The tips on how to keep ice and ice water given above apply to styrofoam. Also note that polystyrene is sensitive to many acidic foods and juices. Lemon oil, for instance, will eat its way into polystyrene very quickly.

Cross-Country Skis

CROSS-COUNTRY SKIS are made of wood laminates or fiberglass. The bottoms may be smooth (wood), smooth with strips of mohair attached to provide one-way traction (wood or fiberglass), or patterned in the familiar "fish-scale" pattern, also to provide one-way traction. Each has advantages and disadvantages.

WOODEN SKIS

Wooden skis need waxing and, depending upon your point of view, that can be a challenge or a nuisance. Probably more has been written about waxes, and how to use them, than about any other single aspect of cross-country skiing, so we won't go into the pros and cons of the various waxing methods.

Preparation for waxing, though, falls into the category of maintenance and refurbishment, so we'll deal with how to get a pair of wooden skis from the scrap heap to the trail, and how to keep them from going back to the heap.

Moisture is wood's big enemy, and wooden skis are just as susceptible to rot and separation of the plies as any boat or canoe. Actually, warping and separation aren't usually a problem because of the resins used to bind the laminations together. But rot, especially inside where the softer wood is, is a definite problem.

Refinishing and Sealing Tops and Sides. You must seal wooden skis and keep them sealed during the entire season. The top and side walls should be varnished—either marine varnish or polyurethane varnish will do. If the old finish has orange-peeled or shows cracks, work the surface over with steel wool—the finer the better—before refinishing. Inspect the surface carefully for deep scratches, nicks, gouges, and cracks. There is no need to take the entire coating off the ski unless there are deep scratches that penetrate the entire coating. In most cases, all you'll need to do is steel wool the ski until smooth, then reapply varnish or polyurethane.

You can, of course, strip the entire finish off the top and sides, and should do so if you need to fill gouges, patch edges, etc. In that case, you may want to apply an oil finish instead of a protective coating. Two parts of linseed oil mixed with one part turpentine used with light (double-O) steel wool will remove a varnish or poly coating and saturate the wood.

Treatment with boiling-hot linseed oil, or more of the same 2-to-1 oil and turpentine mixture, will take oil back into the wood, provide an effective moisture barrier, and, most important, allow the wood to breathe. You'll have to do this a couple of times a season, but you won't have the annoying task of trying to fix scratches in a tough varnish finish.

If you varnish, and the finish is later scratched or cracked, you should try to get oil into the crack as soon as possible, or at least fill the damage with wax to prevent moisture from entering the wood.

Of the two options, oil or varnish, the second will probably be better in the long run, unless you really beat up ski tops.

Care of Binding Screws. The binding screws are the point of greatest wear on wooden cross-country skis. Make sure the screws are tight and stay tight. Often, the flexing action of the ski will loosen the screw in the hole so it can't be kept tight. If that happens, set the screw with epoxy cement. Make sure the hole is clean and free from oil and wax; if you're refinishing the tops, stuff the holes with matchsticks to keep the oil-and-turpentine mixture or varnish out, or simply put the screws back into the holes without the bindings while refinishing.

After you've refinished the tops and sides, replace the bindings and set the screws with epoxy. (If the screws haven't worked loose, white glue will work as well and make the screw much easier to remove.)

If the holes have expanded too far, or if cracks around the screw holes have admitted water and rot has begun, carefully drill a larger hole, removing the damaged wood, and fill with epoxy filler. Once the filler has set, it can be drilled to screw size. You must be very careful not to drill too deep, nor to drill on an angle. A small drill press is an excellent tool for this job.

Remember that epoxy won't stick to oil or turpentine-soaked wood. If you've had to fill a gouge or scratch with wax, you can get it out with heat from a propane torch, steel wool, and turpentine, which does a better job of dissolving hard wax than alcohol. Don't remove the wax, of course, until you're ready to take more permanent measures to seal the ski.

Patching Damaged Edges. The bottom is the business side of your wooden ski, and the edges are the business part of the bottom. Lignestone, a compressed, chemically impregnated wood, is used for edge strips. (The bottom itself is hickory wood in most cases.) It is very hard to keep the edges from wearing down, but they are somewhat brittle and will chip rather than crack. The most common problem, then, is for a chunk of the lignestone edge to break out.

If you're on the trail and you break an edge, you can keep going by swapping your bindings to put the good edge on the inside, which is the most important edge for control. If the edge break has exposed wood, get some wax into it before allowing it to contact the snow; this is a very vulnerable area of the ski, and you don't want any moisture creeping into the wood. Of course, you'll have to torch-and-turpentine the wax out of the break to repair it permanently.

Edges should be patched with epoxy filler, not plastic wood. Epoxy is more flexible than plastic wood, and it doesn't shrink, so you're less likely to lose an epoxy patch. Make sure you get the right kind of epoxy filler— the two-part, long-curing kind seems best for this job—and make sure you follow instructions exactly, particularly those pertaining to application and set-up temperatures and times.

Before patching, you must get out *all* the dirt, wax, lint, etc., including the temporary wax filler you put in on the trail. For ski bottoms, lighter fluid, alcohol, acetone, and wax removers are all good, as they leave little residue to interfere with the epoxy. There has been a lot of research into waxes and wax removers lately, so check with a ski shop for the latest products. Removing wax can be tedious without the right chemical assistance.

Remove any splinters of wood or lignestone, but do not smooth the rough edges of the break because the epoxy will grip better on a jagged edge. Build the epoxy up above the surface of the ski bottom and let it set at the proper temperature until completely dried, then scrape and sand it to level. A steel cabinet scraper is the best tool for this job, but be careful: you don't want to gouge the wood. Finish with progressively finer grades of sandpaper.

Cracked edges can be patched the same way, with epoxy, but make sure you're not patching a piece that's getting ready to break loose—otherwise you'll just waste your efforts.

When repairing an edge, try to get the edge as sharp as possible. You can clamp a piece of metal or smooth plastic alongside the ski to provide a form for the epoxy.

Inspect patched edges from time to time to look for gaps around the patch due to shrinkage or flexing. Fill these with more epoxy. If you notice one of these on the trail, fill with wax to keep moisture out of the wood.

Replacing Base Wax. Removing and replenishing bottom wax is time-consuming but necessary. It should be done whenever the bottoms are scratched or gouged beyond your ability to fill them with wax, at the end of each season (before storing the skis), and whenever you want to experiment with new waxes.

First, remove the binding and place the ski in a vise padded with cardboard or cloth. You need to have a solid grip on the ski for the scraping that lies ahead, otherwise you'll be likely to put more gouges into the bottom than you take out.

Next, scrape all the wax you can off the bottom with a plastic or metal scraper. Use a plastic scraper if you're new to this, as that won't scratch the bottom as severely if you mishandle it. A spring-steel cabinet scraper will do a superior job, but can cut into the wood if it slips.

Following this scraping, use wax remover on a soft rag to rub off as much wax as possible, then take a propane torch equipped with a flare tip and heat the bottom to melt the remaining wax. You must move the torch rapidly, not letting it sit in one spot long enough to scorch the wood beneath the wax. Go over the entire ski, then start at the tail end and go over it again, this time wiping the melted wax off with a clean rag as you go.

Another application of wax remover should be sufficient to remove all the wax, but if not, keep alternating torch and wax remover treatments. Finish with wax remover.

When you have all the wax off the bottom, check for warpage. Modern laminated wooden skis seldom warp—that's one reason they're laminated—but sometimes a slight cupping will occur, either concave or convex. You can—carefully—scrape them even.

Remember, though, that the bottom ply is only about ¼ inch thick, and, even though it's hickory and therefore pretty hard wood, you can scrape through it if you're not careful. Use the steel scraper or a block of hardwood with medium-grit sandpaper wrapped around it to level the bottom. Don't be too persnickety, though; you won't get the bottom perfect no matter how hard you try, and you'll never notice the difference on the trail.

With the bottom scraped clean and leveled, check for cracks in the wood and fill them with epoxy if they're deep or threaten to splinter. Otherwise, the base wax you'll apply will be sufficient to fill them.

After the bottom is as clean and level as you can get it, you're ready to prepare it for waxing. Pine tar—the same stuff baseball players use on their bat handles to improve their grip—forms a tough, sticky, flexible coating which will hold the base wax to the ski and also keep moisture out of the wood.

There are two kinds of pine tar available. One, designed to dry quickly in all kinds of temperatures, can be used on the trail or when time does not permit use of the slower-drying kind. Either will do a good job of forming a base for the wax coating. Liquid pine tar is available at hardware stores.

To apply pine tar, first heat the ski bottom with a torch. This should be done carefully, since the bottom is now bare and easily scorched. Use a propane torch with a fan tip and keep the flame about one inch away from the wood. Keep it moving.

Next, apply a very thin, even layer of pine tar with a one- or two-inch brush. The ski will stay warm while you do this, so there's no need to rush. Make sure you have an even coat of tar on the ski with no runs, thin spots, or puddles.

Following this application, warm the ski again with the torch. The purpose of this second warming is to open the pores in the wood so that the pine tar soaks in as far as it can. Work rapidly and don't keep the torch on one spot too long; if you overheat an area, the pine tar will bubble and run. You'll be able to see the difference as the pine tar soaks in.

With the ski still warm, brush on a second, somewhat heavier coat of tar and warm it once more. This second coat will not soak in as readily, but take your time and warm the ski bottom evenly and completely to get as much of it into the ski as possible.

When you're satisfied that no more tar will soak into the ski, wipe the excess tar off with a soft, lint-free cloth and let it cool. Polish the dry, tarred bottom with wads of newspaper to smooth out the surface and make it ready for base wax.

The subject of waxing is one for endless debate, so we'll not get into the pros and cons of various brands, hardnesses, combinations, and "systems" of applying wax to wooden skis. Once tarred, your skis should be base-waxed promptly, and it is preferable that you do this as soon as the pine tar is cool enough to handle. Otherwise, the tar will collect dust, lint, etc., which make waxing more difficult. Always apply base wax before storing skis.

Base-waxing is pretty simple, requiring only wax, an electric clothes iron, and a scraper. With your skis set firmly in the vise, bottoms up, set your iron on its lowest setting and let it warm up.

Starting at the tip, lay the point of the iron on the ski bottom and hold the wax against it. When the wax starts to melt, move the iron and wax together down the ski, allowing a steady stream of molten wax to flow onto the ski bottom. Don't let the iron rest too long in one place, since you can burn the bottom or start the pine tar flowing and smoking. Work on one side of the tracking groove only, and don't be too concerned about excess wax flowing into the groove—you can easily scrap it out later. Work steadily toward the tail, laying a smooth, even layer of wax on the ski, ironing the wax onto the ski much as you iron a garment.

When you reach the tail, work on the other side of the groove back to the tip. Don't be concerned at this point if the wax is somewhat uneven. It's better to get too much on the ski than not enough.

Once you've gotten the entire bottom coated, work with a plastic or steel scraper to even the wax layer. Be careful not to gouge the ski with the edge of the scraper; if you're unsure, use a plastic windshield scraper or similar appliance. Use the scraper edge to remove wax from the groove. After getting an even finish, you may go over the bottom with a piece of cork to further smooth it, but this isn't absolutely necessary.

Storing Skis. The repairs and tarring described above should be done soon after the ski season, when springtime "mud runs" have taken their toll. Don't delay—moisture will creep into your skis and shorten their life. Even if you're storing your skis for a few weeks during the season, inspect them for flaws in the wax or varnish coating and touch them up with, if nothing else, some wax. (Here, the benefit of using an oil finish on the tops and sides is apparent. It is much easier to rub in some oil or oil/turpentine mix than to sand down and touch up varnish.)

The ideal storage space for wooden skis is not too warm, not too cool, not too dry, not too damp, and not too hard to get to. In other words, it probably doesn't exist. But try to find a place away from direct heat and especially direct sunlight which will work on poly and varnish and evaporate oil. Look for a place away from heat sources such as furnaces, too. An unheated attached garage or an uninsulated attic will do.

The classic method for storing skis is to tie the tips and tails together —a rubber band will do this nicely—and put a block of wood between the skis to preserve the curve. Before modern laminating techniques were perfected, this was necessary to avoid warping, which is less of a problem now. Such a rig does make it very easy to handle a pair of skis, though, and it provides protection for the bottoms, so why not?

Otherwise, store your skis bottoms up, supported at the tips and tails. Laying them across exposed rafters is good, or make a rack to keep them out of harm's way.

FIBERGLASS SKIS

"Waxless" fiberglass skis, with either mohair strips attached or fish-scale pattern, require little year-to-year maintenance. Deep gouges in the tops or sides of fiberglass skis should be patched with an epoxy filler *compatible* with the ski. Check the manufacturer's recommendations or ask at a good ski shop before buying the filler.

Ski makers also may have matching paint or colorings to add to fiberglass filler. If you want to take the time to check, you may find enough material available to completely refurbish a beat-up pair of fiberglass skis at little cost.

Fiberglass bottoms get scuffed and gouged with depressing regularity, but there is a handy way to fix them. "Candles" of polyvinyl chloride (p-tex is the commonly used term) are cheap and easy to use.

Begin your bottom repair by inspecting the edges of the skis for gaps or separations in the lamination. If the bottom layer is beginning to separate, reattach it with epoxy glue, clamping the ski firmly until the adhesive has set.

Next, shave off any slivers, strings, etc., hanging from the bottom. Use a razor blade to get as much off as you can. Leave the rough edges on any deep scratches, though, as they will bond to the p-tex better than a smooth edge.

Clean all debris and dirt out of the scratch or gouge, then light the candle and allow enough p-tex to drip into the scratch to fill it completely. Overfilling is better than underfilling, so don't be stingy. Let the p-tex cool down completely, then scrap off the excess with a scraper or knife blade. Sand with progressively finer grades of sandpaper until the bottom is smooth and even. If you work carefully, you won't be able to notice any difference in the patched area—it will literally be as good as new.

We call fiberglass bottoms "waxless," but you can wax them to great advantage. Again, there's a lot of research going on in this area, so any products or procedures we might mention here may be dated. Check with your ski shop operator for the latest product. Fish-scale bottoms or bottoms with mohair strips can benefit greatly from the application of common paraffin to the tips. Research has shown that the tails of the skis are most important for speed and control, so don't apply any wax there. You can spray silicone lubricant on the fish-scale section with good results.

Transporting skis is easier if you've tied them together, tip and tail. For shipping skis, the cardboard tubes that carpeting is wrapped on are ideal, but you may have to use two different diameters to accommodate the upturned tips. Pack the tubes with newspaper or excelsior and wrap the ends tightly with tape. Ski racks for automobiles are excellent, but don't let the skis sit in the sun.

BINDINGS

There's not much you can do to improve or harm cross-country ski bindings. After using your skis, clean as much dirt and debris out of the bail and hinge as you can and apply a penetrating oil. The bail will eventually wear out, and, unless you've got the type of bindings for which you can buy replacement bails, that means new bindings, which aren't that expensive.

Keeping the screws tight is essential. Not only will loose screws throw you for a loop in the snow, they'll work on both the wood (or fiberglass) and the metal binding and wear it out much faster than normal. Set screws with white glue or epoxy as described earlier.

Decoys

DECOYS RANGE FROM the handcarved masterpieces turned out by a few dedicated artisans to foam plastic "one-season wonders" available at the bargain counter. Constantly exposed to the elements, decoys need care to last.

Molded hard-plastic decoys are very popular because of their low cost, durability, and ease of cleaning and repair. These decoys are constructed of hard plastic, usually in two halves which are cemented together, and get their flotation from the air trapped inside.

PLASTIC DECOYS

Hard-plastic decoys are usually set and left for a long period of time, so they invariably get mucked up with algae, oil film, and just plain dirt. They should be cleaned with a stiff brush and hot soapy water; if they are really dirty, a little chlorine bleach should be mixed into the soapy water.

Cracked seams are easily mended with household cement. Wrap the decoy with bands cut from old inner tubes to keep the halves together until the glue sets. Shot holes, small punctures, and cracks can be fixed with glue or filled with melted plastic from a retired decoy, but you must use the same material for filling. File off any excess glue or plastic with a medium file, taking care not to cut into the shell, finish with sandpaper, and paint to match.

Another kind of plastic decoy is made of lightweight foam, either in a half-decoy or full-decoy configuration. The quality of these decoys varies, with the most durable being the ones that have the smallest, most dense foam. These materials are not particularly durable, and foam decoys are most often used when hunting remote areas, where their lightness makes packing them in easy.

Clean foam decoys with mild detergent and water only. Never brush them, as that will loosen the foam particles and abrade the surface, and keep all solvents, bleaches, and thinners away. Take care not to store foam decoys where they may be kicked around or have gasoline spilled on them. If hunting from a motorboat, keep the decoys out of the bilge water if possible.

Broken foam decoys can be repaired with epoxy cement, which bonds foam better than any other adhesive. Deep gouges can be filled with plastic wood filler or with epoxy to which is added fine sawdust. Build up such patches in layers, letting each dry before applying the next. Lightly sand and paint to match, using a paint designed for use on plastics. Latex house paint will work, but epoxy-based paints are best.

The anchor cable screw eye may work loose from foam decoys. Repair it by liberally coating the threads with epoxy, let it set halfway, then screw it firmly back into the decoy.

WOOD AND CORK DECOYS

Wooden decoys are often real works of art and artifice, but you pay a maintenance penalty for their beauty and authenticity. As with any wooden object subjected to the elements, they must be protected from soaking up moisture. This is best done with an oil treatment, as protective coatings are invariably nicked up and gouged during a season and thus lose their ability to keep water out of the wood. Also, an oiled decoy can be touched up with paint; a varnished decoy cannot.

After taking decoys out of the water, clean them thoroughly with a soft brush and warm, soapy water containing a small amount of bleach. Rinse and allow them to dry completely in a well-ventilated place. Don't let them dry near a heat source.

Inspect the decoy carefully for cracks, open grain, or small "checks" which indicate the wood is drying out. If you intend to repaint the entire decoy, strip the paint with chemical paint stripper and sand all the old finish off.

Fill any nicks or deep gouges with plastic wood or with a mixture of cyanoacrylate glue (super glue) to which you've added a little baking soda. To do this, fill the gouge three-fourths full of glue, then quickly sift the soda into the glue, moving rapidly to keep the glue from setting up before you've completely filled the gouge. A chemical interaction between the two materials will cause the glue to set up immediately into a hard, yet easily sanded, filler.

Broken bills, heads, tails, and other parts can be glued with marine glue.

Next, treat the decoy to a warm bath in boiled linseed oil. The oil should be heated to near boiling and maintained at that temperature in a double boiler. Don't just put it into a pot over a flame or electric coil. While the decoy is in the oil, use a soft paintbrush to work the oil thoroughly into the wood. The decoy can be handled with a spring clothespin on the bill.

When the decoy is well saturated, remove it, wipe off excess oil with a lint-free cloth, and place it in a warm, well-ventilated place to dry. Inspect the decoy periodically and wipe off any oil that hasn't soaked in.

Decoys should dry thoroughly before they are painted with decoy paint or flat latex house paint. For authenticity, a decoy-painting kit with detailed instructions on each species' coloration is a good bet. Let freshly painted decoys weather in the outdoors for several weeks before using them.

You still see a few cork decoys around, particularly the homecarved kind made out of laminated pieces of granulated cork board. The big disadvantage of cork decoys is that they soak up water and become waterlogged. They should be painted with several thick coats of latex house paint before the final coloring is painted on. Repairs are similar to those made on wooden decoys, but don't use the super-glue-and-soda treatment—the glue will eat cork.

Profile decoys made of plywood need to be painted to seal them from the elements. Pay particular attention to the edges of the plywood, where moisture can easily penetrate.

Down and Synthetic-Fill Clothing

CLOTHES THAT MAKE you look like the Michelin Man are ubiquitous. Whether expensive, twenty-below-zero-degree-rated parkas filled with 100 percent prime goose down or cheap, badly sewn synthetics from the Orient, the "down look" has taken over outdoor wear. Obviously, the performance of both down and synthetic fills warrants this popularity. Many people, through fear of ruining their clothing or through ignorance of proper cleaning and storing methods, take years off the usable life of their garments.

Down can mean 100 percent goose down (the best), or a mixture of goose and duck down, or a mixture of down and feathers. "Legal" down —which may be *called* down—may contain up to 20 percent feathers. There's nothing intrinsically wrong with mixing feathers and down, except that feathers insulate less well, have less loft, and possess sharp quills which can puncture fabric. Cheaper down/feather fill is usually placed in cheaper garments, with poorer overall construction, flimsier zippers, etc. In general, a 100 percent goose down garment is a quality garment.

Which is not to say that down is the ideal insulation material. It has certain advantages over synthetic fill—it is less likely to lose its loft, for instance—but it also has several disadvantages. Although down is lighter than synthetics, its physical properties make it hard to contain, so it must be sewn in such a way as to prevent clumping. That means quilting, which leaves many "cold lines" of stitching through the shell and lining. If the garment is double-quilted, the weight advantage disappears.

Down garments will keep their loft longer than synthetic-fill garments if both are compressed and stored that way. Down can be compressed much smaller than synthetics of comparable weight. However, both down and synthetic-fill manufacturers tell you not to compress your garments any more than necessary—and in fact, not to store either kind in stuff sacks or similar small packages. Down, then, will "bounce back" easier than synthetic fill, but you shouldn't force either kind to prove itself in that way.

Also, down is organic and subject to harboring various microorganic growths. While down and feathers must pass rigid sterilization processes to be used in clothing, improper or infrequent cleaning can make it unsanitary. Many people are allergic to down and feathers.

The negative features of synthetics are well known. They will not stand constant compression without losing some of their loft and therefore some of their insulating properties. Nor will they stand up to dry cleaning or drying with heat. Most are sensitive to petroleum compounds.

Pound for pound, new synthetic-fill garments provide greater insulation than down garments. Over the years, though, down will probably retain more of its power to keep warmth in. The choice of one over another boils down, then, to a consideration of price/weight/maintenance.

A common misconception about down and synthetic fill is that the synthetics keep you warm better than down when they're wet. This isn't true, as neither kind of insulation will keep you warm when it is soaking wet. Synthetics, however, retain their loft better than down and so dry much faster (using your body heat to do it, of course), so you'll be warmer faster with synthetic-fill garments, but not until the fill is dry. You can speed up drying by exposure to moving air.

You've probably heard it said that detergents "strip the oils" from down, leaving it lifeless and matted. Or perhaps you've been warned that heat causes down to wilt. Both these stories are false. Down is extremely resilient and able to stand up to both heat and detergents—the best evidence of that is given by the people who import and process down for use in garments and bags.

Down and feathers come from China, chiefly, where the poultry industry thrives. Shipped straight from the slaughterhouse on the proverbial "slow boat from China," down is "a bloody, dirty, stinking mess," in the words of one outdoor gear expert, when it arrives in this country. To make it suitable for use in clothing, pillows, comforters, and sleeping bags, it is treated very roughly indeed.

The down arrives in tightly packed bails, complete with blood, pieces of skin, goose and duck bills, feet, and various other contaminants such as molds, mildew, and dust. It is immediately agitated and vacuumed to remove most dry contaminants, then washed vigorously in hot water with powerful detergents.

After rinsing, the down and feathers are whirled in a centrifuge to remove water, then baked for several hours at 212° F to complete drying and to kill germs. After cooling, the feathers and down are separated by being stirred and blown about in the air, the down floating to the top, the heavier feathers sinking. It is then packed, mixed, and stored until used.

The purpose of this explanation is to demonstrate the resiliency and durability of down. If detergents and heat harmed it, it would never get out of the factory.

WASHING AND DRYING DOWN

You can't harm down garments by washing them in warm water with household detergents, nor by tumbling them in a large dryer at moderate heat settings. Where people get into trouble in cleaning their down garments is in rinsing, handling, and drying.

Down garments with baffles are rather fragile. They should not be washed in top-loading machines, period. The agitators twist and turn the garment, stretching and pulling at the baffles, inevitably breaking them down. Down garments tend to float on top of the water in top-loaders, too, making it much more difficult to clean them well. And the agitators force the fill into clumps.

Commercial front-loading washers are ideal—the larger the better. Hand-washing in a bathtub is also great.

The question of detergents is open. There are plenty of "down soaps" on the market, usually touted as "specially blended for down" and sold at premium prices in small packages. You can find as many people swearing by them as swearing at them, depending on their particular experience. John Rutkowski of Mountain Mend, a Colorado company that cleans and repairs all sorts of outdoor gear, refuses to recommend any such product, saying the effectiveness of detergents depends upon their solubility, the amount used, and the temperature and mineral content of the water.

According to Rutkowski, most people use too much detergent and don't rinse sufficiently. He says whatever detergent gets your clothes clean will work on down gear, as it is obviously suited to the particular water conditions in your area. If it doesn't work on cotton, it won't work on down.

Whatever soap or detergent you use, use less. Don't be misled by the absence of lots of suds. The detergent is getting inside where it belongs instead of foaming on top of the water. Rinse, rinse and rinse again. If you can't rinse by hand, run the garment through a complete cycle without soap to get every last bit of soap film out of the down. The same physical properties that enable down to hold air make it hold detergent film. When people speak of detergents "breaking down the oil" in down, they're really speaking about the tendency for soap and detergent film to clump down fibers together.

If you're able to wash your down gear in a bathtub equipped with a hand-held shower head, use it to rinse the garment. The spray is especially useful for breaking up clumps of down and for driving water through the shell. Neither wash nor rinse temperature should exceed 120° F, not because the down is threatened, but because the shell material, especially internal baffling, can be weakened by higher temperatures.

Handling wet down gear properly will keep it around much longer. Don't twist, squeeze, wring, or otherwise stress down garments. Shells and linings are sewn together and it is easy to pop internal seams. The spinning action of a front-loading washer is less harmful than hand-wringing, but some manufacturers say down gear should be draped over a rack and allowed to drip dry. Don't attempt to speed up the process by pressing water from the garment.

Down garments can be dried in a large, commercial dryer, if you can control the heat. The 30-pound size common in laundromats is ideal; a 50-pound capacity dryer is even better. The heat setting should be below 120° F. A good way to test the temperature is to start the dryer and, after a few minutes, check the garment. If you can hold the metal parts—zippers or snaps—in your hand, the dryer isn't too hot. If you can't, it is.

The problem isn't necessarily heat, it's uneven heat. In a small home dryer, the garment will not move around enough to heat evenly. Hot spots will develop, harming the shell or lining or, even worse, melting plastic parts or making metal parts hot enough to melt through material. Some manufacturers go so far as to recommend NO HEAT settings to prevent overheating, but it is hard to completely dry down without some heat, and wet down is prone to mildewing.

If you use a commercial dryer, make sure the inside is free of foreign objects, snags, etc.

Manufacturers and the Feather and Down Association advise against drying down gear in the sun. They do say, though, that in humid conditions dry down gear should be placed in a dryer at low heat to remove humidity that may cause mildew.

You may have heard that you should put a tennis shoe in the dryer with your down garment to "break up" clumps of down and restore loft. This works, as would a tennis ball, tennis glove, or a tennis racket cover, by beating the clumps of down apart—not a very good thing to subject your garment to.

The reason that sneakers seem to have such a good effect is that the friction between the tumbling rubber-and-nylon sneaker and the nylon shell material creates a static charge which causes the down to fluff up. Just about anything other than another piece of nylon will cause the same thing to happen—tennis balls, for instance, or a large terrycloth towel. In fact, a tennis shoe is one of the worst items you can put in the dryer with your down gear because its metal eyelets can snag and its plastic can melt and stain your bag.

It's just not necessary to beat up down gear to make it loft. You can carefully work clumps out of wet or partially dry down garments with your hands and should inspect down gear as its being dried for clumping.

Those metal parts we mentioned as being dangerous when hot are also dangerous, period. If you can, remove the zipper slider before drying in a machine. If not, close the zipper and turn the garment inside out and back again several times during the drying cycle to dry it evenly.

DRY CLEANING DOWN

Since washing and drying down garments is so labor-intensive, you may consider having your down garment dry-cleaned. Go ahead, but make sure the dry cleaner knows what he's doing.

Commercial dry-cleaning fluids are used over and over again, and become quite greasy and dirty before they're changed. Most fabrics will do fine in such circumstances, but not down. The detergent-film problem mentioned above applies as well to dry-cleaning fluid: if it's dirty, it will actually carry more dirt into the down than it takes out.

Check on your dry cleaner's methods and understanding of this problem. If he charges you extra for cleaning down garments, he may have recognized the problem and solved it by using fresh fluid on down. He will probably also use a milder fluid if he can, and subject the garment to a shorter cleaning cycle and a longer drying cycle.

Garments that have been dirtied by dry-cleaning fluid have a characteristic shine—much shinier than when new. Sometimes a dry cleaner will claim that that's because the garment is finally *really* clean. Not so. The shine is caused by grease, and you can bet that the inside is as dirty or dirtier than before.

The down inside a poorly dry-cleaned garment will have lost most of its loft, due to grease contamination. Again, don't believe the dry cleaner when he says that kind of condition is inevitable—down will withstand high temperatures and harsh detergents without losing its loft. You can immediately spot greasy down by grabbing the garment and rubbing the fill between your fingers—through the shell, naturally. If it feels slippery, it's greasy.

If you can't talk the dry cleaner into giving you your money back or cleaning it over, take it home and wash it—and, if you feel like it, take a gallon of dirty wash water back to show him!

WASHING AND DRYING SYNTHETIC FILL

Synthetic fill cannot be dry-cleaned, according to the manufacturers of the major types. So you're stuck with hand washing, and several of the warnings given above washing down should be applied to synthetic fill.

Avoid top-loading automatic washers and overheating in too-small dryers. With synthetic-fill overheating will harm not only the shell and fasteners but also the fill itself.

Heat really kills synthetic fill, so dry it on the AIR ONLY setting, period. Now, you probably know somebody who took their synthetic jacket, washed it in a top-loader, and dried it in a home dryer with heat and had it come out great. Well, it will—once.

Synthetic fill is treated with water-soluble resins to make it easier to handle during manufacture. When you wash a garment the first time, the resin is removed and the fibers puff up beyond their original size. Your synthetic jacket will look full and fluffy, like down, but it has begun to deteriorate with the removal of the protective coating on the fibers. The next time, it won't look so good, as water and detergent—and heat—combine to matt the fibers and make them stick together. When that happens, there is nothing that will restore the loft.

Heat is really the culprit here. Polarguard, a common fill material, has kinked fibers which give it loft. When heated above 120° F, the fibers lose their kinks permanently, and the garment comes out flatter than a mackerel.

If you must machine-wash your garment, use a front-loading automatic, warm water (below 100° F), and mild soap or detergent. As with down, use much less detergent than normal and don't bother with special soaps and detergents.

Rinsing is essential for the same reasons as mentioned in the section on washing down. So is careful handling—never pick up a saturated synthetic-fill garment by the shell only. Support it fully from beneath, and drape it over a rack to drip dry. The internal baffles and seams are really quite fragile on these garments, no matter who made them, and once torn, they're nearly impossible to repair. You end up with the worst case of sagging fill you can imagine.

REPAIRS TO NYLON SHELLS

Any garment used in the outdoors will need patching or repair from time to time, and down garments are no different. It's a pleasure to tell you, though, about a kind of damage you *don't* need to repair. From time to time, a quill will stick through the outer or inner shell. The worst thing you can do if this occurs is pull it through and stick a piece of duct tape over the hole. Instead, pull the protruding quill back through the hole from the inside. This will take a little feeling around, but you can find the particular feather or piece of down and yank its quill back inside. The tiny hole that's left in the shell probably will close itself in time. Usually the hole isn't a hole at all, merely a misplaced nylon fiber.

Actually, nylon shells are pretty "downproof" with the threads woven tight enough to keep tiny quills inside. Taffeta, especially, is resistant to penetration because it is pressed flat. That's another reason to avoid overheating: at temperatures above 120° F, the nylon strands will lose their press and become round once more, leaving space for quills, and dirt, to penetrate.

As for duct tape, it's probably the worst thing you can put on any nylon shell, no matter what the fill. The adhesive will penetrate and stain the garment permanently, leaving a dark sticky patch where you once had only a protruding quill.

For that matter, no iron-on or other adhesive patch is worth the trouble. Iron-ons risk damage to the fill and/or shell from heat. They tend to roll up at the corners, too, and leave—you guess it—a messy stain. If you must use an adhesive patch, try to make it fit the seams for later permanent stitching, or at least, make it fit so that a permanent patch will conceal its stain. And round the corners so they don't roll up.

Permanent patches of nylon stock—either taffeta or ripstop—can be sewn to down and synthetic-fill garments if you take care not to create baffles where you don't want them by sewing into and/or through the fill.

It's best to try to fit a patch to an existing seam so cut the patch to fit from seam to seam if you can. Fuse the edges of the patch with a candle flame. Usually, you'll be able to sew only one or perhaps two edges to existing seams, so you've still got to sew the other sides without stitching into the fill.

With the patch secured at one or two sides, pinch the shell and edge you wish to sew together and lift it away from the fill. You may need to pull the fill down from the inside to avoid catching some of it with the needle. A whipstitch around the edge of the patch is quick and secure, and will leave a small, raised seam—about the best you can hope for sewing from one side only.

You can add down and synthetic fill to garments that have been torn or mishandled, but it isn't very easy, especially with down, which is very hard to handle and will quickly fill the air with floating fibers. Any good outfitter can refer you to a repair shop that will restuff garments.

Information on repairing zippers and snaps is found in the *Backpacks* entry. See *Nylon* entry for removing spots.

STORING

Even though down is renowned for its ability to retain its loft, it shouldn't be stored in a stuff sack or other container. Store down gear hanging up, in a cool, dry location away from sources of heat and especially sunlight. Humidity will cause musty odors and mildew, so if your down garment gets damp, put it in a tumble dryer for a few minutes at moderate heat, or hang it near a source of moving warm air, as over a heat register.

Mice like to nest in down garments, so mouse-proof your storage area. You shouldn't have any trouble with moths or other insects.

Synthetic-fill garments are very sensitive to heat and humidity. Never store them wet, especially in a closed, warm container. Keeping a garment in the back of a car or car trunk invites trouble—it can literally cook down, and once that happens, you can't restore the loft.

Fiberglass Canoes

FIBERGLASS CANOES AND kayaks have several distinct advantages over both aluminum and plastic. Fiberglass can be made into a more efficient shape—sharper bows, lower freeboard—than plastic, and it is as strong as aluminum. It is as puncture resistant as plastic, and resists tearing better. It is quiet, is easily repaired by amateurs, and needs little maintenance.

On the minus side, fiberglass will "nickle and dime" you with small cracks and abrasion wear, and it will shatter rather than dent—no "popping back" after a hard pin against a rock. Also, it is possible to make a weak fiberglass canoe out of sprayed chopped glass fibers bonded together with resin and most "budget" fiberglass canoes are made this way.

You get what you pay for in canoes, and it pays to do a little research into how a fiberglass canoe or kayak is made before you purchase one. Find out how heavy the cloth layers are. Fiberglass cloth can be as light as 4 ounces per square yard or as heavy as 20, with strength correlated to weight. Manufacturers should be eager to give you specs and discuss construction and maintenance. Canoes made of sprayed and molded chopped matting can be recognized easily, as they have a "waffle" effect on the inside, where cloth-and-resin types will clearly show the cloth weave.

Fiberglass canoes require periodic cleaning and little else. You can scrub the hull with a mild abrasive household cleanser or strong detergent to remove scum, algae, and stains. Fiberglass hulls can also be painted with anti-fouling bottom paint to discourage algae growth, although this is only advisable if your canoe is going to be in the water continually for long periods of time. Otherwise, it's better to scrub off the hull occasionally. Automobile paste wax will give it a nice shine, too.

The smooth, abrasion-resistant exterior layer is called the "gel" coat, and it is vulnerable to tiny cracks from impact, as well as gouges. Fortunately, gel coat repair kits are very commonplace and easy to use, involving little more than brushing a liquid filler into the cracks and letting it set up. Clean the area thoroughly and follow instructions for temperature and set-up time. One of the nicest things about fiberglass is that it can be sanded smooth, so you can clean up any excess without undue effort.

FIELD REPAIRS

Because fiberglass repairs are best done under conditions of controlled temperature and drying time, and with the proper tools, most canoeists make field repairs with duct tape, which sticks extremely well to both interior and exterior surfaces. You can make a pretty tight patch with duct tape and silicone sealant, though of course it won't have any structural strength.

Field repairs for small cracks, punctures, and gouges can also be made with plastic putty, caulking compound, or liquid gel coat if you have the time to let it set up. The usual procedure is to lay several strips of tape on the inside, if accessible, then fill the exterior hole with putty and cover with a piece of fiberglass cloth. Another layer of putty spread over the cloth will set up quickly, and you can be on your way. This kind of emergency patch can be removed easily for permanent repair.

A "temporary/permanent" repair to cracked fiberglass can be made with ground glass mixed with quick-setting epoxy resin to form a putty, which is then spread into the crack and allowed to set up. This shouldn't take as long as the resin-and-cloth repair described under permanent repairs. This patch can be applied and let dry overnight and sanded smooth in the morning. Or it can be left alone and sanded down in the future.

PERMANENT PATCHES

There are numerous books available on repairing fiberglass boats, and before tackling a major, permanent repair job, you might want to read up, talk to a repairman, or contact the manufacturer of your canoe for his recommendations. Although "fiberglass" is now a generic term, there are many different combinations of resin and cloth, gel coats, and coloring agents included under that rubric. Also, as mentioned earlier, chopped glass fibers pressed together with dried resin to make "fiberglass matt" is used in some cheaper canoes. Before tackling fiberglass repairs, therefore, find out as much about your canoe as you can.

Some definitions that may be helpful:

Cloth is twisted strands of glass and resin woven into a cross-hatched pattern. It comes in various weights per square yard, with 7.5- and 10-ounce cloth used in the best canoes. You shouldn't use any cloth lighter than 7.5 ounces for repairs. Cloth has as much glass as resin, and so is strong for its weight.

Roving is an extremely coarsely woven cloth. It is stiffer than cloth, and so is hard to form over curved surfaces. It has great impact resistance, however, when used on flat surfaces.

Matt is a "cloth" made up of chopped glass fibers held together with dry resin. It is much weaker than woven cloth, but more flexible; hence, it can be used in certain repair applications, such as applying a patch inside the narrow bow or stern.

Resin is the bonding agent for fiberglass repairs. There are polyester and epoxy resins of various types, some of which require mixing two chemicals, some of which are self-activating when exposed to air. "Slow-cure" epoxy can take hours to dry, especially if exposed to damp conditions, but it produces an extremely strong bond. There are "quick-setting" epoxy resins available, and these should be used for field repairs to epoxy boats. A fiberglass boat made with polyester resins can be fixed with either polyester or epoxy resins, but only epoxy will bond to an epoxy boat. Again, find out as much about your canoe as you can before attempting repairs.

A cautionary note: fiberglass resins and hardeners are noxious and should be used in well-ventilated areas. Fiberglass fibers can penetrate the skin, causing irritation and rashes. Some people are even allergic to the fibers. Wear long sleeves, use a dust mask, and keep your hands away from your eyes and mouth.

For the sake of this discussion, we'll differentiate between "functional" and "cosmetic" patching. Understand, though, that both are functional in the strict sense of the word: they'll keep water out and maintain the canoe's structural integrity. Cosmetic patching simply means that the finished patch will closely approximate the original finish. In fact, if done well, a cosmetic patch can be nearly invisible. A purely functional patch is not pretty; it just works.

We'll also differentiate between areas accessible from two sides and areas accessible only from the outside. Patching a hole in the side of a canoe is one thing; patching a hole in the narrow bow or stern is quite another.

Tools and supplies you'll need for patching include a sabre or keyhole saw with a fine-toothed blade, sharp scissors, a 1-inch paintbrush, several sheets of sandpaper, duct tape, and backing material consisting of aluminum foil, cardboard, plastic wrap, etc.

You'll need a few paper cups for mixing, some popsicle sticks or short pieces of lath, 1 foot of copper or aluminum wire, and, of course, the cloth and resin (either fast-curing epoxy or two-part polyester and hardener). You may also want a can of gel coat (color-matched to your hull) or some epoxy paint, and if you're going for a real cosmetic patching job, a grinder/- buffer and a medium-fine cut flat file.

Functional Patching. For a functional patch in an area accessible from both sides, cut out all splintered glass with the saw and sand off the gel coat about 2½ inches around the hole. Also sand the inside edge of the hole, and 2½ inches around the hole on the inside of the hull.

If the hole is large—3 inches or more across—cut several strips of duct tape (trimmed to ½ inch wide) and tape them inside the hull, crossing the hole at right angles. These pieces of tape will provide support for the patches and prevent them from sagging. For holes smaller than 3 inches, the cloth itself will usually provide enough support.

Cut a rectangular patch from the cloth large enough to extend 2 inches beyond the hole in all directions, mix the resin, coat the patch, and lay it over the taped hole on the inside of the hull. Add another patch to the inside, being careful not to press hard enough to push the patches into the hole.

Now cut several patches to fit the hole as nearly as possible. Coat these and put them in the hole, from the outside, against the tape and cloth you just put on from the inside. These will fill the hole and prevent the inside and especially the outside patches from sagging into the hole. Handling these small patches can be a bother. Try using a board as a "palette" to coat them and hole them ready while you manipulate each into the hole.

Cut a large rectangular patch to extend 2 inches beyond the edges of the hole, coat it and smooth it over the hole. Smooth the resin out from the center and take care not to leave blobs of it on the hull. You can add a second outside patch and should if the hole is large or if the first patch shows signs of sagging into the hole. Leave plenty of resin on top of the patch, as you'll be sanding it down when it sets.

After the patch has dried thoroughly, it can be sanded and finished with epoxy paint, or left alone. This functional patch will never be very pretty anyway; no matter how much sanding and painting you do, you'll still know there's a patch there.

Making a functional patch from one side is a bit trickier, but if your canoe has flotation chambers at the bow and stern, that's where you'll need to do it. Cut out all splintered glass and sand the gel coat and edges of the hole as described above. Take care not to cut out any more of the flotation material than absolutely necessary to provide working space.

Prepare four strips of cloth about 2 to 3 inches wide and long enough to extend at least 2 inches beyond the edges of the hole in either the horizontal or vertical direction. If the hole measures 3 inches high by 5 inches long, for instance, prepare two strips 5 inches long (for the vertical) and two 9 inches long (for the horizontal). Wet these strips with resin and work them through the hole with your fingers so that they lay half on the fiberglass and half on the hole, in a criss-cross pattern. You'll have, then, a small, rectangular open area in the center.

Make sure you smooth the patches as best you can onto the inside surface of the hull. This is difficult, especially with oddly-shaped holes, but it is essential. You should have the strips positioned so that at least 1 inch is on solid fiberglass.

Let these strips set up and become stiff before you proceed, otherwise further patching will push them away from the inside of the hull, with no way to push them back against the hull surface. When they've set up, cut several small patches to fit the hole as closely as possible. Soak them and place them in the hole, against the strips you put in first, covering the small rectangular gap left in the center of the hole.

Seal the entire patch with one or two large outside rectangular patches, smooth the resin, and let dry. Sand and finish as for a two-sided patch. A note on these large outside patches: resins will not stick to smooth gel coat, so you should not cut and lay on a patch larger than the sanded area. Smaller, in fact, is preferable, as you can then "feather" the resin out to meet the gel coat and have room to sand without roughing up the edge of the cloth patch. Always sand at least a 2½-inch margin around the hole.

Cosmetic Patching. Making a pretty patch is a whole other ball game, since you'll be working with gel coat, which is tough to get right, and especially tough to sand.

With both sides accessible, begin by preparing the hole as described for a functional patch. Then "dish" it, that is, with a rotary-type grinder and medium-grit paper, or the file, taper the edges of the hole on the inside of

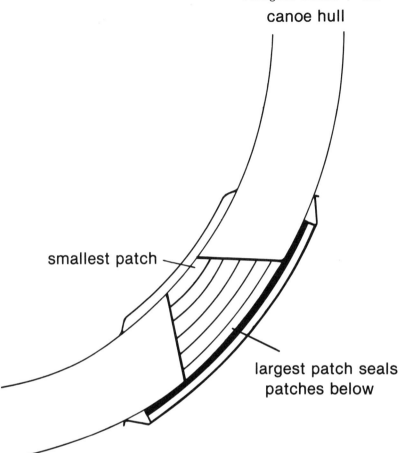

canoe hull

smallest patch

largest patch seals
patches below

outside

To make a functional patch for a fiberglass canoe, you first secure the inside of the hole with two resin-coated patches extending two inches beyond the hole on all sides, then fill the hole with as many small patches (cut as close to a fit as possible) as necessary. Finally, secure the outside of the hole with one or two resin-soaked patches cut to extend two inches beyond the hole on all sides.

the hull. (A cross section of the hole after dishing would resemble a funnel, with the small end at the outside of the hull and large end inside—you tapered the edges, in other words.) Sand a 2½-inch margin around the hole on both inside and outside.

You'll be applying most of the patches from the inside of the hull, so you'll need to construct a backing board from cardboard covered with foil, plastic wrapping, wax paper, or another smooth material. Make sure it is *smooth,* with no wrinkles or creases. The cardboard should be fairly flexible and about 3 inches bigger all around than the hole. Secure the backing board to the outside of the hull, with the plastic or wax paper surface facing *in.* Duct tape will keep the backing board in place.

Cut several patches out of cloth, each one slightly bigger than the last, beginning with one the exact size of the small end of the hole and working up through three or four layers until you have one the exact size of the large inside edge of the hole. Soak these with resin and carefully position them in the hole, smallest one first, against the backing board.

Seal these patches with one large patch on the inside. Let everything dry.

When dry, remove the backing board, and apply a patch, about 1 inch bigger than the hole, to the outside. Let it dry. When dry, carefully sand the edges, "feathering" them out smoothly. Wipe the dust off, mask around the sanded area with duct or masking tape, and apply gel coat with a paintbrush. Smooth it on carefully, drawing the brush from the center out to the edge. Let dry.

Sand the area, using progressively finer grits, and finish with a buffing wheel.

You can finish the inside patch with gel coat, too.

A variation of this method, which is much harder to get right but which will look great if you do, is to apply the gel coat from *inside* the hull, against the backing board. You'll need to take extra care with the backing board. It must be wrinkle-free and firmly attached to the hull—firmly enough to resist gapping when you apply the gel coat from inside.

After the gel coat has completely dried, build up patches inside as described above. When everything has set up, a light sanding or buffing on the gel coat side will make it look (we hope) as good as new. (Matching hull colors is tough, though—colors fade, paint batches vary. For this reason, a lot of experienced canoe repairmen eschew gel coat patching completely and just finish the cloth patch as best they can and paint with epoxy paint.)

For a cosmetic patch with only the outside accessible, you'll need a piece of cardboard, some wire, and a piece of lath or popsicle stick as long as the holes longest dimension.

Prepare the hole as above, sanding a margin on both sides of the hull. Cut away as little flotation material as possible to provide working space inside the hull. Prepare a backing board as follows: Cut a piece of cardboard about 1 inch bigger all around than the hole; an oval shape is best. Cut two cloth patches the same size and shape, wet them with resin, and put them on the cardboard. Make two small holes in the cardboard/cloth assembly near the center, about 1 inch apart. These need only be large enough to allow the wire to pass through.

Pass the wire through one hole from the front (cloth patch) side, hold the lath strip against the cardboard and loop the wire over it and back through the other hole. Twist both ends of the wire together.

Push the whole assembly into the hole, bending the cardboard as little as possible, and position it against the inside surface of the hull so that the twisted ends of the wire protrude from the center of the hole. The wet patches should be firmly against the inside of the hull, where you sanded the margin around the hole. Pull the wire to hold the patch/backing board against the hull, wrap the wire around another piece of lath at least 6 inches longer than the longest dimension of the hole. Tie the wire to the lath, then rotate the lath to wind the wire onto it, keeping pressure on the backing board all the while.

When the wire is wound down to within a couple of inches of the end (and the lath is within a couple inches of the outside of the hull), pad the ends of the lath and with strips of cardboard make a couple more turns to tighten the wire even further. This is tricky: you don't want to pull hard enough on the wire to buckle the backing board, nor do you want to release tension on it too soon, for the patch can slip at this point. The idea is to wrap the wire tightly enough to keep the patch in place with the tension provided by the lath resting against the hull.

When the patch has dried, snip off the wire, and proceed as above with a series of patches of increasing size, a sealing patch, gel coat, etc. The cardboard, lath, and some wire will remain inside the hull.

Repairing major damage is an acquired skill, but fiberglass is forgiving: you can always sand it down or, at worst, cut it out and start over. Kevlar, a "new, improved" fiberglass, is repaired the same way as fiberglass except that it doesn't sand well. You can use regular fiberglass cloth and resin to repair it, and should.

Fiberglass canoes often sustain damage at the bow, along the stem-band, where chunks of glass are knocked out. It's impossible to patch this area well, due to the sharp angle of the bow and the internal supports and flotation. To fill in missing chunks, make a paste out of chopped cloth and resin and fill it in with a putty knife. Remember you can sand away any excess.

Firearms

GUNNING REMAINS ONE of this country's most popular sports and firearms one of the most used—and, unfortunately, most abused—kinds of outdoor equipment. Volumes have been written on gun safety, technique, design, and mechanics, and nearly every gun owner at one time or another contemplates modifying or repairing his own gun.

It is not the intention of this book to provide a practical course in gunsmithing, nor to lead the gun owner into attempting modifications or repairs that should properly be done by an expert. You won't find information on replacing firing pins, rechambering for different ammunition, or modifying trigger pull, for instance, as we feel that is beyond the "keeping it alive" focus of the book.

In this entry, you will find detailed instructions on cleaning and refinishing the metal parts of a gun because we feel these are well within most readers' skills and can contribute to the longevity of standard firearms. For information on care and modification of stocks, see *Gun Stocks* entry.

SAFETY AND STORAGE

No writing on guns of any kind should neglect safety rules. Although you've probably heard it many times before, we'll repeat the dictum that a gun must be loaded and it must be pointed to harm. There's no such thing as an "unpointed" gun; *what* it is pointed at is what matters. Similarly, "I didn't know it was loaded" is merely the rationalization of "I didn't know it was *un*loaded," which is what the careless gunner meant to say. *Prove* your gun's unloaded status every time you pick it up.

Some rules that will minimize the need for excuses: don't trust automatic weapons to unload completely, especially the kinds with tubular magazines. Working the action several times is merely the first step. Inspect the chamber: look for the "follower" which pushes the ammo into the chamber. Look at the lifter on lever-action guns. Work the bolt on bolt guns, and check the chamber with your finger on large-bore rifles to make sure.

Break shotguns and single-shot rifles and inspect the chambers. Don't trust revolver ejector rods to completely empty the cylinder; more than once, live rounds have remained in the cylinder after the ejector was worked. Similarly, work the slide on automatic pistols several times after removing the clip, then inspect the chamber to make sure. Never force a jammed automatic pistol.

Handguns should never be kept in open or unfastened holsters, as they can easily be knocked to the ground with resulting damage or discharge. Never let a revolver's hammer rest on a live round. If a firearm hangfires or shoots a "squib," or underpowered, shot, wait a full ten seconds before inspecting it, then open the action and remove the clip or magazine. Squib shots can leave a slug or debris in the barrel, so don't fire the gun until you've check that. Make sure you've got the right ammo for your gun.

Safe storage means locked storage, period. Keep ammunition and firearms under separate lock and key. To be doubly safe, dismantle firearms before storing them, with pieces in different places.

Security from theft is improved by keeping guns out of sight—no glass-front display cases, please. Dismantling firearms and storing the pieces in different places will discourage thieves, few of whom want to bother with half a gun.

Register and insure your weapons, and mark them with your name or social security number in an inconspicuous place. Some suggestions for marking spots: under the floor plate or under the butt plate on rifles and shotguns; under the grips on handguns. Tell the local authorities where and how you've marked your guns.

Proper storage also affects your firearm's performance and longevity. Long guns should always be stored horizontally to prevent oil from running down the barrel into the chamber and collecting there. If you must store a long gun vertically, store it muzzle down.

Leather cases designed for transporting rifles and shotguns make poor storage containers—condensation and subsequent rust is the problem. Saddle scabbards are likewise poor storage containres. Condensation damage can be minimized by opening or removing the bolt or magazine, making sure you wipe the gun thoroughly before packing it, using silica gel packets to dehydrate the package, and letting guns warm up before packing them. Some gun owners like to plug the barrel to keep oil from running out the muzzle during transportation or storage, but this is not a wise practice, as condensation will occur more readily in any closed space. Handguns can be wrapped in wax paper to forestall condensation.

The ideal storage arrangement, then, is a locked case with ventilation in which long guns can be racked horizontally. A rigid case is most sturdy for transporting any firearms.

CLEANING GUNS

Never store a dirty gun. Modern ammunition, though providing much more "bang for the buck" is surprisingly dirty, requiring more frequent and more energetic cleaning efforts of guns than did earlier ammo.

There are two main reasons for this. Shells are softer, containing a higher percentage of copper than before, and powders, though powerful beyond the dreams of sportsmen of a few decades ago, contain additives that coat barrels with hard-to-remove lacquers.

High-velocity handgun loads are unlubricated for the most part, increasing the heat and friction in the barrel, leading to increased likelihood of lead and/or copper fouling. High-velocity, center-fire ammunition often leaves a lacquer coating in hunting rifle barrels, and rimfire .22 ammunition is especially prone to lead fouling.

Shotgun shells, too, have become more powerful but dirtier. Old-style wax-coated paper shells lubricated and waterproofed the chamber; modern plastic shells do not, and without the protective coating, powder fouling and rust are more likely. This is especially hard to spot in pumps and automatics.

These conditions can seriously shorten the useful life of any firearm, and necessitate intense cleaning with proper equipment. An unclean gun is an unsafe, inaccurate, deteriorating gun, and responsible ownership of firearms mandates frequent and thorough cleaning.

To clean firearms you need cleaning rods, brushes, patches, rod guides or plugs for certain rifles, tissues, and tweezers for manipulating patches into tight areas. A bulb-type syringe, hair dryer, or photographer's aerosol "air bomb" is also helpful, and, of course, you'll need solvent and lubricant.

Solvents are available, but many gun owners feel they're too weak to do the job on severely fouled guns. Particularly, commercial solvents are said not to cut metal fouling, one of the most serious problems with modern ammunition. It is possible to clean a barrel and have it look clean and shiny but in fact be coated with lacquer or even metal which didn't loosen in the solvent. You can find evidence of such fouling by inspecting the tops of the rifling grooves for lumps of metal. Inspect from the muzzle end, of course.

Since commercial solvent is found wanting, you may want to make your own (or buy some homemade from a fellow gun owner or gunsmith). A solvent formula credited to one P. O. Ackley is easy to make and store. It is rather noxious however and should be used in a well-ventilated area.

Mix the following ingredients in a glass beaker with a tight-fitting lid: 1 ounce ammonium persulphate, 200 grains ammonium carbonate (both these ingredients are available from gun shops or chemical supply houses), 4 ounces distilled water or rainwater, and 6 ounces ammonia (clear, not detergent-mixed or "perfumed").

This powerful solvent will work on lead and copper fouling, and is recommended for all types of cleaning where the gun is not totally dismantled, as, for instance, you might do prior to reblueing or to restore a badly neglected gun. For dip-cleaning and soaking firearms and parts, other solvents discussed below are more effective and easier to use.

Solvents powerful enough to dissolve metal fouling will naturally destroy the finish on wooden parts. For this reason it is recommended that you mask the stock before cleaning, or at least be ready to wipe off any spillage promptly.

For cases of severe barrel fouling, abrasive pastes may be needed. Since these are a last resort and will rarely if ever be needed, there's little reason to discuss them except to note that any abrasive should be used with extreme care in or around the chamber or barrel of a firearm. If your gun is so badly fouled that treatment with solvent, brushes, and patches won't clean it, you'd benefit from expert advice and aid.

We'll first discuss cleaning rifles and shotguns, then add information on special procedures for cleaning handguns. Some general rules for cleaning both long guns and sidearms are: keep the piece horizontal to prevent solvents and oils from running into trigger mechanisms and onto stocks, (automatics should be cleaned upside down). Secure the piece in a padded vise to free your hands and prevent gouging, dropped guns, etc. All rods and brushes should be inspected for burrs, rough edges, loose bristles, and rust spots, and cleaned before introducing them into a barrel or chamber.

Rods should be hard steel; a rod that flexes can scar a barrel, or at best make thorough scrubbing difficult.

During cleaning, you should be alert for signs of undue wear, loose screws, and similar indications that minor repairs are needed. Shiny spots on a bolt, for instance, indicate a poor fit with resulting friction.

Rifles and Shotguns. Clean rifles and shotguns as follows: first, remove the bolt, if any, and magazines, clips, etc., before securing the gun in the vise. Single and double shotguns and rifles are easiest to clean, since the breech opens fully. Autos should be secured upside down to prevent contamination of trigger and feed mechanisms, and that can hinder access to the breech.

Rifled barrels should always be cleaned from the breech end; while this is less critical for shotgun barrels, it is a policy that should be followed if possible. Most pump guns dismantle easily for cleaning from the breech end. Bolt-action guns should be fitted with a rod guide—a "plug" that fits into the chamber and has a hole somewhat larger than the bore—to prevent damage from inserting brushes, rods, and other tools.

With the gun set up, begin by wiping out the magazine and chamber area with a patch soaked with solvent. This may be a bit difficult to do thoroughly, but it is essential. Use tweezers to hold and manipulate tiny pieces of patch. For autos and pumps, which have many nooks and crannies, consider using a commercial spray solvent with a plastic "straw" attached to the can to direct the solvent into tight places. Your homemade solvent can also be delivered with a straw: dip one end into the solvent and put your finger over the other to carry a few drops in the straw; release it by removing your finger. Toothbrushes and scrapers made from plastic toothbrush handles can help you get into tight spots. Never use nails, pins, or other pointed objects to scrape out deposits.

Next, the barrel. If it's badly fouled, you may want to soak the barrel in solvent before using brushes or patches on it. If you're not sure, it's a good idea to try the brush-and-patch cleaning method first, then inspect the barrel for undissolved metal or powder fouling. (More on soaking in the next section.)

There are several types of tips available for gun-cleaning rods. Most are designed to hold a patch securely even though the patch is soaked with solvent or oil and is being pushed through a tight bore. The most common types are the slotted, button, and jag tips, all of which will work well. Experiment.

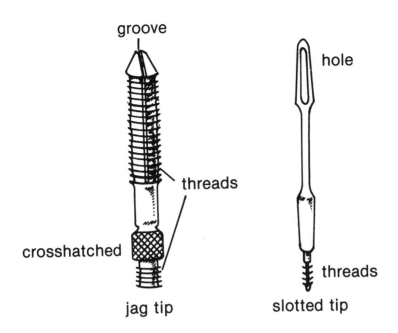

groove

hole

threads

crosshatched

threads

jag tip

slotted tip

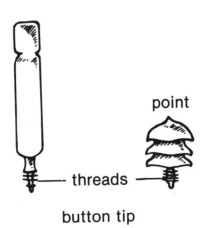

point

threads

button tip

The most common types of tips found on gun-cleaning rods: slotted, button, and jag.

In general, slotted and button tips are good for general cleaning; jag tips, which resemble augers, are better for removing metal fouling. Whichever tip you use, make sure the patch is centered on the tip, otherwise you'll miss sections of the bore and make thorough cleaning impossible.

Brushes are usually brass-bristled, spiral-patterned, and threaded for attachment directly to the rod. Make sure you have the proper size brush for your gun. A gun shop can set you up with the right tools. Chamber brushes—short, flexible handled brushes designed for use on shotgun chambers—are a good investment if you do a lot of shooting with a scattergun.

The proper sequence for cleaning a barrel is two or three passes with patches soaked in solvent, followed by a couple of passes with the brush, followed by clean patches, then finish with an oiled patch. Working always from the breech end, you must take care not to allow the rod to contact the breech or bore.

A common mistake most beginners make is trying to pull a patch or brush back through the barrel, thereby either losing the patch or banging the rod against the muzzle. Never do this. Always push the patch through, unscrew the tip, remove the rod by pulling it back through the breech end, and replace the tip of brush. The most critical part of the rifled barrel is the muzzle, and you can easily ruin this area by gouging it with a rod tip or brush.

Button tips won't pull back through, which is a safety feature, but jag tips will. A jag tip used with patches *can* be push-pulled in a barrel, though, if you're careful not to let the tip protrude past the muzzle. Some gunners rig rubber or wooden stops on their rods to prevent the jag tip and patch from going the whole way through the bore. You may want to use this system for working on badly fouled barrels. Shotguns may, of course, be push-pulled without fear of harming the muzzle or bore, since they have no rifling.

This is as good a time as any to address a problem common to neophytes and veterans alike: a stuck patch. No matter how carefully you've secured your patches, you're going to lose one from time to time, usually when you're in a hurry. Your first impulse will be to try to push the stuck patch through from the muzzle end. Don't do it, as you'll most likely get it stuck worse, and may scar the bore trying to manipulate it.

The best solution is to make a special patch-catching tip by soldering a sheet-metal screw to a piece of cleaning rod, point first. (You solder the screw head to the rod tip.) This can then be used to "bite" pieces of the patch off by inserting it into the breech end and twisting into the patch. If the patch is dry, you may have better luck by soaking it with oil overnight —or at least for several hours—to soften it. Some gunners report good results in removing stuck patches with a double-corkscrew tip usually used on muzzle-loading arms.

After the cleaning sequence is complete, wipe out any debris you've allowed to accumulate in the chamber area, and inspect the barrel—especially the rifling grooves at the muzzle—for fouling. Remember that a shiny bore is not necessarily a clean one; you may have merely polished the lacquer or metal coating. The ends of the grooves will reveal fouling.

If this cleaning procedure doesn't remove fouling, you can soak the bore, and follow with a standard cleaning.

Soaking the barrel is easy if you can obtain or make a cork to fit the breech. Cork the breech securely and fill the barrel with solvent. (You need to have the muzzle pointing up, naturally.) Let it sit for at least a half hour; then empty the barrel and run several patches wet with hot water through from the breech end, followed by several dry patches to get the water out. For severely fouled barrels, several soakings may be necessary, but don't give up too soon. The next step would be abrasives, and they're tricky and hazardous.

The above procedures concentrate on cleaning the interior of the gun. If, however, your gun is rusted or caked with grease or mud, you'll need to deal with exterior cleaning as well. One of the best and safest ways to loosen rust on the exterior is to spray the metal parts with WD-40 and work it into cracks and tight spots with a toothbrush. Let the gun sit overnight, then wipe off.

Immersion Cleaning. A gun which is very badly corroded or fouled, or one which you plan to reblue, can be cleaned by soaking the pieces in solvent. This is also advisable for easily removed pieces such as revolver cylinders, trigger assemblies, and others which you may have occasion to remove for repairs and modifications. Naturally, you must remove all wooden and plastic parts before immersing a handgun.

Gun solvent is satisfactory for soak-cleaning, as are lacquer thinner and acetone. All are flammable, however, and take a long time to work, especially on really dirty firearms. A better chemical, perchlorate ethylene, is a commonly used dry-cleaning fluid. It is poisonous but nonflammable. Its effect on metal fouling, old grease grime, and rust is rapid and complete. "Perk" doesn't harm wood or plastic, so you can use it on grips and stocks; you can even immerse a handgun, grips and all, without fear. Perk is not usually sold over the counter due to its toxicity, but dry cleaners can obtain it and you may be able to persuade one to sell you a few quarts. Caution: perk will dissolve synthetic plastic bristles, so use natural bristles.

Another benefit of using perchlorate ethylene is that you can mix liquid silicone with it to leave a rustproofing film on the gun when the perchlorate has evaporated. Liquid silicone is easy to get—just spray an aerosol silicone spray into a glass jar. Mix one ounce of silicone with five quarts of perk to make an effective immersion bath for rifle and pistol parts.

Silicone is, by the way, an excellent rust preventive coating for any firearm. It is especially handy to use in its spray form, and for a "quick fix" prior to storing cleaned guns in humid surroundings, it can't be beat.

For sidearms, immersion in carbon tetrachloride or water is also effective. You can put a handgun in a plastic bag, fill it with carbon tetrachloride, and agitate it to dissolve old grease and oil. Caution: carbon tetrachloride fumes are noxious and possibly dangerous. Use it in a well-ventilated area only.

A surprisingly effective immersion-cleaning method for handguns is a hot bath. Simply remove the grips and put the gun into a pan of boiling water to which you've added a capful of detergent. The agitation of the boiling water will carry the detergent into tight spots and loosen caked oil and grime. (This is also a very effective way to clean black-powder arms.)

Of course, you'll want to dry the gun as soon as possible to prevent rust. A hair dryer is a good tool for this, and you can also use it to blow oil into internal spaces, which you should do after cleaning. Since solvents and detergents dissolve oil, you should never let a just cleaned firearm sit around. Once rust begins, it is difficult to stop without a complete stripping and reblueing. There are a number of fine gun oils, greases, and silicone- and graphite-based lubricants on the market in handy containers. A gun shop can advise you as to the latest and best.

Special Cleaning Techniques for Handguns. The cylinder area of a revolver poses special cleaning problems which must not be neglected, since built-up oil and grime can seriously affect performance and safety. The chambers themselves aren't too difficult to clean with patches and solvent; neither is the barrel, which can be worked over effectively with a short-handled brush made especially for handguns. You can push one of these through from the muzzle end, as it is difficult to insert a brush through from the cylinder opening on all but fixed-cylinder guns.

The barrel itself isn't as much of a problem as the cone at the breech end. Revolver barrels are flared slightly at the breech to accommodate slight misalignment of the cylinder—a bullet fired slightly off-center is "funneled" into the bore by the cone-shaped breech. Naturally, this is a prime spot for lead fouling, and it can be difficult to clean well.

The best way to clean the cone is with a tool specially made for it, resembling a breech plug. You may be able to find one made for your particular gun, or at least for the proper caliber. These plugs are designed to be wrapped in brass screening which acts as a brush when inserted into the cone and rotated. You can use solvent and patches to clean the cone thoroughly.

If you can't locate a cone tool, you can improvise. Cut a threaded rifle barrel cleaning rod down to handgun barrel size. Insert through the muzzle and push the end into the cylinder opening. Then screw on a brush larger than your pistol's bore. Pull the brush back into the cone and twist. You can wrap a smaller-diameter brush with patches soaked in solvent to work on this area also, or use handgun brushes of a larger caliber than your gun. One handgun-cleaning outfit has patches made of brass screen with holes in the center to fit onto the spike tip of the cleaning rod. (It also has a cone tool.) If you do a lot of revolver shooting, you may find such a setup worth buying.

The ejector/ratchet mechanism on revolvers is a critical area for dirt, grime, and powder residue. There's no easy way to clean this area, so go to it with tweezer-and-patch, toothbrush-handle scrapers, solvents, etc. Never use steel scrapers of any kind to remove fouling from this area, and be careful not to leave any lint or pieces of patch there.

Automatic handguns are particularly troublesome to clean well, and there's no shortcut. Plenty of time with tweezers, patches, scrapers, and the like is required. Pay particular attention to the slide, as fouling or debris can build under it, causing jamming and wear. The soaking methods described in the section on immersion cleaning are particularly suited to badly soiled automatics.

CARE OF GUN SCREWS

Other than cleaning, the most frequent maintenance chore on guns is tightening screws. The recoil shock of repeated firing is taken up almost exclusively by the several screws that secure the frame and stock, but since gun screws are usually considerably softer than the frame and barrel metal, they tend to stay tight once set. However, their softness works against them during removal and replacement. Too often, a neophyte will strip threads or ruin slots when dismantling a gun for cleaning or repair, and reap a harvest of loose screws ever after.

Gun screws are made to very close tolerances and have fine threads, so it takes surprisingly little overtightening or cross-threading to strip the threads. Never force a screw that doesn't want to eat, and never try to use an oversized screw to replace one that's stripped. Frame steel is easily retapped to accept a larger screw should you ruin the threads in the hole, but this should be done only by a gunsmith. A broken screw can be removed by drilling into it and using an "easy-out" tap to remove the broken piece, but, again, extreme care is necessary.

Screws can be secured with Loc-tite or a similar product. This is preferable to continued tightening, which in time is sure to damage threads, slot, or both.

More gun screws are damaged by bad screwdrivers than anything else. Since gun screws are soft, a standard screwdriver with a tapered blade will chew up the top edges of the slots. You need screwdrivers that fit the slot exactly—not only side-to-side, but top-to-bottom. In other words, the blade of the screwdriver must resemble a squared-off bar. This is especially critical for removing very tight screws, since a tapered blade, when tapped, will break down the top of the slot without touching the bottom, which is where you want the loosening force to be applied.

Gunsmiths' screwdrivers are hollow ground, much like some knife blades. This merely means that the edges of the extreme tip of the blade are parallel to each other for a short distance—just enough to allow the squared bottom of the blade to reach the bottom of the screw slot.

You can easily modify a standard screwdriver to fit gun screws with a bench grinder. Rig a tool rest as a guide to ensure that both sides are identical, and dip the heated blade in water to preserve the temper. If you plan to do a lot of work on your guns, a set of hollow-ground screwdrivers is a worthwhile investment.

It is possible to restore a screw slot that's been chewed up. Remove the screw from the gun and secure it, head up, in a padded vise. With the round end of a ballpeen hammer, strike the edges of the slot firmly to flatten the burrs and drive them into the slot, but don't hit hard enough to dent or flatten the screw head itself. Then cut the burred metal away from the slot with the edge of a flat file, making sure you don't widen the slot. Once polished and blued, a restored screw is nearly indistinguishable from a new one.

JAMMING AND OTHER FIRING PROBLEMS

No matter how well cleaned and maintained your firearms are, you may still experience jamming or difficult ejection, chambering, or feeding from time to time. In 90 percent of the cases, the ammunition is at fault.

Always make sure the ammunition you buy is correct for your firearm. Never carry two different kinds of ammunition of the same caliber—say, .22 shorts and long rifles—together. Reloaded cartridges and shotshells are big offenders, only because many reloaders can't or don't recognize potential problem cartridges or fail to understand the importance of proper measuring, crimping, etc.

The combination of reloaded ammunition and automatic weapons often results in jamming. Preventive measures, in addition to knowing exactly what's in the shell or cartridge you're loading, should be second nature to any automatic owner.

Before taking reloads into the field, work them through the magazine, chamber, and ejector mechanism. Shotshells in particular will change shape somewhat from this treatment, and you'll be able to spot and reject problem shells quickly. Automatic shotguns are often equipped with power adjustment knobs to accommodate different loads, so make sure your gun is set for the load. Some automatic rifles with bolt actions must be loaded through the magazine, not at the chamber. Check.

The variety of "jams" affecting automatic pistols is great. Most can be attributed to improper ammunition or accumulated dirt. Some typical types of malfunctions are:

Failure to feed. This is caused by bent lips on the clip, more often than not. All automatic owners should have a clip on hand, if for no other reason than to compare a new one against a used one. The old one can easily be rebent to match.

Failure to chamber. Either the lips of the clip are too tight, or the magazine is not firmly seated in the frame. Both are easily repairable. Again, you may need a new clip to compare and use as a pattern to rebend the old one.

Failure to fire a full magazine. The magazine spring may be weak.

Failure to eject. The recoil spring may be too strong for the ammunition being used. Different loads require different springs. Match loads, for instance, are much weaker than military loads, and will not operate an automatic pistol set up with a stiff recoil spring. Failure to eject is also caused by a very dirty, worn, or damaged ejector.

Failure to close. The slide is probably dented or bent, although a very dirty gun may not close.

A jammed automatic pistol is a dangerous weapon. If your automatic jams, point it in a safe direction and work the slide, if possible. If the slide is jammed do not under any circumstances try to free it by pushing on the muzzle or pushing the slide from the muzzle end. A sudden release could fire the entire magazine through your hand!

If you can't get the slide to work, remove the magazine and try to pry the jammed cartridge loose from below with a screwdriver. If neither of these tactics work, take the gun to a gunsmith.

Bolt-action automatic rifles sometimes jam with the bolt closed. There isn't a lot you can do about this except whack the bolt with a piece of wood to free it. As always, be conscious of where the gun is aiming when you strike it.

Revolvers have their own ejection problems, usually due to swelling of the cartridge upon firing, or build-up of oil in the cylinder. If not all the empty shells eject when you work the ejector rod, tap the forward end with a block of wood. You can also work a screwdriver blade—carefully!—underneath the cartridge rim and pry it out.

A similar problem is wedging of some or all spent cartridges against the recoil plate, freezing the cylinder. You can loosen these shells by tapping the cylinder with the muzzle pointed down; use a block of wood and tap lightly. Another method for freeing stuck shells is to place the firearm in a freezer to make the metal contract a bit.

Once you have the cylinder open and have extracted the shells, inspect the charge holes. Chances are, you'll find fouling, debris, or, most likely, deposits of gun oil which have prevented the cartridge from fitting in properly. Clean out with solvent or, in the field, with lighter fluid.

Never try to force a revolver cylinder to turn. If it is wedged, tap it as described above. Place a single-action revolver on half cock to do this.

Rimfire rifles should never be dry-fired, as the firing pin can strike and dent the edge of the chamber, causing misfires and extraction problems. This is very expensive damage to repair. Actually, dry-firing any weapon is not only pointless but likely to cause problems with the firing pin. Similarly, don't pull a trigger against a safety, as you may pull hard enough to bend the trigger mechanism or the safety itself.

Rimfire .22s sometimes develop problems when used with both short and long or long rifle ammo. Rifles chambered for longs should never be loaded with shorts. The problem occurs in the chamber, where the short cartridge doesn't fit the whole way to the end of the bore. When fired, some of the explosive force is thus directed against the walls of the chamber, and in time a ring will be burned into the chamber at that point. Subsequent use of long ammo is likely to result in the cartridge case expanding into the ring, in which case it will be very difficult to remove. Firing shorts in a rifle chambered for longs will ruin the gun, and there is no cure.

Sometimes a cartridge case will come apart in the chamber at firing, either splitting lengthwise or, more likely, separating into two pieces, one of which is ejected properly, the other staying in the chamber. This is a touchy situation, but working carefully, you can push the remaining piece of brass through the bore with a cut-off cleaning rod.

First, though, you must provide something for the rod to bite into. A tap worked carefully into the chamber and twisted a few times should "thread" the stubborn case enough to provide purchase for the threads on the cleaning rod. If this seems too difficult—and it is a very delicate operation—take the firearm to a shop, where a gunsmith may have a set of taps for standard-caliber bores. Carefully inspect the barrel after any work on or around the bore.

REFINISHING METAL PARTS

A firearm that's been neglected or abused will show rust and corrosion on the outside. Once begun, rust is impossible to stop without complete reblueing or plating. (For this reason, always wipe the metal parts of your gun with a silicone-treated cloth after handling, as fingerprints are notoriously corrosive.)

Reblueing not only halts and prevents rust, it also beautifies and increases the worth of the firearm. Factory blueing is done with heat (hot blueing) and that can be a messy, time-consuming, and difficult chore requiring experience and special equipment. Cold-blueing kits on the market will provide a finish almost as good, and certainly adequate for any but collectors' pieces.

The cold-blueing kits often advise you to clean the gun with a degreasing solution included in the kit, followed by steel wool or emery paper on tough spots, then more degreaser. This procedure will give a mediocre finish, however. You can improve the performance of blueing kits by adding an acid bath as described below.

Before working on the finish at all, repair damage—grind down burrs, fix broken screws, etc.—and thoroughly clean the interior. Completely dismantle the gun and degrease it.

Bathe the dismantled gun in a 50 percent solution of muriatic acid, available at chemical supply houses and from some gunsmiths. You don't need a lot of this: a pint in a coffee can or wide-mouth jar will do. It is strong enough to remove the finish from steel in 45 seconds, so take precautions: wear gloves and glasses, wipe up spills, etc. Small parts can be dipped by wrapping a piece of wire around them and moving them back and forth in the acid bath. The frame and barrel should be swabbed with the solution —a cotton dauber or paintbrush will suffice. Rinse with water.

While rinsing look for corroded spots or places where the old finish did not completely come off. Work these over with extra-fine (4/0 if possible) steel wool and rinse again. Dry with soft cloths—lint-free cotton is preferable. Inspect the inside of the frame for rust spots that weren't loosened by the acid bath. Work on these with steel wool. Rinse again, this time in gun solvent. Dry.

From this point on, do not touch the metal with your bare hands, as skin oils and acids will promote rust rapidly. The metal is now unprotected. Wear gloves—soft cotton preferably.

This ends the preparation phase. You can store the gun and finish it later (or you may decide to take it to a hot-blueing shop or electroplater instead). If you want to store it, wipe it with gun oil and put it into a plastic bag which can be sealed. Store in a cool, dry place.

A word about hot blueing and electroplating. In the long run, either a professional blueing job or a chrome finish is preferable to a cold-blueing treatment. Electroplating in particular is relatively cheap and especially durable. Look for a shop that specializes in chroming motorcycle parts or replating bumpers. Such a shop can *de*plate a gun, too, so if you have a beat-up nickle-plated revolver, for instance, you can take it to be deplated, then smooth out the rough spots, and have it replated to look like new. It's an option.

Let's assume, though, that you want to do it yourself. The kit should include blueing and "rust preventive" liquids, and perhaps some swabs or steel wool. You'll need a couple of cotton swabs, some 4/0 steel wool, gloves, and wiping cloths.

Warm the gun and blueing solution to 75° F. This can be done easily by putting the gun and solution beneath a heat lamp or near a radiator or heat vent. Make sure it is warm and stays warm.

Swab the entire surface of the gun with blueing, taking care not to miss any sections. Make the coat as even as possible and do not overlap. Work the solution into all the nooks and crannies. Let it stay on for about three minutes, or as the directions advise, then wipe off the surplus.

Burnish the entire exterior with steel wool and wipe again. This treatment will lay a good base coat of blueing on the gun and bring out the shine of the underlying metal.

Apply additional coats, burnishing and wiping as you go. Do not overlap or miss any spots, otherwise the finished product will show quite clearly where you do. Each coat should be complete. Three or four coats should do it. After the final coat, wipe on the rust preventive solution provided with the kit as instructed on the package. This will halt the blueing action and set the finish. Let the gun dry overnight, away from dust.

By the next day, the finish should be hard and dry, and the glow of burnished metal should shine through. The gun should be oiled before being handled with bare hands. After oiling, reassemble.

First Aid Kits

A COMPLETE FIRST aid kit should be part of every outdoorsperson's baggage, and that kit should contain medication and bandages sufficient to bandage sizable wounds, prevent infection, and stop pain for up to a week, depending upon the length of the intended sojourn. It should also enable you to splint broken bones.

A suggested inventory for a backwoods first aid kit includes adhesive tape, sterile gauze pads (either nonstick or regular), butterfly closures and-/or large, sterile adhesive strips, a roll of two-inch gauze, pain medication (in capsule form), hydrogen peroxide, an antibiotic/antibacterial ointment such as Neosporin, and at least a seven-day supply of a broad-spectrum antibiotic (seven days worth of the maximum allowable dosage).

Optional supplies include a burn ointment or general skin irritation ointment, an eyecup and boric acid eyewash, cotton swabs, tweezers, scissors, a razor, Ace elastic bandage and closures, and an anti-bacterial soap, such as phisoDerm.

Pay attention to the shelf life of all medicines in your kit. Antibiotics and hydrogen peroxide will be labeled with an expiration date. Never keep "leftover" antibiotics. All sterile bandages should be kept wrapped in plastic, and pill and capsule containers should be kept sealed. It is better to have pain medication in capsule or coated-pill form than in soft-pill form, as moisture will soften and deteriorate soft pills. Toss in a few silica gel packets to control humidity.

First aid supplies should be kept in a hard metal or plastic container, sealed with tape, and kept out of children's reach. If you're traveling afloat, secure the kit to the craft and wrap the supplies in several layers of plastic (zip-lock bags are ideal for this). Taping a piece of foam flotation material to the inside of the lid will help keep the kit from sinking.

Fishing Line

THE DEVELOPMENT OF nylon and other synthetics for use in fly, casting, and spinning lines has revolutionized the sport and simplified line care and maintenance. Aside from heavy braided linen lines occasionally used by surf casters, most fishing lines today are nylon, which is virtually maintenance free.

That doesn't mean it lasts forever. Nylon deteriorates with exposure to ultraviolet light. Knots can weaken it and rough surfaces abrade it. Exposure to strong acid can dissolve it. And, in time, it will just lose its strength from a combination of the above and the normal friction of casting and retrieving.

You can keep nylon monofilament line in service, however. DuPont, leading manufacturer of nylon fishing lines, provided much of the following information, including excerpts from a report written by the research manager of their fishing line division, Dr. John E. Hansen.

Line replacement depends on how much the line has been used, not the age of the line. You could store a spool in its original package for years and it would be just as good as the day you bought it. Same goes for a reel of line that has been properly stored. (That line could last indefinitely if it never saw the light of day.)

How much a line has been fished is the key to replacement. The less frequent angler might need to replace his line only once a year, while the avid bass fisherman who gets out on the water every chance he gets ought to respool his reel at least once a week.

The kind of fishing is another key. Fishing in deep, unobstructed water can call for line replacement once a year. But, surf casting subjects the line to more punishment, so the line may have to be replaced once a month.

Fishing around rocks in a stream bed or stick-ups in a reservoir might call for line replacement every trip.

Most bait casting, spin casting and open-face spinning reels are designed to work best when filled to near capacity. Consequently, as a general rule, line should be replaced whenever it no longer fills the reel properly and casting distance has shortened.

One thing that will cause nylon line to deteriorate is prolonged exposure to the ultraviolet rays of sunlight. Day-to-day fishing under bright sun has negligible effect, but continuous exposure for several months may weaken line. Consequently, when reels are not being used they should be stored in a dark place, such as a tackle box, boat locker, or garage. New spools of line should be stored in their original boxes on a closet shelf, or in the basement.

If you have line on a reel or spool that may have received an overdose of sunlight, check its strength. The surface of the line may feel dry. Or it may seem brittle. Tie an overhand knot and determine whether it cuts the line under reasonable pressure.

Only the outer coils may be damaged. Check along the line until you reach a point with normal condition and strength. Then cut off the bad line. If the remainder fills the reel properly, it is probably safe to use.

Be sure to store your filled reels and extra line in a cool, dark place. Don't store line on the deck inside your car's rear window or in the truck.

Besides ultraviolet light, nylon monofilament appears to have only one other enemy, and that's battery acid. Sulfuric acid found in most batteries will destroy nylon.

Test results have shown that nylon monofilament is not damaged by exposure to salt water, gasoline, motor oil, insect repellent, sunscreen lotion, detergents, rust inhibitors, or lubricants. However, you wouldn't want to be careless in exposing your line to materials such as gasoline or motor oil which might give your line an odor and affect your fishing.

Nylon monofilament can be cleaned in warm water and detergent, and should be rinsed thoroughly afterward. Cleaning gives you an opportunity to inspect the line and, more important, to reverse it.

Usually only the first one-fourth to one-third of a spool of line is in use. Under unusual circumstances, perhaps half the line is off the reel. What's left on the reel isn't really subjected to any stress, although it may develop a severe set from being kept on the reel. It's a simple matter to reverse the line, using the strong, virtually new line on the "business" end.

COILS, TWISTS, AND BALLOONS IN LINE

Like most plastic materials, nylon has "memory"—the characteristic of returning to its original shape. In fishing line, that results in coils from the reel or spool. It is the nature of nylon to take a set ("remember") a position it has been in for a period of time.

The degree of set is directly related to the amount of moisture in the line and the amount of tension on the line. Nylon absorbs water. Both the diameter and the length of line will increase with increasing moisture content. When the line is stored on the reel for several days, the absorbed moisture evaporates and the line shrinks back to its original length. This causes tension on the line and forces it to set in the curvature of the reel. It doesn't harm the line, but on the first cast of the next fishing trip, the line will usually fluff up on the spool and come off in wide loops like a "slinky."

Line curl is not a permanent problem. It is easily solved by adding moisture to the line by soaking the reel in a bucket of water or trailing the line through the boat's wake for a few minutes. Nylon absorbs water quickly under all fishing conditions. Some monofilament takes up water more rapidly than others, but ultimately all nylon lines attain approximately the same moisture content. Within about an hour of fishing, the nylon line will absorb from six to eight percent water, depending on the pound test. Water makes the line softer, limper, and easier to handle. It also makes the line thicker and longer—as much as two percent longer by the end of the day of fishing.

That first cast after fishing gear has been unused for a period of time can often result in snarls, bird's nests, or at best a series of stiff coils in the line. New line off a spool will often present the same problem. Soak the line for an hour or more before that first fishing trip. As it absorbs moisture, the line will relax and gain limpness.

Tension can also remove these coils. Tie the line to a tree or other stationary object. Let the line off the reel as you back off about the distance of a long cast. Use your rod to put strain on the line, as though you were setting the hook. Apply this tension, short of the breakpoint in the line, a dozen times or more.

Several elements of your tackle, plus the way you handle the crank on the reel, can put twist in monofilament line. Fishing with a twisted line can hamper casting and damage the line.

With spinning gear, never crank the reel when the fish is pulling line off the spool. Every turn on the handle puts more twists in the line. If your terminal tackle—lure, spoons, or bait—spin when the line is being retrieved, use a swivel that you're sure turns freely.

If you get twist in the leading end of the line, raise the rod tip and let the dangling lure or bait unwind the line. If the twist extends well up the line, and you're fishing from a boat, remove all terminal tackle and troll the line behind the boat for a few minutes. Or, if you're on a stream bank, let the line pay out downstream and the current will unwind those kinks.

If the line twist is so bad that these remedies won't remove it, strip it off your reel and put on fresh line.

Filling your reel properly can help prevent line twist and increase the working life of your line. The following procedures for major types of reels will assure a smoothly wound line.

When filling a revolving-spool bait casting reel, insert a pencil into the supply spool to allow the fishing line to feed smoothly off the spool. Have someone hold each end of the pencil while you turn the reel handle. Keep proper tension on the line by having the person holding the pencil exert a slight inward pressure on the supply spool.

You fill an open-face spinning reel differently than a bait casting reel because you must allow for the rotation of the pick-up bail which may cause the line to twist. Follow these steps: Have someone hold the supply spool as shown in the illustration or place it on the floor or ground. Pull the line so that it spirals (balloons) off the end of the spool. Thread the line through the rod guides and tie the line to the reel with the bail in the open position. Hold the rod tip three to four feet away from the supply spool. Make fifteen to twenty turns on the reel handle, then stop.

Check for line twist by moving the rod tip to about one foot from the supply spool. If the slack line twists, turn the supply spool completely around. This will eliminate most of the twist as you wind the rest of the line onto the reel.

Use this same procedure for a closed-face filling a spinning reel. Remember to partially remove the reel cover so you will be able to see the spool and the rotation of the pick-up pin as shown in the diagram. This is critical to insure that you do not underfill or overfill the spool.

Always keep a light tension on fishing line when spooling any reel. Do this by holding the line between the thumb and forefinger of your free hand.

While casting with spinning gear almost guarantees freedom from bird's nests and line snarls, three conditions can cause loops of line to balloon or plop off the fixed spool on the reel.

Line filled too close to the lip of the spool can cause several loops of

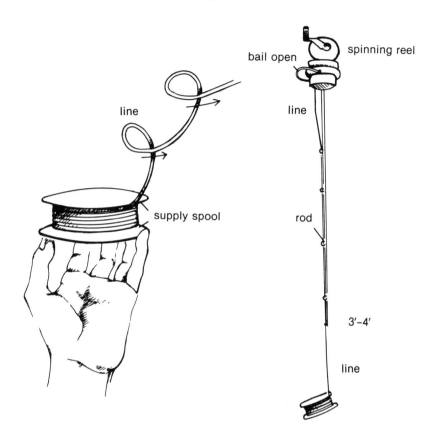

To fill an open-face spinning reel, have someone hold the supply spool as shown and pull the line so that it spirals off the end of the spool. Thread the line through the guides and tie to the reel with the bail in the open position. Then carefully begin to reel in.

line to come off simultaneously as you cast. Recheck spooling instructions for the reel. Normally, the spool should not be filled beyond an eighth to a quarter of an inch of the lip.

Unless moderate tension is applied to the line when filling the reel, it may be too loosely wound and loops will entangle as they come off the spool. A long cast downwind, or paying the line out into a current, will free these coils so the line can be rewound properly.

In rare cases, the diameter of a spinning reel spool causes loops to flow off that are too large to pass through the first guide on the rod. Line spirals will either slap the guide, cutting casting distance, or pile up causing a great snazzle. The answer to this problem is to use the proper reel on the proper rod; for example, always use a spinning rod with a spinning reel.

LINE BREAKAGE

Repeated line breakage, well above the terminal tackle, can often be traced to rough metal surfaces on rod guides or reel parts. Even small burrs on the inside surfaces of guides can nick or rip small shavings off the line with every cast. Rough and worn spots on bait casting reels or on bail pick-ups on spinning reels can do the same sort of damage.

Periodic inspection of such metal parts with a magnifying glass can spot these problems before fish are lost due to frayed lines. Some types of metal guides will groove after months of fishing. Since it's difficult to see inside guide surfaces, pull a piece of material—like a nylon stocking—through the guide. Even tiny rough spots will snag the fabric.

Premium lines have built-in abrasion strength to reduce the wear caused by dragging the leading end of the line across rough bottom or brush. But this line property provides little protection against the cutting action of such rough metal surfaces on rods or reels.

Many strong fish have snapped good line and escaped because the drag was too tight on the reel. After the line absorbs the impact of the strike the drag must permit the fish to take line off the reel as it makes its run, yet be tight enough to slow it down and eventually tire it out.

To accomplish this, a good rule is to set the drag at no more than half the pound/test of the line. Remember that the braking action increases as the spool empties. When fishing deep, or in heavy currents, set the drag to about a third of the line's pound/test.

To set the drag, attach the line to a reliable spring scale, apply tension, and check the pounds of force required to pull line off the reel. Then adjust the drag control to give the desired value. (For more on adjusting drag, see section on spinning reels in *Reels* entry.)

Dragging line over rocks, rough sandy bottoms, submerged tree trunks, and other underwater obstructions can nick and fray monofilament. Line abraded by these obstacles is weakened in such properties as knot strength and impact resistance. A fast strike or the struggle with a hooked fish can cause the line to snap in these worn sections.

A good rule is to check the leading end of the line every two or three casts by running it lightly between thumb and forefinger. If the line feels rough, check along the line to the point where it becomes smooth, then cut off the worn section.

KNOTS AND LINE STRENGTH

Line manufacturers classify lines by several factors, including the familiar pound/test rating. Another rating factor is knot strength, which is defined as the property in line that provides insurance against breakoffs in the knot, particularly when the knot is improperly tied. It's a fact that knots weaken fishing line. Consequently, the knot is usually the weakest link between the fisherman and the fish. The type of knot used and and the way it is tied directly influence the breaking strength of a knotted line.

Most line manufacturers have emphasized this in the way they have chosen to evaluate knots. Knots are rated according to how much they diminish the strength of the line. That's calculated using a laboratory machine called the Instron tensile tester, first to measure the breakload of an unknotted line, then to measure the breakload of the line with a knot tied. The breaking point of the unknotted line is divided into the breaking point of the knotted line to produce a percentage measure. The formula:

$$\text{Knot Efficiency} = \frac{\text{Knotted Breakload}}{\text{Unknotted Breakload}} \times 100$$

For example, the two most popular knots for tying terminal tackle—the Palomar and improved clinch knots—are rated at 95 percent to 100 percent. Lines with these knots won't usually break in the knot. Other knots, however, have far lower knot efficiency, like the dropper loop which is rated at 80 percent to 90 percent.

The problem with knots is that nylon monofilament is such tough stuff that it tends to cut through itself. Good knots have ample cushioning against that cutting action. Poor knots, like the simple overhand knot many of us tied as youthful anglers, don't have that cushioning. The overhand knot, for instance, has a rated knot efficiency of about 50 percent to 70 percent. That means the line will probably break more often in the knot than it does in the unknotted line.

If you've been losing fish due to breaks in the knot, you can use a simple test to check your line's knot strength. Tie an overhand knot in the line a foot or two from the terminal end. Wrap the line around your hands on both sides of the knot and exert a steady pull. If the line breaks, move up a yard and try again. Unusual abrasion or general line wear may have weakened the leading section of line. When you reach the point where no further breaks occur, cut off the weak section and check to be sure the existing line still fills the reel properly. (Better wear gloves when making this test. Monofilament can cut your hands under this sort of pressure.)

With ordinary monofilament, the overhand knot will cut through the line at about 50 percent of the rated pound/test. Premium lines withstand this cutting action up to a minimum of 70 percent of the line's pound/test. If you're checking small diameter line (2-pound through 8-pound test), keep in mind that only light pressure is required to break it.

Even the strongest knot—one that will hold to the full pound/test rating of the line—can be weakened when tied hurriedly and without proper attention to basic details. Heed the following tips when tying knots:

Avoid twisting lines. Where the knot is tied with a doubled line, keep the two lines parallel rather than twisting them together.

Pull loops slowly. When tightening coils or loops of a knot, such as the improved clinch, be sure they pull up in a neat spiral. If these loops are pulled up quickly and cross over each other, the upper turns may cut the ones beneath when tension is applied.

Pull all knots tight. Slippage in a loosely tied knot can cut the line and cause breakage in the knot.

Practice tying your favorite knots. It's just as easy to tie them right and the results in terms of handling the big ones will pay off.

SPECIAL CARE OF FLY LINES

Most of the above information about spinning and casting lines can be applied to fly lines as well, although due to their different structure— a plastic coating over a braided core in some cases—and shorter length, line curl is less of a problem. Even so, fly lines should be used with a "backer" to fill the reel and provide a safety margin in case you hook a long-running fish. Fly lines require some special handling and care. Cortland Line Company, a leading manufacturer of fishing lines, offers several care tips.

In normal use, microscopic particles of dirt and debris will adhere to the surface of a floating line, adding weight that eventually overcomes the natural buoyancy of the line. The tip section of a tapered line will begin sinking first, indicating that the line should be cleaned.

Use line cleaner before each use to remove surface residue and to provide lubrication that allows the line to move more efficiently through the rod guides. Avoid leaving an excess amount of the cleaner on the line. Sinking lines do not normally require application of the cleaner.

Don't let the surface of a fly line come into direct contact with chemical substances that may be harmful to the fly line finish. Chemical substances in some brands of insect repellents are harmful. So are gasoline, detergents and some brands of fly line dressing. It is good practice to protect your line from these liquids.

Excessive heat can be responsible for rapid deterioration of synthetic fly line finishes. One should be especially careful about leaving a reel filled with line in direct hot sun. Lines can be ruined by even temporary storage on dashboards or rear ledges of automobiles where direct sun rays are intensified.

Sharp projections on fly reels and worn fly rod guides can slice and ruin a line very quickly. Examine carefully at least three or four times a season and replace or repair.

During the off-season, line should be removed from the reel and hung in loose coils over a large wooden peg. Avoid storing in an area subjected to extreme temperatures, either hot or cold.

Beginners at the sport of fly fishing often have loops of line over, under, and around their bodies, trees, etc., etc. (Experts never do, of course!) If you're prone to let line loose, carry some two-sided tape with you on your fishing trip and, just before you begin, wrap a piece around the handle, out of your way. It'll provide a handy place to stash line while you unsnarl your tangle.

Fishing Rods

TUBULAR FIBERGLASS RODS have nearly taken over the market from bamboo. The reasons are obvious: glass rods are cheaper, easier to repair, and less likely to need maintenance. Their action is, to all but a few dyed-in-the-wool purists, satisfactory—or at least getting there—and the chemists' magic can produce nearly any degree of flex an angler might require. And, of course, the potential for technological improvement is limitless—witness the combination glass and graphite rods, which at this writing are the highest of high tech.

BAMBOO RODS

Despite the inroads of modern technology, many anglers still prefer bamboo rods. And why not? Bamboo is, after all, the material that made fly fishing the art it is. Bamboo is durable, sensitive, and beautiful. Most important from the point of view of this discussion, you can work on it without having a degree in chemistry.

Bamboo is wood, and the greatest enemy of wood is water. Keeping a bamboo rod in service, then, is a matter of keeping moisture from entering the cells of the wood, where it contributes to rotting and eventual disintegration. Any quality coating will achieve this, but the harder varnishes and lacquers will resist scratching better than softer polyurethane. Of course, an oil coating is best of all from the standpoint of cost, simplicity, and renewability.

If you're considering buying a bamboo rod, inspect it carefully for evidence of rot and splitting. Check the wood around line guides, ferrules, and handle closely. Are there soft spots, dents, or cracks which might indicate internal damage, or damage that's been covered with fancy winding thread? If you can, remove a guide and a ferrule. Look for dry rot in the portion of the wood covered by the thread or metal. Serious deterioration of the bamboo in this area means that the rod is on its way out—or at least that section of it has trouble. You can, of course, shorten individual sections, albeit at the cost of modifying the rod's action. Handles, line guides, and ferrules are all replaceable.

Preparing a Rod for Rebuilding. To rebuild a bamboo rod, first strip the entire rod of its guides, ferrules, handle, and windings. Cut wrapping thread with a razor blade and peel it off in one piece. Don't try to loosen it by sticking a knife underneath it or attempt to find the end and unwide it. Just slice it off.

Ferrules are secured to rods with ferrule cement, which will melt with heat. Apply the flame of a butane lighter or torch to the ferrule until glue begins to run, then grip the ferrule by hand and tug it off smartly—no prying, twisting, or squeezing the rod with metal tools.

If you can't pull the ferrule straight off by hand, and you're sure no one has stuck it on there with epoxy or cyanoacrylate or another space-age adhesive, tap the end of the ferrule smartly on a solid surface, keep heating and try once more. In a real pinch, grip the ferrule with a vise grip and pull straight off—no twisting!

With the ferrules, guides, and handle off, begin working on the wood. If you find rot or splitting at or near the end of a section, cut it off and taper the end to accept another ferrule of the same size. This means removing wood with abrasives or blades. You can use a simple pencil sharpener to remove large amounts of old wood, but of course you'll have a pencil-pointed rod section. Still, that's better than whittling; it's nearly impossible, unless you're a skilled woodcarver, to whittle an even taper on the end of a cylinder. Make sure the end is perfectly square. Remember: you can always take more off, but you have a hard time putting wood back once it's gone—and fillers are expensive, messy, and at best a poor compromise.

Once you've gotten the rod end to size, strip the rod of its earlier finish. For lacquered rods, use lacquer thinner and steel wool (00 grade is fine enough). For a varnish finish, use turpentine.

You'll need a rod holder for the rest of the project. There are several commercial holders available. One made by Featherweight Products is part of a thread-wrapping system and is a worthwhile investment if you're serious about rebuilding rods. If you're just doing it once, though, you don't need to buy a holder.

You can make an adequate rod holder from a few 1-inch by 6-inch pine boards. Envision an upside-down bench, with the "legs" notched to hold the rod. Cut three pieces of wood, two about 12 to 16 inches long, the other 20–24 inches. Notch the two short pieces and nail them to the ends of the longer board. You can brace these end pieces with wedges cut from a piece of two-by-four, if you wish, or get really fancy and make an adjustable holder by drilling a series of holes in the base board and cutting and inserting pieces of dowel to match in the end boards, but the basic bench is all you really need. Tack a piece of elastic on either or both ends to hold the rod securely.

Coating the Wood. If you've chosen to lacquer or varnish your rod, do so now. Mask the areas you shaved down to accept the ferrules so that you won't get lacquer or varnish on the rough wood.

Follow directions given on the varnish or lacquer container. Use a small brush; spray finishes are hard to apply evenly to a curved surface. Allow plenty of set-up time and a warm, dry place for curing.

If you put an oil finish on the rod, you needn't mask the areas you shaved for the ferrules, as the oil will soak in without affecting the bonding of the ferrule to the rod.

Heat boiled linseed oil in a double boiler and apply it as described in the section on refinishing in the *Gun Stocks* entry. You don't need to seal the bamboo beforehand, of course, and you'll probably not need as many coats, but the procedure is the same. Again, allow the rod to dry completely before proceeding to mount the ferrules and guides.

Before installing ferrules, though, take one more rot-preventive measure. Inject linseed oil into the end of the rod using a short, stiff hypodermic needle and a syringe filled with a couple cc's of oil. Push the needle into the wood but don't force it farther than it wants to go, otherwise you'll have a bent or broken needle stuck in the rod. Slowly inject oil into the wood, letting it soak in as you go. This small extra bit of care can pay off in extended rod life.

Mounting Ferrules and Guides. Glue the ferrules to the rod with ferrule cement, which comes in handy stick form and needs only to be heated over a candle flame or other heat source and applied to the wood. Twist the ferrule to distribute the cement evenly and to make sure the ferrule is all

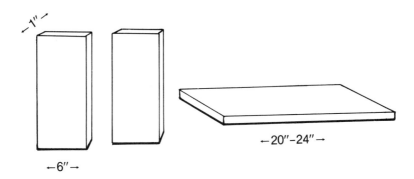

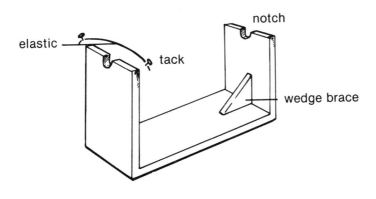

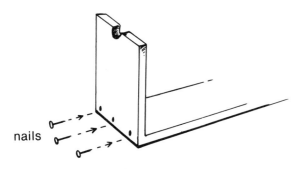

Make a simple rod holder from pine boards. You can make it adjustable by drilling a series of holes in the base board and inserting corresponding pieces of dowel in the down ends of the upright boards.

the way on. Check it with a straightedge to make sure it is absolutely straight—you cannot be too careful with this! The ferrules must line up exactly or the rod won't fit together.

Hold the rod and ferrule firmly in hand until the cement sets. Don't worry about drips and spills, as you can scrape them off later with a knife.

After the ferrules have dried, mark where you want the line guides. Usually, you'll just put them back where they were. Rod guides come in many sizes, shapes, and materials. For fly rods, stick with simple chrome-plated "foulproof" loop guides; for spinning rods, aluminum alloy guides will resist cutting and grooving much longer than chrome; for deep-sea fishing or trolling rods, a ceramic-lined, polyethylene-cushioned guide will give long service. The type of rod guide is important, too, because guides affect the rod's action. The heavier, sturdier braced guides are stiffer than simple loops.

Before installing the line guides, flatten the tips of their feet with a hammer and rough them up with a file. This will insure that the winding will fit smoothly over the tip and will prevent the feet from lifting or the thread slipping during winding.

On bait casting and spinning rods, wrap the rod with thread and seal before putting the guide on (see next section). This provides a cushion for the guide and will simplify placing the guide. On fly rods, you'll put the guide right on the rod. Place the guide on the rod. If you're repairing a one-piece rod or a section of rod with more than one guide on it, make sure they line up. Secure the guide to the rod with a rubber band or piece of masking tape.

Wrapping Bait Casting and Spinning Rods. Wrapping is an acquired skill and you'll probably feel like you need three hands to get it right. One tool is essential to make a tight wrap: a bobbin for the winding thread. You can improvise one from a length of dowel and a rubber band.

Cut a piece of ⅝-inch dowel about 6 inches long. Secure a wide rubber band to both ends of the dowel with thumbtacks, so that the rubber band is stretched fairly tight. (You may have to cut the rubber band if you can't find one to fit perfectly.) The winding thread can now be transferred to the dowel and the rubber band secured over it. The rubber band will prevent the thread from unwinding by itself when you let it hang.

You can also make a simpler version of the professional-quality bobbin holder that comes in the thread-wrapping kit made by Featherweight Products. Take a piece of heavy, stiff wire and bend it into a U shape. Bend

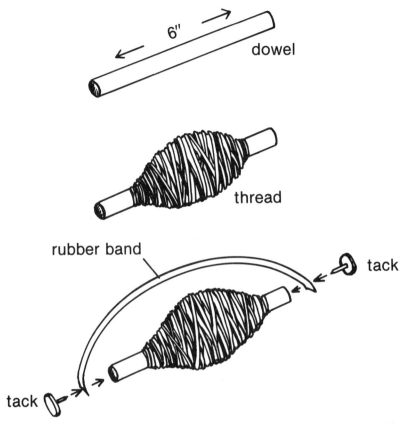

Using a bobbin will help you when you're wrapping the rod. Improvise a simple bobbin with a ⅝ inch dowel about six inches long and a wide rubber band.

a small loop in each end. Insert a bolt through a flat washer, through one loop, through the center of the thread spool and through the other loop. Secure it with a flat washer and wing nut. This will hold the spool as tightly or as loosely as you wish—just adjust the wing nut to close the wire U until it binds against the ends of the spool.

Begin wrapping about three-fourths inch from the tip. Secure the thread to the rod by whipping it (lay the thread along the rod and take several turns over it) and wrap tightly and evenly over the foot, toward the loop. When about five or six turns from the guide, lay a loop of fishing line on the rod, take the five or six turns and cut the thread off with about an inch to spare.

Put the end of the thread in the loop of fishing line, and pull both ends of the loop back under the wrapping. Pull it tight and make sure the last turn doesn't double over the next to last. Once you're satisfied with the wrapping and all the turns seem tight and even, snip off the thread close to the wrapping.

Coat the thread with color preserver and/or winding finish, both of which are available at sporting good shops. There are several different kinds available; some involve mixing, some not. An epoxy one-coat finish, which requires mixing a catalyst and resin, is a good bet for the beginner. Otherwise, you'll need several coats of color preserver and clear varnish or fingernail polish. Make sure whatever you use is compatible with the finish you've put on the rod!

Handles and Finishing. Preshaped rod handles, with reel seats, caps, and ferrules, are available in a variety of configurations. You can make rod handles from cork rings or handle stock of cork, wood, or plastic. Unless you have some experience, you're probably better off buying a prepared handle for your bamboo rod. You can learn to make your own handles by practicing on old bait casting rods following the procedure explained in the next section.

With the handle, guides, and ferrules in place, and the windings dressed, your bamboo rod is ready for one final coat of varnish or lacquer, if you desire, or a final wiping with oil.

FIBERGLASS RODS

Guides and Guide Spacing. Mounting guides on fiberglass rods is done in much the same way as described for bamboo rods, except that you have to know where the rod's "spine" is to properly place the guides.

Tubular glass rods are made by forming cloth around a metal rod. The glass is then glued, sanded, and finished, making the joint nearly invisible. It's there, though, and the slight overlap and adhesive makes this side of the rod stiffer than the other. Thin-walled rods have a more pronounced spine than thick-walled ones. Graphite and hybrid rods have a very stiff spine and you must locate it to place the guides properly, otherwise the rod will cast off to one side.

You can probably assume that the manufacturer placed the original guides correctly. However, if you don't know where they were, or if you are building a rod from parts, you'll need to find the spine.

To find the spine, lay the end of the rod in your left hand, with the hand placed about two feet from the tip. Support the butt on a table or work-bench. With the other hand, grasp the top and bend it down several inches. Now rotate the rod with your right hand, holding the bend, until you feel resistance—the rod doesn't want to rotate any more, or will do so only with a slight increase in pressure.

Try it again. There, feel the difference? It may be only a slight hesita-tion, but when you feel that resistance, the spine is at that moment facing down, resting in your left palm. Mark it.

If the spine is very hard to locate, it probably isn't stiff enough to make any difference. In such cases, guides may be placed anywhere, especially if the rod has a slight curve, as many do. It's advisable to place the guides where they will tend to straighten the rod. The guides have stiffness and their feet will add rigidity to the rod. You can use this rigidity to help offset a slight bend in a glass rod. If the spine is very pronounced, however, you should place the guides either exactly on it or exactly opposite.

Guide spacing is important. The following chart gives spacing for casting and spinning rods. It was printed in "How to Build Custom Quality Casting, Spinning and Fly Rods," copyright 1976 by Featherweight Pro-ducts, a fine source of rod blanks, handles, ferrules, guides, and necessary supplies for building or rebuilding rods.

Handles. We recommend prepared handle kits for most beginners, simply because building handles from stock and fittings takes time and practice, and most often the hassle isn't worth the savings in cost. Feather-

SUGGESTED GUIDE SPACING   All measurements are from the tip of the rod toward the butt. (casting rod lengths include a 12″ handle)

CASTING RODS

5′ ROD	5 GUIDES	5″	10½″	16½″	23¾″	32¾″	
5½′ ROD	5 GUIDES	5″	10½″	18½″	27½	36½″	
5½′ ROD	6 GUIDES	4½″	9½″	15½″	21½″	28½″	36½″
6′ ROD	5 GUIDES	5″	10¾″	19½″	30½″	43¼″	
6′ ROD	6 GUIDES	4½″	9½″	15½″	21½″	28½″	36½″

SPINNING RODS

5′ ROD	5 GUIDES	4½″	8¾″	14½″	21½″	33½″		
5½′ ROD	5 GUIDES	4½″	9½″	15¼″	23¾″	33″		
6′ ROD	6 GUIDES	4½″	10″	16½″	24½″	32″	39¼″	
6½′ ROD	6 GUIDES	4½″	9½″	16″	24″	35⅝″	44¾″	
7′ ROD	7 GUIDES	4½″	9″	14″	21″	29½″	38″	51″
8′ ROD	8 GUIDES	4″	8″	13″	19½″	27″	35″	44″ 55″

weight Products has many kits available, one of which is sure to fit your rod.

Making a simple rod handle out of cork rings may be within your abilities, though. It's not that hard, just messy. Begin by removing the butt plate, if any, on the old handle.

Now get all the cork off the rod butt. Messy, like we said. Resist the temptation to burn it off, otherwise you'll ruin the rod before you get it all off. Just whittle and shave it off as best you can with a knife. Save the cork scraps, by the way, because they can be mixed with white glue to form an excellent filler for cracks and holes in your handle.

Once you've gotten the old cork off, you're ready to install the new handle. Check the opening in the center of each ring. Most likely, you'll have to increase the size of this opening. Cork is tough to drill, but that's how to do it—drill it with a wood bit. Soaking the cork in water first can help prevent splitting, but nothing will make this an easy job. Keep at it and try to get the openings in all rings as close as possible to the size of the rod butt.

Coat the butt liberally with waterproof adhesive (a neoprene-based one-step glue will do fine here) and slip the rings on the butt. Slather glue between them—don't miss a spot. The more glue between the rings and on the rod butt, the better. Don't worry about drips and runs on the outside, as you'll be shaping the handle to your specifications anyway and will remove the excess glue.

Once the glue has set, shape the handle to fit your hand with a razor knife, rasp, and sandpaper. Get creative if you wish; you have a lot of cork to work with and can get the handle to fit like a glove if you take your time.

Handles that are merely dirty can be washed with soap and water, or sanded down to restore their appearance. You can coat the handle with polyurethane varnish, but this leaves a shiny, slippery coating on the cork. There are several other materials you can use to cover a dirty or unsightly handle. One new product called Qoro Grip is ¾-inch wide tape with a feltlike surface advertised to be waterproof. Fastened with double-edge tape, it provides an attractive, comfortable, nonslip grip for any rod. Foam weatherstripping tape can also be used to cover a rod handle.

Repairing Breaks. Fiberglass rods are so strong and flexible they seldom break. In fact, some graphite-glass hybrid rods are offered with unconditional five-year guarantees. That's a pretty good indication that the manufacturers feel they've solved the problem of making a light rod strong.

Sometimes, though, tubular fiberglass rods break, usually at or near the tip. Although you can't make the rod as good as new, you can fix a broken tip and stay on the water.

If the rod is broken within six or eight inches of the tip, you can easily remove the tip guide and replace it on the shortened rod. Most tip guides are held in place with ferrule cement, so begin by heating the guide with a lighter or torch until the cement begins to run. Pull it off and keep heating it until all the cement has run out of the guide. If the guide has been cemented on with a more permanent adhesive, break it off and dig out the fiberglass with a knife.

Now test the fit. You may have to sand the rod a bit to get the guide on easily. You can open the end of the guide a bit with a knife and/or sand the rod to make the guide fit.

After you have a reasonable fit, simply heat some ferrule cement, smear it on the rod and put the guide on. You can use other adhesives of course, but you shouldn't if you plan to make more permanent repairs later on. Rubber cement, duct tape, or electrician's tape all can be used to hold the guide on the rod for a short time.

A break farther from the tip is a problem. You don't want to just slap the tip guide on a shortened stub. It is possible to splice a fiberglass rod; it won't look great, but it will keep you fishing.

All you need to splice a broken rod is aluminum or steel tubing and ferrule cement. There are rod repair kits available which contain tubing, tape, and cement, but you don't need to buy one if you can get some scrap metal tubing. A good source is a radio/TV antenna shop. Get a scrap telescoping antenna of the kind found on FM radios. For larger diameter rods, try outdoor antennas. In a pinch, you can use automotive fuel-line tubing, brake-line tubing, or plastic tubes used to carry wires through the firewall. Nearly anything rigid enough to resist bending when you cast or play a fish will do.

Begin by cleaning the inside of the tube with solvent to remove all grease, oil, and debris. Boiling the tube in soapy water will help, too. Dry it thoroughly.

Prepare the pieces of rod by removing any splinters or loose pieces of cloth from the ends. If the rod is cracked, sand off the cracked areas. You want good glass for the joint.

Take a piece of tubing as close to the diameter of the rod pieces as possible and insert both pieces of rod to judge the fit. You can build up the rod with winding thread if you have any handy, but resist the temptation to wrap tape around the rod, as the cement won't stick to it very well. When you have a fit you like, remove the tube and mark the center with a nail. Use a center punch or sharp nail to dent it slightly at the center—just enough to keep the rod pieces from slipping past.

Heat ferrule cement and apply it to one rod piece. Insert the piece into the tube and hold until cool. If your fit isn't too great, melt more ferrule cement and allow it to run inside the tube from the open end; then, working quickly, cement the second piece in place.

Remember that ferrule cement can be melted and remelted without losing its adhesive qualities. Don't be afraid to reheat the tube a little to get things tight. Avoid overheating, of course, since you can melt the rod that way.

Once everything has cooled, a couple of turns of tape around the end of the tube will finish the job. You're back on the water with a functional, though somewhat stiffer, rod.

Cases and Holders. A tubular case isn't much good without its cap. Secure the cap to the case by drilling a hole and tying a piece of monofilament fishing line through it. Remove burrs from the hole with a rat tail file. Secure the other end of the line to the plastic cap by making a similar hole in it and taping a button inside the cap to prevent the monofilament from enlarging the hole. An easy way to make a hole in plastic is by heating a needle and pushing it through the cap.

Many rod guides are damaged by careless insertion. Hold the case with your thumb and forefinger at the opening and insert all the rod sections at one time, using your fingers to cushion the edge.

You can make a case for storing or transporting your rod from a cardboard mailing tube. A more ambitious project is making a case for a couple of rods from an electric guitar case, which you can pick up at a secondhand store or pawnshop for peanuts.

Begin by removing all the foam or rubber padding from the interior of the case. Cut a piece of cardboard to fit inside the case. You'll use this as a template. Arrange your rods and mark the cardboard by outlining each rod with a marking pen. Be careful not to space the rods too closely together.

When you have the cardboard template marked, make small holes all along the lines you've drawn with a nail or knife point. Keep the holes small, but open them up enough to allow a pen point to pass through.

Lay the perforated template on a piece of three-inch thick rigid foam cut to size. Mark the foam by pushing a pen point through the holes. Remove the template and begin cutting the foam to accept the rods. Careful —don't yield to the temptation to use heat. You'll have a much neater job if you cut the foam with a razor blade knife and straightedge.

When you're satisfied with the fit, cut a piece of canvas to fit over the foam and fasten it to the inside of the case. Actually, nearly any material will do; all you want to do is have a secureable flap to hold the rods in place. Rig Velcro strips along the edges for a tight fit. Cut another piece of foam to fit the lid and glue it into place.

Large, one-piece rods are difficult to transport and store. In most cases, they're safer outside an automobile than inside. Roof racks and ski racks are likely places to rig them. Use a couple of screw-type hose clamps padded with cloth or felt and wrap the rods in paper or plastic before mounting.

One of the safest places for a long surf casting rod is on the front bumper, pointing up. You'll soon get used to seeing it there, and you're unlikely to forget it and carelessly bump into it there. Any welding shop can help you rig up some sockets and clamps to hold rods in place.

Goretex

GORETEX IS A trademark for a laminated fabric having extraordinary properties of water repellency combined with breathability—the ability, in other words, to keep drops of water out while letting water vapor in. A similar fabric is named Klimate. Both are three layers thick, with a layer of a Teflon derivative in the middle, a layer of nylon taffeta on the outside, and a layer of nylon tricot on the inside. Goretex has found its way into sleeping bags, shoes, tents, and especially raingear.

Goretex has drawn both praise and criticism from outdoorspeople who expected it to be perfect. It isn't—no fabric is—but if cared for properly, it comes close to being a perfect foul-weather outer garment material. The problem seemed to be inconsistency. When Goretex first came on the market, reports were mixed. Some found it ideal; others claimed it let them down, keeping rain out for awhile, then failing to do so. Gradually, the solution emerged. Gortex will work well if kept clean and free from contamination by oil (including body oil), detergents, and salt water, and if its seams are sealed.

"Second generation" Goretex and its cousin Klimate have proven themselves in countless hours afield. Goretex garments must have their seams sealed. Although the laminate itself won't let drops of water pass through, the threads and the holes they pass through will. Seam sealants like Gore's Seam Stuff, made by Goretex's manufacturer, and Kenyon's K-kote have been developed to seal Goretex seams. Most garments manufactured of Goretex have sealed seams, but some older ones may not. Use two coats of sealer, applied at least one hour apart.

Goretex should be washed in soft water using a mild soap or detergent.

It must be thoroughly rinsed, since detergent residue will tend to break down water drops and allow moisture to pass through. Prewash agents, usually marketed in aerosol sprays, can be used to pretreat stubborn soil, but should be washed out completely for the same reason.

Aerosol prewash agents are excellent for removing oily stains and grease from Goretex, and should be used as soon as possible after the material has been soiled.

Goretex cannot be dry-cleaned, as the oily fluids leave a residue in the fabric which destroys its water resistance. Klimate is said to be dry-cleanable, as long as its seams aren't sealed. Oil contamination from insect repellents, lotions, etc., will also break down the water barrier, as will oils from your skin. Don't wear Goretex over nothing.

Denatured alcohol can remove severe oil contamination. Sponge it on and rinse thoroughly in cold water before the alcohol has time to dry.

Saltwater contamination is a bit of a mystery. No one can figure out why saltwater residue should help water get through this fabric, but it seems to. The answer is to rinse saltwater-wet Goretex in fresh water as soon as possible after it is exposed and not to let salt water dry on it if possible. For more information on water repellent gear, see *Raingear* entry.

Pinhole leaks in laminated-fabric garments should be patched with seam sealant. Larger tears and punctures are a problem. You can sew nylon patches to either side of the garment, but each pass with the needle opens another hole. Seam sealing is about the only solution.

Gun Stocks

A LOOSE STOCK is a common problem on rifles and shotguns, but one that's easily remedied. Most long guns have a large bolt running through the center, which screws into the frame. It's a simple matter to remove the butt plate, if any, and tighten this bolt with a large screwdriver. Loc-tite can help keep it from loosening, which it will tend to do. (See information on butt plate/recoil pad installation in the next section.)

SHORTENING

A commonly attempted modification/repair is stock shortening. We say "attempted" because too many misguided gunners hack off a piece of the stock without measuring and calculating just what they want to do. You can't put it back on once it's off, so "measure twice and cut once," as they say.

Actually, if you're contemplating shortening your stock, you should get expert advice first. Often, shooters will acquire bad postural habits which make them *think* they need to modify their guns. If you can reach the trigger and forestock without straining; if you can hold the gun on target; and if you can lay your cheek against the stock and see both sights, you probably don't need to shorten the stock.

Of course, if you're modifying a rifle or shotgun for a youngster, or if your gun is okay now but you want to add a recoil pad, you will have to cut some wood.

Length isn't the only thing to consider in a stock. If you hold a gun so that the barrel is perfectly horizontal, you'll notice that in some cases the end of the stock is not vertical. The angle the butt and barrel make is called the pitch, and is expressed in inches, not degrees.

Here's how to measure pitch: Stand the gun on its butt, with both the heel and toe touching the floor. Now move it against a wall. The breech end will probably hit the wall first. When it does, measure the distance between the muzzle end and the wall. That measurement, in inches, is the pitch of that particular rifle, with that particular stock. You can change the pitch, of course, by cutting the butt at a different angle or by adding a recoil pad with a different shape.

Another way to determine and measure pitch is to lay the gun upside down on a workbench and hold a carpenter's square up to the butt. If the heel only touches, you have negative pitch; if the toe and heel touch, no pitch.

Most long guns, as we said, have negative pitch. The barrel, that is, stands somewhat away from the wall during the above test. You can have

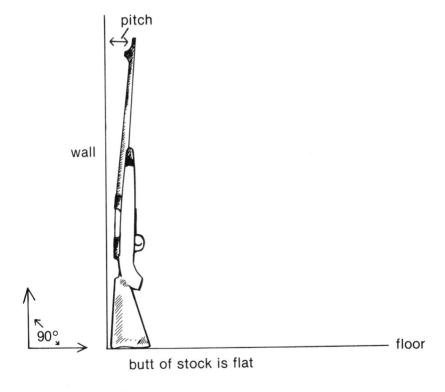

The pitch of a rifle can be determined by standing the weapon on its butt, then moving it against a wall and measuring the distance between the wall and the muzzle end.

positive pitch, but that is rare, or zero pitch, which is possible (usually in match guns with fancy stocks and no or virtually no recoil). The reason for negative pitch, especially in shotguns, should be apparent: it gives you an edge against the muzzle-raising force of the recoil.

You can change the pitch, as we mentioned, but it is not a good idea to mess with it unless you're sure what you want to accomplish. Again, seek an expert's advice and test-shoot the gun over and over with wedges of wood either taped onto the butt or inserted beneath the butt plate or recoil pad to approximate different pitches. When you change the pitch, you change the balance of the gun. It's better to adjust your stance if you can.

Let's suppose, then, that you want to remove two inches from a shotgun stock that now has a recoil pad. Begin by removing the pad, being careful to save the screws, and loosen and remove the drawbolt, which holds the stock to the frame. Remove the stock and put the frame and barrel aside.

You must be careful of both pitch and square, which is the angle of the butt as compared to a line passing through the center of the barrel, frame, and stock. In most cases, you want a square butt, whatever the pitch. Mark the stock $\frac{1}{16}$ inch long; that is, if you want to remove 2 inches in length, mark $1\frac{15}{16}$ inches in from the butt. This is to allow you room to make a mistake without making the stock too short. Again, measure and mark twice before you cut. You're going to be cutting hardwood, which is difficult at best.

You can use any sharp saw to cut a stock, but you're better off with a power saw. A circular table saw with an adjustable blade is ideal. Cut the stock to the mark, and finish with a belt sander, measuring constantly with a level and/or plumb line to check pitch and square.

Now you're ready to install the recoil pad. (Incidentally, adding a recoil pad is the easiest way to *lengthen* a too short stock. You can use the same procedures set down here.) Oh, yes, before you begin on the butt plate, check the drawbolt for length. Chances are it's now too long. You'll have to have it cut and threaded, probably at a machine shop.

Since you've shortened the stock, the recoil pad may not fit. Fitting one is a very tedious procedure, involving dismantling the gun, fitting the pad, and reassembling the gun, over and over until you get it right. This is further complicated by the fact that you don't want to attach the pad until you have it lined up, and so you should avoid drilling screw holes during the fitting process.

A way around this dilemma is to use a temporary adhesive—two-sided carpet tape is one suggestion—to hold the pad on the butt while you mark the areas you need to remove.

Removing material from the recoil pad is best done with a belt sander. If you have access to the upright kind, so much the better. If you only have the portable kind, cut as much of the excess pad away as you can, not worrying about roughness at this point. You can use a disk sander, too, but it's a little tricky.

With the pad roughed in, position it on the butt and mark and tap screw holes. You should tap the holes, since a recoil pad takes a lot of thrust and can easily loosen its screws. Once that occurs, you either have to glue the pad fast to the stock, which makes it impossible to tighten the drawbolt, or drill and tap oversize holes. Tap the holes the first time to avoid the dilemma.

Of course, not all long guns have a drawbolt passing through their stocks. If you don't need to remove the pad, go ahead and cement it to the stock with epoxy or clear varnish, which will do just as well beneath the screwed-on pad.

With the pad screwed into place, though slightly overlapping at one point or another, mask the stock with several layers of tape—maybe five or six—with one edge of the tape at the butt/pad joint and the other several inches up the stock. Don't skimp on this wrapping: you're going to be sanding the pad down to size with the belt sander, and you can easily mar the stock if you don't protect it.

Use the sander to shape the pad to the stock. If you have a portable sander, secure the stock in a padded vise and work the sander over the pad. If you have an upright sander, manipulate the stock and pad against the moving belt. You need a medium-grit belt to start, then finish with finer abrasives.

You can do all this by hand, of course, but it is tough. You can also mark the pad and remove the excess on a small bench grinder, but that means much refitting and estimating. If you can, find a way to work with the pad on the stock. Keep an eye on the tape layers. They'll get chewed up and should be patched to prevent serious damage to the stock. The idea is that you sand the pad down to stock level without touching the stock. You'll merely wear away the tape.

We should note here that sometimes there will be a gap between the pad and the butt when you try to refit it. If this occurs, it may or may not be because of a poor cut. You can check the new pitch and square by holding the piece of stock you removed against the new butt and comparing

—it should match pretty closely. If it doesn't vary too much, especially on pitch, leave it alone and reshape the recoil pad by soaking it in hot water and shaping it with your hands when soft. Variations in square, of course, should be corrected with the belt sander.

You may mar the stock somewhat in finishing the recoil pad—hopefully, not too deeply. If you're refinishing the entire stock, it's of no concern; go ahead and remove the pad and go to work. If you just want to remove a few scratches, 4/0 steel wool and wood stain can mask the damage.

REPAIRING DENTS AND GOUGES

Damaged stocks can be repaired with a few simple tools and supplies. Fortunately, most factory stocks are finished with tough coatings that resist nicks and gouges, or at least minimize them. Dents, however, are common.

Remove dents by steaming them out. If you picture the wood as being made up of numerous cells, and a dent as being an area where the cells have collapsed, you can visualize how forcing steam into the wood will cause the cells to swell and return to their normal shape.

Steam dents by placing a wet cotton cloth on the dent and applying heat from an electric iron set at "synthetics" or a similar low setting. Keep the iron moving, and don't let the cloth dry out.

Gouges and scratches need a bit more care. Most can be filled with shellac which comes in stick form. Apply the shellac by heating a knife and letting the knife melt the shellac. Work it into the gouge and smooth it out as best you can with the knife, then finish with fine steel wool or wet/dry sandpaper soaked with oil. Blend in the filled area and apply wax or polish to shine it up.

REFINISHING

Total refinishing of your rifle's stock can be extremely difficult or moderately so, depending upon the nature of the existing finish. Varnish and acrylic finishes are relatively easy to remove with solvent or varnish remover. Oil finishes, though, are so tough as to be nearly impossible to remove; but that's good, because you can sand and polish a rough-looking oil-finished stock and not disturb the finish enough to require resealing.

Of the various finishes, oil is hardest to put on, but it wears like iron and can be refurbished with just an additional wiping of oil from time to time. A wax coating over the oil is especially attractive.

Varnish and lacquer finishes are quickies—particularly if you have a spray system. Their shiny, brittle finishes are more showy than practical, they need to be polished to look their best, and their fumes are noxious.

Acrylic coatings are tough and flexible and easy to put on, but also need polish and are noxious.

Polyurethane varnish is rather soft and easily marred—not up to tough field use.

Whatever the finish you select—and we vote for oil as the longest wearing and least likely to be marred—the quality of your finished product is largely determined by the preparation. Sand carefully with the grain, leaving no edge marks or skips. Seal the wood after sanding with a commercial sanding sealer compatible with whatever finish you choose. (This is not necessary when putting an oil finish on a stock previously finished with varnish or lacquer.) Be sure to provide ample drying time between coats, and keep dust and dirt away from the drying stock.

Preparation includes removing all the old finish. Commercial stripping compounds should be used with care; do not let them soak into the wood. Varnish remover will do a good job, but should be followed with a washdown in acetone, alcohol, or lacquer thinner.

Acrylic and varnish finishes are best sprayed on in several thin, yet even, coats. Sand the stock with #400 or finer sandpaper between coats, and buff the finished stock with a soft cloth. A wax coating will help protect the shiny finish.

Finishing a stock with linseed oil is a time-consuming but rewarding project which will give your stock lifetime protection that looks good. After sealing the wood, in the case of new stock, apply oil to a small portion of the stock and sand lightly with fine sand paper. This wet oil sanding (use #400 or #600 wet/dry paper) should be done in small patches all over the stock. The idea is that the oil and wood dust will fill the grain. Wipe across the grain with a cloth and repeat this sanding over the entire stock until you see that the grain is full and the surface smooth. Let the stock dry overnight.

Next, wipe an even coat of oil onto the stock with your hand, covering the entire stock with a thin coat of oil, leaving no drips, runs, or thin spots. Keep wiping until the oil soaks in, then set it aside to dry for at least 24 hours. Repeat on subsequent nights, each time applying the oil with your hands and letting it sit for a day. Three or four of these treatments should suffice. After the final coat is thoroughly dry, wipe the stock with a piece of burlap, polishing it until the shine is to your liking. (Note: sometimes you'll have a stock that's *too* shiny after oiling. Work on it with 4/0 sandpaper and oil, then finish with burlap.)

The oil finish can be touched up with applications of oil from time to time, or you can apply a paste wax.

ADDING A SLING

A sling is a valuable addition to any rifle. Attaching sling swivels is easy. Begin with the rear (butt) swivel. Locate a spot at least two inches forward of the butt and mark a spot for the swivel. Keep it at least that far from the butt to avoid interfering with the screws that hold the butt plate or recoil pad in place. Drill and tap a hole as deep as the screw, then turn it in with a lever passed through the swivel.

The front swivel is a little tougher. The forward swivel is attached with a bolt rather than a screw, so you have to remove the forestock from the frame, or remove the barrel, depending upon the construction of the gun.

Locate and mark the spot for the swivel before dismantling the gun, then take it apart. Drill a hole large enough for the swivel bolt entirely through the forestock. There will be a nut on the bolt inside, so you've got to cut away enough wood from the bed to accommodate it. This can be done with a wood chisel or gouge, or even a sharp knife if you're careful. Don't cut too much wood away—just enough to allow the barrel to clear the nut and bolt. Push the nut into the hole you've cut and screw the bolt in from below.

Hammocks

HAMMOCKS ARE ENJOYING a comeback, thanks largely to the development of lightweight, synthetic backpacking hammocks. Made of nylon, these one-piece, knotless net hammocks offer the advantages of nylon fabrics: lightness, quick-drying, mildew-resistance, soil-resistance, and strength. They can be compressed into a tiny package, and some come with their own small stuff sacks. Nylon hammocks sometimes have nylon ropes, which can stretch, but more often have polypropylene ropes. See the *Rope* entry for the advantages and disadvantages of these ropes and their care; see the *Nylon* entry for information on care of the hammock itself.

Other common materials used in hammocks are cotton, polyester, and polypropylene.

Cotton hammocks are made with either heavy canvas or braided cotton cord, with the former becoming extremely rare. Cotton canvas is cool, soft, and easy to clean, but doesn't have the mildew- and weather-resistant properties of synthetics. The *Canvas* entry contains information on cleaning, patching, and storing canvas. Cotton canvas hammocks shouldn't be left outdoors over an entire season, as dirt will soak into the fabric with dew and rainwater and foster mildew growth. Since cotton will grow mildew itself, it should never be stored wet or dirty. Cotton can be bleached and treated with fungicides or waterproofing to help retard mildew growth.

Net hammocks made of woven polyester ropes are soft, comfortable, and weather-resistant. They can be washed with mild detergent and water, but not bleached, and they will gradually become yellowed with exposure. Polyester is mildew resistant.

Polypropylene is not as soft as cotton or polyester, having a scratchy texture. Polypropylene netting will deteriorate with exposure to sunlight, and so should not be used in direct sunlight.

Most net hammocks use wooden spreader bars at each end to give the hammock its shape. These bars need periodic oiling with linseed oil to forestall rot, but you don't want to stain the ropes with oil. This presents a dilemma, for the hammock is usually woven in such a way that the amateur will have a lot of trouble getting it back together once he gets it apart. A solution is to pull the bar toward the fastening point as far as possible, then wrap the part of the ropes normally beneath the bar with tape. Using a rag to soak up excess oil, you can then carefully oil the inside of the holes as well as the exterior of the bar.

Inflatable Boats

INFLATABLE CRAFT HAVE come a long way from the toy rubber rafts and life rafts of a few decades ago. Now, highly sophisticated motorized dinghies, rafts, and runabouts with all the comfort and convenience of more conventional craft are available in a variety of styles, sizes, and prices.

The advantages of inflatables are their light weight, large capacity for their weight, stability (they're hard to tip), and easy portability in the deflated state.

On the negative side, inflatables are vulnerable to puncture; they deteriorate with exposure to sunlight and heat; and with wooden accessories such as decks, floorboards, and transoms, they need quite a bit of maintenance. But, as with every item of outdoor gear, the trade-off is acceptable if you have the means and knowledge to perform the needed maintenance. Inflatable boats are thus a reasonable alternative for many boaters.

Inflatables are made of coated fabric. Usually, baffled tubes made of nylon or polyester fabrics are joined with glued seams, then impregnated with neoprene or Hypalon plastic. Polyvinyl chloride (PVC) is also used on some craft, and at least one manufacturer uses a fiberglass-type fabric coated with PVC.

Naturally, there is a good deal of variation in construction methods used on these craft and, as usual, each manufacturer touts his product as superior. The prospective buyer has little to go on, as you can't look inside the tubes to check on baffles, seams, and attachment points for fittings. You can, however, inspect the outside, and here there are clues to the overall quality and attention to detail—as well as indications of potential or actual trouble. Fittings such as oarlocks and grab rope attachment rings should

179

be made fast to the hull with large, cemented on patches—the larger the better. Look for hot-cut patches that are not fraying or lifting at the edges. There should be no adhesive smeared sloppily around the patches.

There should be some reinforcement at the sides and bow, where the boat is most likely to rub against or bump into other boats, docks, or obstacles. Most good-quality inflatables have a bumper built into the hull at the "impact line".

The inflation valve should be sturdy and set into the hull with a large-radius patch. The valve should have a cap. Beyond these criteria, you need to judge the valve on its location, ease of operation, and materials. It should have brass or other noncorrosive metal parts (if any).

Wooden parts need careful scrutiny. Look for rounded, smooth edges on transoms, seats, and floorboards. The wood should be varnished or otherwise coated and should fit the hull precisely because any sloppiness in the fit can cause damage to the hull. Inflatable seats should have attachment points that enable them to be secured firmly to the hull. They should be substantial—high enough and wide enough for comfortable seating.

Accessories such as ropes, oars, lights, and controls should be made well. Two-piece oars should slide together easily and well. Cables and wires should work smoothly and easily.

Look for a full accessory package: a well-designed carrying case, rain cover, emergency CO_2 inflation system, air pump (either electric or hand), mast, and sail. Try all of these and judge their ease of operation.

INFLATING AND DEFLATING

The most unlikely accident to an inflatable is one that engenders the most concern: puncture and total deflation. Good-quality boats have at least three air chambers, separated by strong fabric baffles, so total deflation is unlikely in any but the worst of circumstances.

Small punctures can occur, of course, but they are usually the result of careless handling, especially when inflating the craft. Be sure the boat has room to inflate without coming in contact with sharp objects. If you inflate the boat on the deck of a larger craft, take care not to set it on deck fittings, cleats, etc. Never try to inflate a boat with objects in or on it—no free rides for the kids, in other words.

Proper inflation procedures are important. Starting at one valve, put enough air into each chamber in sequence to give your boat shape and firmness, but do not fill to full pressure. Now, reverse the sequence starting with the last air chamber that you put air into and top off the chamber. Continue this procedure with all the air chambers. By doing this, the bladders that divide the main air chambers are aligned so that there is equal pressure on each side of the bladder, and they are not all pushed in one direction.

It is important to reduce air pressure when the boat is exposed to the sun for long periods of time or pulled out of the water.

A foot- or hand-operated pump is preferable to an electric pump because you will have greater control over the rate of inflation. Automatic inflation/deflation pumps which operate off a 12-volt battery offer one big advantage, however. They will completely deflate your boat without any pressure being applied to the hull. One manufacturer has a reversible foot pump available that will do the same thing.

Deflating a boat without a reversible pump involves pressing the air out of the tubes, which should be done carefully in order to prevent damage to the baffles. One wag has suggested letting the kids roll on the raft until all the air is pressed out, and there's nothing wrong with this but make sure they don't have any metal objects on their clothes that might puncture the skin.

REPAIRING SMALL LEAKS

Although careful use can prevent most punctures, small leaks from abrasion are possible. Makers of inflatables have complete repair kits available which include the proper adhesive and patching material. Small leaks need not be patched with fabric. All that's needed is to coat the area with the sealant.

The procedure to repair a small abrasion leak begins with finding it. Swab soap suds onto the hull in the suspect area. The bubbles will indicate leakage. Mark them, wipe the hull, and allow to dry completely.

Deflate the hull completely. Wipe the area to be coated with the thinner supplied with the repair kit. It will evaporate quickly. Next, coat the area with three or four coats of sealant. The first coat should be brushed into the fabric well and the next couple applied in quick succession, before the previous coat has dried.

You can thin the sealant with the thinner supplied in the kit, but this should be done only if the sealant has thickened or if the area to be covered is so large that you cannot begin applying subsequent coats before the first has set up. If you thin the sealant, you'll need to use more coats to get the same thickness.

After this application, the raft should be let dry for a week or even longer. Reinflate it, and if the first treatment did not stop the leak completely, repeat the entire procedure, thinner and all.

The sealant can also be used to coat the entire hull, and should be. After all abrasion damage and small leaks have been sealed, wipe the entire raft with thinner, using a clean cloth. Immediately apply several coats of sealant. It is important that this be done while the solvent coat is tacky, otherwise the sealant will not bond to the fabric. Be careful, too, not to apply a successive coat of sealant over one that's already dried and especially avoid letting the sealant pool or run over dried sealant. The best waiting time is one hour between sealant coats. If let dry more than that, you may have to wipe with thinner once more to make adhesion possible.

You must leave the boat inflated until the coating dries. The minimum waiting period is one week, and longer is advisable under conditions of high humidity. Don't be fooled by an apparently dry hull; the sealant coating will set up and be dry to the touch, but will not withstand pressure or folding.

If absolutely necessary to deflate the craft, try not to fold it or roll it too tightly, otherwise the hull will stick to itself, pulling off sections of sealant. You can prevent this by sprinkling talcum powder liberally over the entire surface before deflating and rolling.

For small punctures, injecting sealant with a hypodermic needle is an effective way of getting the material exactly where you want it. A #3 plastic syringe and a #10 needle work well with slightly thinned sealant. (Don't add more than 10 percent thinner.)

To inject sealant into the interior of the hull, first deflate and position the boat so that the puncture is on the bottom. Putting the boat on a plywood platform with the area to be repaired hanging over the edge is one good way. Simply inject a small amount of sealant through the hole, at the same time pulling the skin down so that no sealant sticks to the opposite side of the hull.

Allow the sealant to pool at the puncture site and remove the needle slowly. The sealant should flow into the hole and stay there—possibly with one or two drips. You can repeat this procedure several times to fill the hole completely, but if you can't get the sealant to completely close the hole, you'll have to patch it.

PATCHING

When patching a small tear or puncture—say, two inches long or round— on an inflatable boat don't sew the fabric together. For anything larger, pull the torn edges together as best you can and stitch with nylon monofilament or a nylon/cotton thread. Take care not to create more damage while doing this; make sure, for instance, that you're not perforating an internal baffle.

Hypalon and PVC-coated boats have different adhesives, and you should not use anything on Hypalon hulls not specifically recommended for them. The instructions below apply in general to all kinds of inflatables, but you should check the instructions with the repair kit for modifications or revisions, since manufacturers constantly find new products and materials to use on their boats.

Before patching, wash the area with soap and water. Rinse well, and let dry. Clean the area thoroughly with the thinner supplied with the kit, toluene, or other solvent such as petroleum spirits or acetone. Do not use oil-based solvents such as paint thinner. From the material in the repair kit, cut a patch to cover the damaged area; then place it over the puncture and outline with ballpoint pen, making sure all edges of the patch are at least two inches from the hole. (Avoid overlapping a seam, as a patch over a seam most likely will leak.)

Using coarse sandpaper, buff the area inside the pen marking and one side of the patch. Care must be taken not to remove so much rubber that the nylon core is exposed, but all traces of old glue must be removed, and the surfaces must have a matt appearance with a fine-grain texture. Buffing must be done on a flat surface.

Apply a thin coat of adhesive to the hull and patch and let both dry until it no longer feels tacky. Apply a second coat; while the glue is still tacky, press the patch onto the hull, starting from the center and working toward the edge. The edge of the patch must rest on a buffed and glued area otherwise it eventually will lift.

Press the entire patch very hard with the edge of a blunt, round tool, or roller. A large spoon will do nicely. Clean excess glue from around the patch with solvent and at the same time smooth out the edges of the patch. Let the patch cure at least four hours, but preferably 12 to 24 hours.

USING AN OUTBOARD MOTOR

More and more inflatables are being used with outboard motors. While it is beyond the scope of this section to discuss the proper size motor for various size boats, the owner who wants to motorize his craft should be aware that inflatable boats handle much differently than their conventional counterparts. Most manufacturers will set weight and horsepower limits for their craft and caution against exceeding those limits. Following their instructions can increase safety and utility and add to your enjoyment of your inflatable craft.

Inflatables designed for use with outboards have wooden transoms and most have inflatable keels. The keel is, in effect, a separate hull tube attached to the bottom of the craft, and its purpose is to add stiffness to the hull and also to aid in steering the craft. Since this keel is out of sight and exposed to hazards from shoals and debris, you should check it frequently for abrasion damage and proper inflation. Evidence of an underinflated keel is excessive hull flexing.

Weight distribution is vital. If too much weight is placed toward the aft, the boat will plow rather than plane. If too far forward, the boat will dig in and the motor will race as the propeller refuses to "bite." Before adjusting the transom height or motor angle, check weight distribution. The transom may be cut to accommodate an outboard motor, but this should be considered carefully.

CLEANING AND STORING

It is advisable to wash your boat off after every trip, being sure to get any sand off the inside floor next to the tubes. Turn the boat on its side or upside down, and use a bucket to wash out the boat. Bleed off excess air as necessary, then allow the boat to dry inside and out. Check the valves for sand or debris. Finally, let the remaining air out, and roll or fold up the boat.

Roll the boat up loosely, not tightly, and store in a cool, dry atmosphere, with some air in the chambers. Keep your boat out of the sun whenever possible, because sunlight speeds up fabric deterioration. Do not roll the boat up tightly. Although they can be a hassle, the carrying cases supplied with inflatable boats should be used when transporting the craft.

Insect Repellents

THE MOST COMMON ingredient in commercial insect repellents is something called N,N-diethyl-meta-touluamide, also known as DEET. No one is quite sure why bugs don't like it. It may mask the smell of carbon dioxide, which animals breathe out and which may be an attractant for bloodthirsty winged critters; or it may in fact have an odor of its own that drives bugs buggy. Whatever the reason, DEET works. And it's pretty nearly foolproof: it doesn't separate, spoil, break down, burn, or evaporate (if kept in a closed container). You'll probably degrade before it does. Keeping it, then, is pretty easy: just don't spill it.

DEET-doused lotions, sprays, and sticks are meant to be used on you and your clothes, but they can cause some problems. Nylon fabrics, especially, react to insect repellents, and the fabric will deteriorate from exposure to them. Aerosol sprays are particularly hard to control, and so shouldn't be used around tents and backpacks. Keep lotions off Goretex, nylon, and nylon-blend garments.

Insect repellents also cause nylon monofilament fishing line to deteriorate and have a similar effect on some finishes used on gun stocks.

Aerosol sprays should be kept away from sources of heat and flames, and should never be used in a closed space such as a tent. Never puncture or incinerate spray cans, and store them upright.

Some alternatives to commercial repellents are chamomile tea, which will repel mosquitoes if used as a lotion; garlic, which is reputed to keep flying insects away when eaten in large doses; and vitamin B1, said to make you smell unattractive to mosquitoes when eaten at the rate of 100 milligrams every six hours. Yellow sulfur powder is an effective repellent for ticks and chiggers.

Citronella candles are an old-time method of chasing flying bugs. Keep them away from direct heat sources, and wrap them in an airtight wrapping when not in use to preserve potency. Punks, incense, and mosquito coils also produce smoke offensive to flying bugs of all kinds. Keep such items dry and packed in a sturdy container to protect them from breakage.

Kayaks

THIS ENTRY DEALS with traditional folding kayaks made of wood with a flexible fabric covering, rather than modern thermoplastic kayaks, which can be repaired and maintained using the procedures and materials covered in the *Plastic Canoes* entry.

There is only one kayak for the purist, and it is made by the Hans Klepper Company of West Germany. If you have a Klepper "foldboat" or are considering acquiring one, the company's New York office is an excellent source of parts, materials, and advice on maintenance and repair. Like Old Town canoes, Klepper has an extensive parts list available and will assist in any restoration project involving one of its own craft.

Klepper boats have a stressed rubber and canvas outer skin with flotation sponsons built in, stretched over a knock-down hardwood frame consisting of over thirty pieces. Over the years, Klepper has changed materials on their hulls and sponsons, so before attempting repairs you should find out definitely what material you're working with. If you know how old or approximately how old your craft is, Klepper can advise you on this.

The following information covers all types of Klepper kayaks and the kinds of injuries most common to them. References are made to materials and kits available from Klepper. These include a general repair kit and a keel-strip kit for reinforcing the keel area. Klepper also has various waxes, paints, and cleaners in stock.

CARE OF UPPER DECK

Repairs to the upper (blue canvas) deck are seldom necessary. Occasionally a squirrel or mouse will make a small hole, or perhaps careless use of a knife or sharp tool will puncture the canvas. For this, a simple sewing job as described in the Canvas chapter will do. Use a piece of the deck material provided in Klepper repair kits, sewn to the inside of the deck with heavy thread.

Klepper sells Deck Impregnation Blue, a coating/filler which they call "not a covering paint." The idea is that you should not use it to touch up small patches or stains, but should apply it to the entire deck at once.

First clean the deck thoroughly with a medium-bristle brush and warm soapy water. This should remove the whitish spots caused by saltwater spray which has been left to dry. If the deck has not faded drastically, this may be all you need to make it look like new.

If you want to reblue, first mask the red trim where the deck is joined to the hull, then apply the entire contents of the can with a medium brush. Shake the can first, and stir it frequently while using. Make sure the coating is even, without drips and heavy spots. There is a quart of blue deck dressing in the can, plenty to give a heavy soaking to the entire deck. Let it dry in a protected spot away from direct sun for a day or two. When completely dry, brush over the deck with a dry paintbrush to remove any dressing that didn't sink into the fabric.

PATCHING HULLS

For temporary repair of minor damage to the grey Hypalon or rubber hull, Klepper recommends tape which they supply in their service kit. Duct tape will also do a serviceable job, provided that you first roughen the area around the damage with some abrasive material. The hull should also be dry.

For long-term repair of a deep scar, gouge, tear, or hole, use a piece of the hull material or keel-strip material secured with cement, which are provided in the Klepper kits. It's best to patch major damage from the inside.

Cut a patch two to three inches larger than the damaged area. Roughen the hull with sandpaper and apply a thin layer of the cement. Allow it to dry for eight to ten minutes, then press the patch firmly into place. If possible, hold it or weigh it down for a few hours to enhance the bond.

Klepper suggests that cements available commercially will not work well on its hulls, and without information to the contrary we pass on that recommendation. It seems, though, that any adhesive that will bond Hypalon (see *Inflatable Boats* entry) should work.

Since most serious damage is likely to occur under the keelboard,

Klepper recommends reinforcing this area with a keel-stripping kit consisting of long pieces of hull material cut to fit and a can of cement. Detailed keel-stripping instructions are provided.

WAXING HULLS

Pre-1967 Klepper kayaks had rubber hulls, and the company offered silver, rubber-based hull paint to protect and beautify them. Newer models have Hypalon hulls, and Klepper warns against using hull paint on them, as it will not stick. If you have an old-timer, you may be able to acquire some hull paint from Klepper, although they list this material as discontinued.

Instead of paint, Klepper sells boat wax, which can be used on the old rubber hulls and the newer synthetics. Here again, you should know the approximate age of your craft, as the company changed the materials slightly a few years back and, with typical thoroughness, also changed the composition of the boat wax.

The new product, Boatwax Neutral, can be applied to all parts of the craft—wooden, metal, and rubber—but not to the blue canvas deck. It is a soft wax which needs only be wiped onto the boat with a rag and left to dry. It is especially recommended for kayaks that will be used in salt water.

For older craft, both Hypalon and rubber, get some Silver Boatwax from Klepper and apply it thinly to the hull. Again, you need not rub it in, buff it or use anything other than a soft rag. Klepper recommends using boat wax after applying a keel-strip kit.

REPAIRING SPONSONS

Damage to the flotation sponsons is rare, but it can occur. The most common problem is a small leak at the stem, and Klepper suggests cutting a half inch off the end of the stem—removing the worn rubber, in other words—and reattaching the stopper. If that doesn't work, the problem may be fatigue in the material around the stem from constant bending or ultraviolet deterioration. A reinforcing patch of hull tape should cure it.

Actual holes in the sponson itself must be patched, and the danger here is that you'll use the wrong material. Klepper's repair kit has black and red sponson material, and you should use them on sponsons of like color only. The older, black sponsons must be patched, but small holes in the newer red ones sometimes can be repaired with just a small drop of the PVX solvent/sealer in the repair kit.

The procedure for patching sponsons is similar to that described above for hull patching: roughen the surface, apply adhesive (black patch takes rubber cement; red takes PVX solvent); and weigh or hold the patch in place.

The trick to sponson repair is in replacing the sponson in the hull. Klepper suggests the following procedure: To push sponson back into chamber, use a broomstick (without the broom). Lay sponson flat, lay broomstick on it, cup the end of the sponson over the end of the stick, about one inch bent over. Tape cupped end *lightly* to broomstick. *You need a helper.* Slide broomstick and sponson gently into chamber, feed it carefully. When at the end, your helper has to grab the hull and *feel* the stick inside. (He has to get a hold above and below the broomstick.) Pull the stick back with a slight twist motion. Then repeat for the other end of the sponson. Afterwards, inflate halfways, and pat the hull vigorously to shake out wrinkles in the sponson. Inflate fully.

REPLACING METAL AND WOOD PARTS

Klepper uses soft rivets to attach hardware to their boats, so replacing or adding metal parts is easy. Just cut the head off the existing rivet and remove it, using a punch or dull nail if necessary. Insert a new rivet and set it, using a ballpeen hammer and backing board or anvil.

Broken wood members should be promptly replaced. If in the field, you can splint, tape, wire, or otherwise secure the broken pieces to preserve the integrity of the hull. Klepper has replacement parts for its kayaks, so you needn't consider fabricating your own wooden parts.

TRANSPORTING AND LAUNCHING

Klepper's kayaks are tough, but you can break them by careless actions, particularly during transporting and loading. It isn't necessary to dismantle the boat for short transports, as you can easily rig a standard canoe carrier to accept your kayak.

Klepper recommends carriers with broad support members, not thin metal poles, and advises against the use of rubber or other stretchable tie-downs and straps. Use nylon straps with buckles and be sure to tie the bow and stern securely to the *car,* not the rack.

The company also recommends that you launch the kayak from a flat spot, even if it is rough, and cautions against launching from a dock or wall —not because the kayak is not sturdy enough, but because many users are

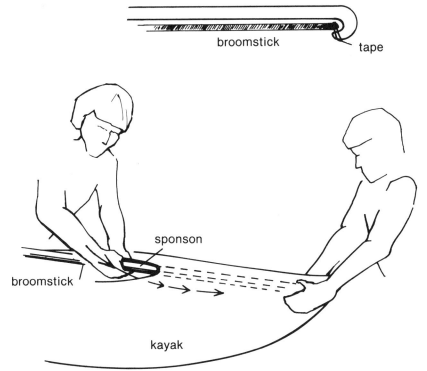

Putting the repaired sponson back in the hull is easier if you cup the end of the sponson around a broomstick and then gently feed the sponson and stick into the chamber.

not agile enough, which can result in a sunken boat! Ideally, you will launch your kayak from a beach, and embark from shallow water.

Klepper offers a sail and mast kit with its larger boats, and recommends that added flotation in the form of air bags, air mattresses, etc., be used to offset the weight of this accessory.

Knives

A KNIFE IS probably the most valuable tool you will carry on a camping trip, and proper care of your knife will assure long life and satisfactory service.

CHOOSING A KNIFE

Getting the most from your knife begins with picking the right knife for the job. For heavy field butchering or skinning, a sheath knife with a hollow ground blade up to six inches long, with a skinner (straight backed, sharp pointed) or clip (a "break" in the blade, tapering to a sharp point) shape will do the job neatly and efficiently. For chopping, kindling, or sawing through tough roots or branches, a V or rolled-edge ground, drop, or space blade will hold up to harder use. The variety of blade shapes is vast, but a few simple rules can help you choose a knife to fit your needs.

First, don't buy more knife than you need. You'll see plenty of weekend backpackers trucking along with a six-inch, razor-sharp, hollow-ground "buffalo skinner" sheath knife bouncing on their belt when what they really need is a good folding knife with a sturdy chisel or rolled-edge main blade and several smaller special-purpose blades. The first time the "Arkansas Toothpick's" point breaks off or punctures a tent flap will give the novice something to think about.

Second, don't go light. The present obsession with lightweight gear often compromises durability in an effort to save a few ounces on the trail, but the weight saved by carrying a thin-bladed, lightweight knife isn't worth the long-term loss of durability and strength. A broken or wiggly blade or a loose handle is annoying and possibly dangerous.

Third, buy the best steel you can. This can be tricky: everyone's knife is "best," according to their advertisements. In general, high-carbon steel is preferable because it holds an edge better. Stainless steel blades have gotten a bad reputation. They're hard to sharpen, won't hold an edge, and usually are thinner than standard blades. Stainless steel is well suited to kitchen use, where its ability to withstand rust is valued, but it won't stand up to hard use in the field.

It should be noted, though, that metallurgy has made great strides in recent years, resulting in high-carbon blades that are nearly as corrosion resistant as softer, traditional stainless steel, yet will hold an edge through sharp use. Chrome vanadium, a stainless alloy, is tough and stain-resistant . . . and expensive.

It should also be noted that corrosion resistance, though a laudable characteristic, is not a necessary one. A tarnished blade can be sharpened as well as a shiny one—and, of course, no blade is *completely* stainless: acids will produce surface corrosion even on stainless steel. (By the way, such labels as "Solingen" and "Sheffield" are as meaningless as "Swiss Made" or "Made in Japan" as an index to quality. The Germans and British produce both good and bad steel.)

Fourth, if you're buying a folding knife, pay attention to the "action." The blade should open smoothly and precisely, with a solid feel. The backspring should be taut; the hinge should be precise and sturdy. If the knife has a locking blade, it should be stiff and precise, with no mushiness. Of course, the blade shouldn't wiggle from side to side, or yield to downward pressure on the tip. If you've opted for a stainless steel blade, make sure all the parts—hinge, backspring, bolster—are corrosion-resistant as well. A folding knife blade should rest in the center of its channel when closed. If you're buying a multi-bladed folding knife, test the punch and screwdriver blades to make sure they won't fold closed when pressure is applied. Try the can opener for effectiveness and strength, and try any other "special" blades: corkscrew, scissors, saw, bottle opener. Listen to the knife: the blade should open with a solid click.

Fifth, make sure the cutting blade(s) have the kind of grind you want. "Grind" refers to the blade's profile, when viewed from the point end. Typical grinds are V, rolled edge (also called cannell), hollow, and concave.

The V and cannell grinds are thicker nearer the cutting edge, which makes them stronger and more suited to chopping and rough cutting. Machetes usually have rolled-edge blades. Naturally, you won't be able to put a lasting razor edge on a machete, nor would you want to: strength and sharpness are trade-offs. The advantage to a rolled edge with a chisel point is that it will hold its edge much longer than a hollow or concave ground blade.

Hollow ground is a compromise between rolled edge and concave, and it is probably the best all-around blade type. A variation called a "Saber" edge actually tapers both ways from a ridge midway between the back and cutting edges, and is found on knives designed for skinning and other field work where sharpness and thinness are desirable blade characteristics. A concave grind is a thinner, gently tapering hollow grind. Straight razors are concave ground, which is one reason they need constant stropping to maintain an edge. Concave grinds are usually too fragile for field use.

"Polished-edge" concave and hollow ground blades are extremely sharp because the edge has been given a final polish on a felt wheel after honing. As will all super-sharp blades, polished edges require frequent and careful sharpening to remain effective.

One more word about blades: if you're buying a sheath knife, try to find one with a thick blade or, better yet, a serrated blade back. Working with wet, cold, or slimy hands is much easier if you can put pressure on the blade without fear of slipping off.

Sixth, if you're buying a sheath knife, make sure the handle and thumb-guard are carefully and securely fastened to the blade. Sloppiness here indicates generally poor quality in a knife, and it is very difficult to correct looseness in such a knife when it inevitably occurs. The point where the handle, thumbguard, and blade tang come together is as critical to a sheath knife as the hinge is to a folding knife.

USING A KNIFE

The first rule of keeping a knife around and in use is don't use it for anything but cutting. This seems elementary, but if you're like most people you've found yourself using a knife as a lever, screwdriver, wire cutter, can opener, fire poker, or—heaven forbid—as a tack hammer. Knives are specialized tools, meant only for cutting. If you use them for anything else, you run the risk of ruining them. Any action that puts sideways stress on the blade tends to loosen the blade and, in a folding knife, that's fatal.

Don't try to force a knife blade through something it won't cut. If you can't get through the material with a sawing motion, you probably shouldn't be trying to cut it. Absolutely never place a blade edge or point on an object and hammer on the blade back or handle butt: no matter how well tempered the blade, it won't take that treatment long, and of course, the handle was never meant to, either.

Throwing a knife is sure to loosen the handle, if not break it. It doesn't do the blade any good either, especially if you miss! The knives circus performers toss are one-piece, specially balanced daggers with no cutting edge. Buy one if you can't resist the urge to heave a blade at something.

Locking-blade knives are much safer to use than other folding knives, but they are prone to wear and, once loose, cannot be tightened. Proper closing and opening techniques will minimize wear on the lock parts. To open a spring-lock blade, fully depress the lock release while holding the knife with the blade side up. Then lift the blade and fully extend it before releasing the button. Never "snap" a blade or release the lock before the blade is fully extended. Never hold the blade side down while opening; if the lock isn't fully released, the action of the blade opening will wear both blade and lock surfaces, eventually rendering the lock inoperative. A drop of oil will keep it working smoothly and minimize friction.

To close a spring-lock blade, hold the knife with the cutting edge up, fully depress the lock release button, and keep it depressed. With the button *fully* depressed, apply pressure to the back of the blade, closing it smoothly. Do not let it snap shut, no matter how much you like the "solid" sound your high-tech knife makes when you do! If you snap it shut often enough, it won't be solid long.

Another type of lock is called a "split scale" lock—the "scale" is the liner of a folding knife; hence, a split scale is an extra liner that slides over to block the blade at the tang and prevent its closing. This kind of lock needn't be released when opening the blade, but must be fully released before applying any closing pressure on the blade back. Otherwise, pressure on the vulnerable hinge area will cause it to loosen in time. Again, don't let the blade snap shut.

CLEANING

Dirt is the biggest enemy your folding knife has. Dirt and grit lodge in the channel, working on the moving parts every time you open or close the blade. Prevention is better than care: clean the blade every time you use it, and keep the closed knife inside a leather sheath if you have one (if you don't, make one).

Clean the hinge area frequently with a toothpick and Gunk engine cleaner, making sure you don't put too much pressure on this vulnerable area. Tiny pieces of gauze bandage pushed into the channel will soak up the solvent better than plain cotton, which tends to leave tiny threads in crucial places. After you've gotten the solvent out, lubricate the hinge(s) and lock with light machine or household oil. Lay the knife blade side down on a piece of rag to let excess oil drain out. Frequent cleaning and re-oiling—or just an occasional drop of oil on the hinge and lock—will keep a knife in service indefinitely.

Many sheath-knife owners neglect to clean the inside of their sheaths, causing unnecessary wear to the blades. All that's really necessary is to apply a good leather oil periodically and wipe the knife blade off before inserting it into the sheath.

Storing a knife in its sheath for prolonged periods is said to cause discoloration of the blade, either from condensation or reaction to the chemicals used in tanning the leather or a combination of the two. This won't harm the blade, but if you want to prevent it, try folding a strip of gauze around the blade before slipping it in.

SHARPENING

A sharp knife is a safe knife. Trying to force a dull knife to cut not only puts you in danger of a cut from a slipped blade, it puts undue stress upon the hinge and spring of folding knives.

If you've never done so, take a "razor sharp" knife and look at it under a powerful magnifying lens or microscope. You'll see that the "perfect" edge is, in fact, serrated and nicked like a miniature saw blade. If the blade is truly sharp, you won't see many burrs or curled slivers of metal, but the nicks and dents will be there. Now take that knife and whittle a piece of wood a few strokes. Return the knife to the microscope and take a second look. You'll probably see many more rough spots and perhaps a few burrs or rolled spots along the edge. The point of this exercise is to show you how quickly an extremely sharp knife, with a razor-thin edge, can be dulled.

If you plan on using your knife for filleting fish, skinning game, or any other use for which an extremely sharp edge is required, you'll need to carry a whetstone and oil with you. If you're just taking a knife along to whittle a few sticks or scare off inquisitive bears, you're better off with a slightly duller edge to begin with. The difference comes from the angle you use when sharpening on a stone. (Here is one good reason for choosing a multi-bladed folding knife over a sheath knife: you can hone different edges on different blades, keeping one razor sharp and one extra strong.)

The tools you'll need to keep a knife sharp are a stone, oil, a leather strop, and perhaps a file. Actually, all you really need is a good combination stone—with "hard" and "soft" sides—and some oil. But for radical refurbishing of a damaged blade you should have a file, and if you desire a shaving edge on your hollow- or concave-ground blade, you'll need a leather strop.

It's a bad practice to use a rotary abrasive wheel on a knife blade. The potential for overheating and consequent weakening of the metal's tempering is great, even if you're careful to cool the blade frequently. If your knife is damaged through abuse to the extent that you need to put a completely new cutting edge on it, use a hand-cranked or foot-pedaled grinding wheel if you have one, and work carefully at low speeds, removing a little metal at each pass and cooling the blade frequently in water. Use a medium stone with frequent oiling. Even then, though, you run the risk of ruining your blade, particularly if it is a hollow- or concave-ground extra-sharp type. Never use an electric grinder.

For such radical surgery, a good metal file will do the job—albeit slowly and with a good deal of elbow grease. You'll be removing a lot of metal, but you must resist the temptation to "take a big bite" with each pass; rather, secure the blade in a vise (pad the jaws so the blade isn't marred) and work from hilt end toward the point, holding the file at a 45-degree angle to the blade, working an equal number of strokes on each side. Follow with work on a stone and strop as described below.

There are three basic strokes for honing a blade: shaving, circular, or figure eight. In each, the important thing is to keep a constant angle between the blade and stone for the entire length of the stroke (and, of course, for each stroke). For a super-sharp edge, the blade should be held at a 10-degree angle to the blade surface; for a heavy brush-cutting or bone-chopping edge, use a 30-degree angle. A good compromise is 20 degrees—the blade will be sharp enough for most camp work, but not so fragile as to require constant touching up.

Before honing, put a few drops of light machine or household oil on the stone and spread it out.

The shaving stroke is the one recommended by most manufacturers because it is the easiest and safest. You work with the stone held flat on a level surface or in your hand and draw the knife blade toward you, "shaving" the stone as if you were trying to remove a light beard from it. Work in a smooth arc from the tang end to the point, applying firm pressure at first and then tapering off to lighter strokes. Count the number of strokes and make sure you hone each side of the blade the same number. Wipe the oil off the blade after each five or ten strokes. (You may have to re-oil the stone from time to time. If you are unable to use oil, by the way, kerosene will do. In a pinch, saliva or water will also suffice.)

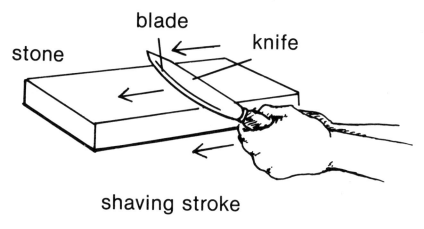

shaving stroke

To sharpen a blade using the shaving stroke, work with the stone held flat and draw the blade toward you.

A combination stone with a hard (coarse) and soft (fine) side gives you quite a bit of versatility. If you just want to touch up an already keen blade, the soft side will do. To sharpen a dulled blade, though, begin with the coarse side and move to the soft—always using an equal number of strokes on each side of the blade, and always using oil on the stone to trap metal shavings and reduce friction and heat.

A coarsely honed blade will show a shiny or "white" area along the blade edge when you sight along it toward a light source. Use the fine side until this area is removed, whetting with ever-lighter pressure until the edge appears even and doesn't shine.

Finish the job with a leather strop (the inside of a belt will do). Hold one end of the belt, stand on the other, and drag the blade across the leather —this time pulling *away* from the cutting edge. Use moderate pressure, with an equal number of strokes on each side.

You've now got a sharp knife. Test it by dragging the edge lightly across your fingernail, not your thumb. It should bite in evenly with just the blade's weight on it.

Before you put your tools away, take a minute to clean the stone. Wipe it with a rag, removing as much oil and grit as you can. If the stone is clogged with grit, clean it with lacquer thinner and a brush, then re-oil it.

The circular and figure-eight strokes are similar to the shaving stroke, in that you draw the blade edge across the stone with a constant angle and even pressure, progressing from heavy to light. For long-bladed sheath knives, a circular stroke is best. It's merely a series of short shaving strokes combined with a light backstroke. Work your way from the point of the blade toward the tang. This stroke is useful on longer blades or when using a small stone in the field. Finish the blade on a leather strop or belt as described above.

The figure-eight stroke is more difficult to master, but probably the best for use with a small blade or when using a butcher's sharpening "steel" of the sort often sold with home carving sets. The figure-eight stroke is an alternating stroke along the length of the blade, with each side getting the same number of licks at, of course, the same pressure and angle. The advantage to the figure-eight stroke is that it's easier to prevent taking too much metal off one side of the edge. The disadvantage is that you can easily get careless and let the angle and pressure vary, thus dulling the blade you've just honed.

A steel, by the way, doesn't actually sharpen a blade in the sense that it removes metal or creates a new edge. The stroke against the steel realigns the extreme cutting edge, straightening the "roll" that develops with use. A steel is particularly useful on a razor-sharp hollow- or concave-ground blade used for filleting or skinning.

The honing action of a stone and the realigning action of a steel are said to be combined in a sharpening rod made of alumina oxide ceramic, a man-made material harder than Arkansas stone, of which honing stones are made. W. R. Case & Sons manufactures two such rods, called the Sharp Stick and Moon Stick. From all reports they're excellent.

We probably don't have to add—but will anyway—that the so-called automatic knife sharpeners on the market are virtually useless for putting a fine edge on an outdoors tool.

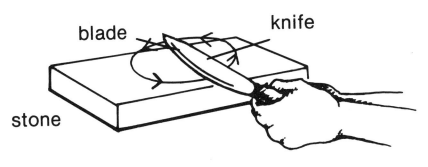

blade **knife**

stone

circular stroke

A circular stroke is a series of short shaving strokes plus a light backstroke.

KNIFE HANDLES

Knife handles are made of wood, leather, cork, plastic, bone, and metal. They're usually one of three styles: two-pieces riveted to a tang that extends to the end of the butt; one-piece with the tang extending halfway into the handle, fastened with some sort of adhesive; and one-piece with the tang extending through the handle, ending in a threaded section to which a butt cap is screwed to hold the handle in place. Each type can be replaced or tightened using epoxy or new rivets.

When working on a knife handle, always secure the knife in a vise with padded jaws for safety and to prevent the blade from twisting or being marred.

A handle made of laminated leather rings stacked one atop another should be coated with clear varnish from time to time to prevent moisture from softening the leather. Cracked plastic handles can be glued, and wooden handles can be fixed with any number of common adhesives.

A handy, quick-setting filler for wood handles can be made from cyanoacrylate glue (super glue) and baking soda. For some reason, baking soda sets up immediately into a hard, sandable, waterproof filler when combined with super glue. To fill a gouge on a knife handle, drop enough super glue into the hole to nearly fill it, then sprinkle baking soda onto it. The glue will "wick" up into the soda, so don't use too much glue. Within minutes, you'll be able to file and sand the patched area. A drop or two of varnish or stain will color the patch.

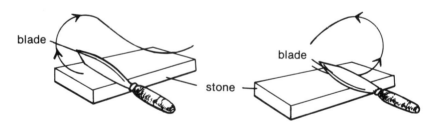

figure-eight stroke

The figure-eight stroke is an alternating stroke along the length of the blade with each side of the blade getting the same number of licks at the same pressure and angle.

Lanterns

CAMPERS USE GASOLINE- and propane-powered lanterns, as well as simpler battery-powered flashlights and lanterns, to light the night. Years of refinement and experience make these appliances safe and reliable, but they need periodic maintenance and are prone to failure if allowed to become clogged and dirty.

Liquid-fuel and bottled-gas lanterns operate the same way. A flammable liquid under pressure is forced through a small tube and mixed with air, forming a vapor. The vapor is directed through outlets to a burning chamber, which is surrounded by an asbestos-fiber mantle (on double-mantle lanterns, there are two burner-and-mantle rigs). Here, the vaporized fuel burns, raising the temperature of the mantle to incandescence. The glowing mantle produces light—much more than an open flame consuming the same amount of gasoline would produce. The mantles are protected, and the light amplified, by a glass chimney, and the vapors given off by the burning fuel exit through holes in the top.

Gasoline lanterns are slightly more complicated than propane lanterns because the fuel is in liquid form and must be pressurized sufficiently to mix with air in the proper proportion. An air pump assembly on the fuel tank accomplishes this. Propane is pressurized in the tank, and vaporizes upon contact with air, so no pump is needed.

On propane lanterns, the cylinder fits directly into a valve assembly and forms a structural part of the lantern. Thus propane lanterns, when the cylinder is removed, are much more compact. With the cylinder in place, they're heavier than liquid-fuel lanterns, due to the need for heavy-walled construction of the propane tank.

GASOLINE LANTERNS

Likely trouble spots on liquid-fuel lanterns are the pump assembly, the generator (which mixes the fuel and air), and the mantles. Before discussing these parts, however, a word about fuel is in order.

Choosing and Using Fuel. Since the fuel/air mixture in a liquid-fuel lantern must be precise, and since adjustments are somewhat limited, you must use the right fuel to begin with. The Coleman company, makers of the most popular lanterns, cautions against using automotive unleaded gasoline in its products. "White gas," which is extremely difficult to find today, is okay, but Coleman recommends that its own product, Coleman Fuel, be used in its products, claiming it has been carefully blended with additives especially suited for lanterns and stoves. Your lantern will run on unleaded or regular gas, but it won't run well or long before it needs cleaning. The slightly higher cost of Coleman Fuel is said to be worth the freedom from maintenance chores and the possibility of equipment failure in the field.

Old fuel, whether white gas or Coleman Fuel, should never be used, as evaporation and condensation will dilute it and cause deposits and poor performance. If still in the original, unopened can, Coleman Fuel may be kept and used for a year or more, but once opened it should never be kept that long. It is better to discard the fuel—or pour it into your car gas tank —and start fresh.

Fuel that's been contaminated by condensation or dirt can be strained through chamois. Coleman sells a custom-fitted funnel with a screen and replaceable filter built in.

Lanterns should be filled with fuel only when cool. Once filled, a lantern should never be tipped over, except to check for leaks as noted below, especially when warm. Never overfill. The tank has a fill tube that should keep you from overfilling, but many people try to tilt the lantern to jam in a few extra ounces and thus upset the fuel/air balance. The lantern won't maintain pressure if there is insufficient air in the tank. Before filling, the fuel valve and the air pump knob must both be closed.

Pump Assembly. The air pump assembly is very simple, using a plunger and leather washer to force air through a small hole in the pump stem and into the tank. The plunger screws in and is secured by a clip to prevent accidental loosening. There is very little to go wrong with this assembly, except a broken spring or clip. The leather washer will sometimes dry out, which is evidenced by a lack of resistance to the plunger's action and a resulting difficulty in pressurizing the tank. To prevent this, you need only oil the washer from time to time with a light lubricating oil (in a pinch, food oil or fat will also do the job).

To oil the leather washer, remove the spring clip from the pump cap by hand, or use a knife blade or screwdriver to pry it loose. This will free the knob to turn counterclockwise, which will loosen the entire assembly for removal. Pull the assembly from the tank, revealing the leather washer. Add a few drops of oil to the washer and work it in with your hands, then reinsert the assembly into the tank. You must be sure not to invert or fold the washer when reinserting it, or the seal will not be good.

The leather washer will, in time, wear out. If, when reinserting the assembly into the tank, you find it impossible to keep the leather washer from inverting or folding, it has worn out and should be replaced. Coleman sells replacement washers ready to slide onto the air stem. To install one, simply remove the retaining nut at the bottom of the stem and slip the replacement onto the stem. Oil it, work the oil into the leather, and reinsert.

If you have no factory replacement, you can make a leather washer from a leather shoe tongue or similar piece of leather. Use the old washer as a pattern to cut the new one, being as precise as possible. Soak the leather in oil for an hour or more and install it as above.

If replacing the washer doesn't allow you to pressurize the tank, you may have a leak in the tank, pump or, fuel-feed system. Unless it's bad enough to hear, you may have trouble finding it.

Start with the pump assembly. Check to see that the assembly has been screwed in tightly, then douse soapy water over the pump. A bad leak will cause some bubbles to appear. If nothing shows, immerse the cold lantern in water up to the level of the air intake (bottom of the glass), and look for bubbles.

A leak in this area can be caused by the leather seal not being seated correctly, or possibly by damage to the threads on the tank or cap. Check the leather, and if it looks all right, inspect the threads for dirt or damage. See if the cap has been bent, or the spring broken. All of these parts can be replaced, including the tank itself if the threads have been damaged.

The threads can be sealed temporarily with pipe dope, Teflon tape, or caulk, but this is only for short-term use, as eventually the seal will begin leaking again.

Another potential leak spot is the fuel filler cap, which can be bent or have its threads damaged from careless handling. Many older lanterns had cork inserts in the filler caps which would dry out and crumble with age. These can be replaced with cork or rubber seals, cut from stock. Nearly any rubber or plastic flexible enough to fit into the cap can be used for a temporary seal, and tape will help seal worn threads. These temporary repairs shouldn't be trusted for long-term use, but can get you through a weekend.

Generator and Fuel-Supply System. If the tank, pump, and filler assemblies are all tight, the leakage could be in the generator, fuel-supply valve, or, less likely, in one of the tubes above them. Best bet is the valve controlling the fuel supply, which can be removed by dismantling the upper assembly and carefully turning the entire valve assembly out of the base. Be careful here, as the threads are easily damaged. The tank should be depressurized before disassembly.

The problem in this area is usually either stripped threads (very unlikely, unless you've been careless in dismantling the lantern) or dirt deposits in the valve, generator, or fittings connecting them to the upper assembly. Using the wrong fuel or dirty fuel is often the culprit. Your first course of action should be to attempt to remove these deposits.

First, remove the plastic knob from the valve assembly and carefully unscrew the valve stem, generator tube, and fuel/air supply tube—be careful with these soft metal parts! The metal parts can be soaked in carbon tetrachloride, lacquer thinner, or white gasoline; for a quicker cleaning, they can be boiled in a detergent solution for fifteen minutes or so. Use noxious solvents only in a well-ventilated place.

The valve assembly includes a cleaning rod which is fitted into the valve assembly at the point where the generator tube fits onto it. This rod is operated by a lever which passes through the assembly to the outside. It is designed to clean the tip of the generator at the point where the fuel enters it. The lever should be rotated several times every time you light the lantern.

Other potential leakage spots in this area are the threads of the valve stem assembly, generator nut, and fuel tube. There's nothing you can do to repair damaged threads, so if cleaning doesn't solve the problem, you'll need to replace the entire assembly. Again, temporary sealing of threads with tape or pipe sealant will get you through the night.

The generator tube becomes sticky with deposits after prolonged use, and if you can't get it perfectly clean, or if it won't fit tightly to the valve assembly or the burner cap, replace it.

To replace the generator, close the fuel valve and turn up the cleaning

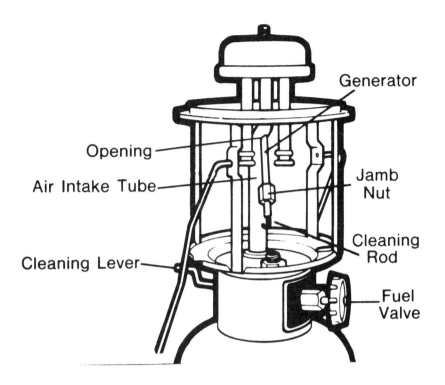

Generator

Opening

Air Intake Tube

Jamb Nut

Cleaning Rod

Cleaning Lever

Fuel Valve

Replace the generator tube when you can't get it clean or when it no longer fits tightly to the valve assembly or burner cap.

lever. Lift the generator tube off its fitting at the valve assembly and remove it. Unhook the generator cleaning lever and remove the cleaning rod with the tube.

Pull the cleaning rod on the new generator down about one inch, and insert it into the valve assembly. Hook the lever to the cleaning rod and turn the lever down and carefully fit the generator tube over the fitting on the valve assembly. Take care not to bend the cleaning rod. Slide the nut over the generator tube and tighten it down firmly. Do not overtighten, but use a small wrench to make sure this seal is tight.

Above the generator tube, there is little to go wrong with the lantern. The fuel and air pass through several holes before being burned, so if the lantern is clogged you might check these for deposits, dirt, spider webs, etc.

Yes, spider webs. For some reason known only to arachnids, the tubes in lanterns are favorite nesting places. Tiny spiders barricade themselves inside, making the lantern burn yellow (if at all) and become fouled easily. Simple dismantling will reveal a blocked tube, which can be cleaned with air pressure or solvents as described above. If you've been burning your lantern for a long time without cleaning it, or if you've used bad fuel, you can boil these deposits out as described above.

Mantles. On older lanterns, a weak or yellow light that can't be attributed to a clogged or fouled fuel tube, generator, or valve might be caused by a clogged screen in the burner assembly, where the mantles attach. This is easily dismantled for cleaning with a stiff brush.

If all is well in the fuel and air systems, but your lantern doesn't give enough light, check the mantle. This fragile screen is easily knocked loose or broken, and once broken it's worthless. You should keep several spares on hand. Taping them to the bottom of the lantern is a good idea, or use Coleman's Spare Parts Kit, which snaps onto the bottom of the lantern base.

The mantle should be tied to the mantle support at the end of the burner tube. First, clean off all residue from the old mantles which may be sticking to the burner. This dirt not only makes it difficult to tie the mantle into place, it may dislodge and fall into the mantle, breaking it.

The mantle should be tied into place securely, with the material evenly distributed around the burner. Snip off the ends of the tie strings. Reassemble the globe and ventilator. The mantle is coated with a flammable waxlike substance which protects the mantle until it is ready to be used. To burn this off, touch a match flame to the bottom of the mantle. Do not allow the matchhead itself to touch the mantle. The coating will flame and burn off, leaving a fragile white ash. The globe and top assembly may now be replaced and the lantern lit.

Storing and Moving. Lanterns should never be stored under pressure, nor should they be stored over a winter with fuel in the tank. For carrying in an automobile or boat, a lantern case is ideal. Coleman markets such a case to fit its lanterns, but there's no reason why you can't make your own. Remember to design it in such a way as to keep the lantern upright to prevent fuel leakage. Pad with foam cut to fit the contours of the lantern.

PROPANE LANTERNS

Bottled-gas lanterns are nearly troubleproof, although they are subject to the same cleaning and spider-removing maintenance as liquid-fuel lanterns. The fuel and burner tubes and the fuel valve are spots to troubleshoot. Leaks can be detected with soap suds—never use a match! (See the section on propane and butane stoves in the *Cookstoves* entry.)

KEROSENE LANTERNS

There are two other kinds of liquid-fuel lanterns sometimes used in the outdoors. The common "hurricane" kerosene lamp (or its sturdier cousin, the "railroad" lantern, which is much safer to use in the field), and the combination wick and mantle lantern made by the Aladdin Manufacturing Company.

Kerosene lamps, whether the common table models sold in hardware stores and gift shops or the rarer but sturdier railroad kind with a protective cap and guard enclosing the globe, are simple machines that require little maintenance beyond an occasional cleaning of the globe and trimming of the wick. They'll burn the crudest, smelliest kerosene with ease, or will happily digest the sweetest lamp oil you can afford. Never try to burn gasoline, lighter fluid, Coleman Fuel, or any other volatile, explosive fuel in one of these lamps.

To keep a wick-type kerosene lamp burning brightly, trim the wick each time you use the lamp. The wick should be trimmed to match the shape of the holder; that is, it should be contoured, not just chopped off square, which will result in a "double" flame and a lot of smoke (and a dirty chimney or globe).

Aladdin lamps have been called the Cadillacs of kerosene lamps, whether because of their elegant design, precision fit, high cost, or appetite for fuel no one seems to know. They are beautiful instruments, but expensive—and thirsty. On the other hand, they produce as much light as a pressurized liquid-fuel lantern and do it with cheaper fuel, so it probably evens out in the long run. And, of course, they give off a considerable amount of heat, and can thus supplement the heating system in a small camper or tent.

These lamps combine the wick of the simpler kerosene lamps with the mantle of the pressurized models, with the obvious advantage that, since the tank and fuel is not under pressure, it is safer and easier to maintain. The tubular wick fits over a central tube which forms the base for a mantle and holder assembly. The mantle and holder, along with the globe, is lifted up and off the wick assembly, and the wick is lighted and adjusted. Then the mantle and globe assembly are replaced. The low flame of the wick heats the mantle, which is just as fragile as any used on pressurized lanterns, until it glows white hot.

These lamps put out light equivalent to a 75- or 100-watt incandescent bulb, and the light is white, not yellow. They do it on cheap yellow kerosene, too, although the better grades of kerosene are preferred since they don't smell as strong or foul the wick as easily.

The wick is the trouble spot. It must be trimmed frequently, and the only way to trim it is with a small plastic tool that Aladdin makes and sells. If you don't have one, you'll probably ruin the wick before you get it right. Not trimming the wick leads to flare-ups and burning mantles.

In fact, the Aladdin lamps are quite delicate, and the parts fit together so well that you have to handle them with aplomb or risk bending or breaking them. Too, the mantles and wicks are frightfully expensive. The mantle cannot be purchased separate from its carrying assembly, which costs several dollars at this writing. As we said, the Cadillac of liquid-fuel lanterns.

Folks who have Aladdin lamps love them, and there are many elegant shade and base variations available to please the stylish homeowner. The one model most likely to be used in camp is a hanging model which is also one of the cheapest. It has an aluminum bail to hang from an overhead hook or nail and a screen cap to prevent bugs from diving down the chimney to their doom (and probably the doom of the mantle). If you can get one of these screen assemblies for use on cheaper, wick-type lanterns or lamps, do so. They're a great addition. You can, of course, make a screen cap to fit any chimney you might have. A ring-type jar lid and a piece of window screen will do it.

BATTERY-POWERED LANTERNS AND FLASHLIGHTS

Since batteries produce a low-power electrical charge which flows over contact points, failure of battery-powered lanterns or flashlights can usually be traced to corrosion or poor fit at those points. If you have to shake a flashlight or lantern to get it to work, chances are there's a poor connection between the battery and bulb or ground. A little snooping can detect this, and springs can be bent to make the connections tight.

Corrosion can be cleaned with a bit of abrasive paper or steel wool, and a dab of light oil can protect the metal surfaces from pitting and corrosion. Never leave a leaking battery in a flashlight or lantern.

Stashing a lantern or flashlight in a pack invites accidental discharge due to inadvertent opening of the switch. Tape the switch closed until ready to use, or better yet, reverse one battery to break the circuit.

Fluorescent lanterns, which operate at extremely low voltage, are sometimes hard to get started, especially in wet weather. The culprit here is humidity, which prevents the charge from building up enough strength to illuminate the gas inside the fluorescent tube. You can help it along by simply touching it or rubbing along it with your hand—you'll be the conductor and carry the charge up the tube!

For further information on battery-powered gear, see the *Batteries (Flashlight and Lantern)* entry.

Leather Boots and Shoes

"TAKE CARE OF your shoes and they'll take care of you" is a lesson learned by most of us, too often the hard way. Leather walking shoes and hiking boots are essential outdoor gear, but frequently outdoorsfolk take them for granted, denying them the little maintenance and care they require, expecting them to last forever. At today's prices, you can't afford to do that.

BREAKING IN, WATERPROOFING, AND CLEANING

Leather boots and shoes need to be broken in to be comfortable. Depending on the kind of leather and the type of construction, this can take a little or a long time. In the course of researching this book, we encountered suggestions ranging from the barely plausible to the patently ridiculous, all of them aimed at breaking in new boots in the shortest amount of time with the least discomfort to the wearer.

A few of them seemed like good ideas. For example, wearing two pairs of socks, the outer pair soaked in neat's-foot oil, sounded effective. Unfortunately, you can't get rid of the oil once it's inside the boot, and your feet will be stained and smelly from it for a long time. Threads will break down, too. Scratch that one.

One suggestion that apparently gets a lot of play is filling the boots with water and letting them stand overnight, then wearing them with two pairs of socks for several hours the next day. Unless broken in means "broken down" to you, don't do this. Water will soak into the unprotected threads in the insole seams and cause them to rot. Mildew will form inside the shoe, where it's nearly impossible to get out.

Boots get broken in—that is, shape themselves to fit your feet—largely from the action of your sweat and the pressure of your foot. Water will mimic this softening action, but your boots will lose many, many miles of service. Wading in new boots is not only uncomfortable, it's downright stupid; you stand a great chance of slipping on rocks in stiff, unfamiliar, new boots.

A way to break in and stretch tight boots was related by a shoemaker who's been repairing shoes for fifty years. Farmers would, he claimed, fill their boots with cracked, dried corn and add water. The corn would swell to many times its original size, pushing against the leather evenly in all directions to stretch and soften it. "Of course," he winked, "you had to watch it so they didn't *explode* on ya!" Uh-huh.

Well, with all that in mind, the bad news is there's no quick way to make new boots fit and feel like old ones. Breaking in boots takes time, travel, and, unfortunately, some pain as your skin and the leather work out an adequate compromise. You can, however, ease the process somewhat.

First, make sure your boots fit, and when you find a brand that fits well, breaks in without undue hardship, and gives good service, stick with it no matter what the "in" boot happens to be. Try on several styles in various length and width combinations. Listen to the outfitter: he can advise you on what boot to buy for your intended activity. Try different sizes on each foot. Few people realize that their feet are probably of slightly different shape and size, and that sizes vary from manufacturer to manufacturer.

Once you've got a pair of boots you like, find out what they're made of. Chrome-tanned leather and oil-tanned leather are very different in their strength, water-resistance, and response to dressing and chemicals. Take the trouble to ask or write the maker before you start slopping goop all over them.

Now you're ready to take them home and break them in. One tactic that minimizes discomfort while breaking in a boot is to use an already broken-in leather or foam rubber insole. These are available from shoe repairmen, and the foam kind can be found at drugstores and the like. Keep a couple of pairs of these in use in various shoes and sneakers, and you'll always be ready to slip a pair into your new boots. Take them along when you go shopping to make sure they'll fit well. Actually, using insoles in all your shoes at all times is a good way to gain miles of comfortable travel.

Before setting out on your first jaunt, apply a waterproofing solution or wax to your boots (see below). Here's where it's important to know what your boots are made of. Oil-tanned leather should be treated with oil—neat's-foot is cheapest, mink oil more expensive—or an oil-based commercial coating. Chrome-tanned leather, on the other hand, doesn't like oil, which clogs the pores.

For new boots, an oil-based paste is probably best for oil-tanned leather, as it will not soak in readily and won't saturate threads. Chrome-tanned leather should be sprayed with silicone spray, or waxed with a good shoe wax.

Many people mistakenly assume they don't need to waterproof new boots; they think the "factory" does it. Well, in many cases they're wrong, and even if they're right, the months those boots spend in transit and storage take their toll on any waterproofing with the exception of silicone. Be safe —waterproof.

With your boots thus protected, get your feet ready. If you wear your boots with *no* socks for a few hours indoors—no heavy walking, of course —you'll soon feel where they're likely to pinch, rub, or bind. Reinforce those places before setting out on your first serious walk by applying moleskin or plastic adhesive bandages.

Next, wear two pairs of socks, both cotton. Avoid wool and synthetic socks in new boots, as they tend to slip and slide inside the boot, and you'll be doing enough of that anyway. Loosen the bottom laces, but keep the top few tight enough to avoid chafing at your ankles.

Now, walk, avoiding tough terrain, steep slopes, rocky hillsides, etc. Gradual, rolling terrain is best. Check your laces once in a while. Your feet will probably swell and the laces will become tight, so loosen them.

Stop and rest your feet from time to time, and take a look at them, too. Patch up any spots that may be becoming blistered with moleskin or adhesive bandages, and promptly treat any broken skin you find.

At some point, you'll notice lots of little aches and pains in your ankles and arches. You'll also feel that blister you've padded and repadded, and maybe your heels will feel like they're on fire. It's time to stop and change socks and shoes—you did bring a spare pair of comfortable shoes with you, didn't you? Oh, well. . . .

Try to spend as much time in your new boots as your feet will allow. The wearing process is slow, but it is better to work on it continually for a week than once a week for a month—the leather will "remember" which way it's supposed to stretch.

If, through vanity or ignorance, you've bought a pair of too small boots, you can stretch them with shoe trees. It's better to find a shoemaker who'll do this for you, though, as he is less likely to split a seam by using too large stretchers.

Most "shoe-ease" products are alcohol-based, which will certainly allow leather to stretch, but will just as certainly hasten breakdown. These products are usually sold in small amounts in aerosol cans, which makes them expensive and hard to apply to the right spot *inside* the shoe, which is where you need them.

A better way is to use a cotton ball soaked in 70 percent isopropyl rubbing alcohol (which has very little water in it). Wring the cotton almost dry, then rub the alcohol on the spot you want to stretch; don't soak the entire inside of the boot. Wearing two pairs of cotton socks, don the boot immediately and wear it for at least an hour. This "shock treatment" isn't good for your boots, but it can help solve problem cases for people with oddly-shaped feet.

Thus far we haven't mentioned "suede" shoes and boots. "Suede" is French for "Swedish" and originally referred to a particular kind of soft goatskin from that country. Modern suede is properly called "roughout" leather: the hide is split, and the inner, rough surface roughed up to give the characteristic napped appearance. This treatment also softens the leather, making suede boots somewhat easier to break in. You have to waterproof them with silicone spray, though, and that does little to soften new boots.

All the care information below calling for liquids being applied to the boots does not apply to suede. All you really need to keep them looking good is a stiff brush and silicone. If you get them really muddy, for instance, just let the mud dry, brush it off, and re-spray.

Once in full-time service, your boots need only minimal attention, unless you get them wet. Too many people apply the "more is better" reasoning when it comes to waterproofing. You really don't need to waterproof any boots more than once a year if you do it thoroughly. In fact, too much silicone, wax, or oil will have a detrimental effect, either clogging pores in the leather, which will make the insides wear out faster, or trapping dirt and water in the leather and stitches, which can cause mildew and rot.

Silicone is probably the most abused waterproofing, simply because it's so simple to spray on and it's invisible. People tend to use more discretion with oil and wax-based products.

The "once a year" rule doesn't apply, of course, to boots subjected to constant soaking or to boots contaminated with salt water (or road salt). You can and should treat boots used under these conditions more frequently. A good way to tell when your boots need help is to look for whitish deposits on the outside. This means the leather is drying out, and while the boots will still keep your feet dry, it's time to treat them again.

Boots must be thoroughly dried before waterproofing. You do much more harm than good coating leather that still has a lot of moisture inside it. (And that means the insides, too, as perspiration contains salts and acids which will work on leather and thread. It should be standard procedure to wipe out your sweaty boots with an absorbent cloth every time you take them off.)

Drying boots that have become soaked or covered with mud takes time. Unfortunately, you don't have much time in the field, and so will seldom be able to properly dry your boots overnight in camp. One thing not to do is try to speed up the process by applying heat or hanging the boots near the fire or stove. This will dry the boots, alright, but it will also crack the leather and cause it to blister and stiffen. Remember, leather is skin. Do you dry your arm by sticking it in an oven?

The best thing you can do with wet leather boots in camp is to wash them off and hang them upside down in an airy place, away from direct sun (which will also dry and crack leather). For such short-term drying, don't fill the boots with newspaper, cloths, or other absorbent matter. Overnight, this will hold moisture inside the boot and inhibit the free circulation of air, which will get your boots as dry as anything.

For camp drying, wash off any mud, dirt, dust, and other debris with clear water. Since your boots are already soaked, a cleansing bath won't do much harm, and it will make drying faster and easier. Mud holds moisture in the leather and inhibits air flow. It also can dry hard as a rock, making your boots very stiff and uncomfortable. It also tends to leach oil out of the leather. Don't try to brush off mud, however, as it will just be forced into leather. If heavily caked, work mud off with a knife or stick.

After washing off the outside, blot the insides and outsides dry with paper towel, chamois, etc., and hang as described above. Oh, yes, if you're in porcupine country, remove the laces and keep them in the tent with you. Porkies like salt, and few things are more salty than much-handled shoelaces. Find a place to hang those boots well out of the reach of raccoons, too—if such a place exists.

If you can, blot the insides of the boots with an absorbent cloth once an hour or so, particularly if your boots have been soaked clear through. Hanging boots upside down allows water to pool inside the uppers, where it gets little if any air.

If you have the luxury of ample drying time, you should modify the above procedures somewhat. Again, wash off all the mud and crud you can with clear water. Use a soft brush this time, however, and an old toothbrush to scrub out the welt. Yes, you'll force some mud into the seams and leather, but since you won't be wearing the boots for a while and will have time to saddlesoap them before waterproofing, this is less of a problem.

If, of course, your boots are just slightly muddy, or if you don't need a saddlesoap and waterproofing treatment yet, just wash them off in clear water.

Once washed, the boots should be blotted dry, inside and out, and placed in an airy place out of sunlight and away from direct heat sources. This time don't hang them up. This will lengthen the drying time somewhat, but will allow water inside the boot to evaporate through the uppers instead of pooling there. Naturally, you'll have to blot out the insides every so often, as water will pool in the heel and ball areas.

The experts disagree on using absorbent material inside boots during slow drying. On one hand, it will definitely act as a wick to draw water out of the leather. On the other, it wicks toward the *inside,* which is where your boots will stay wettest longest anyway. In humid climates, or during warm weather, this can pose a significant mildew problem as well, so we advise against stuffing boots on those grounds.

There's an argument for stuffing that says really wet boots need the internal support of stuffing to keep their form while drying. If you dry your boots slowly, away from heat, they shouldn't stiffen and curl anyway, and even if they do, it's doubtful newspaper would help much. Don't stuff.

Never leave the laces in wet boots. Moisture will collect underneath them, making perfect little mildew incubators. Remove cotton or nylon laces, wash them in soapy water, rinse thoroughly, and hang them up to dry. When dry, fabric laces can be sprayed with silicone, which will help keep them from rotting from absorbed moisture.

Leather laces should also be removed and rinsed in clear water until surface dirt is gone. Hang them up, away from heat, and soak them in neat's-foot oil before replacing them.

Once your boots are thoroughly dry, inspect them for damage or evidence of drying out. If you've recently waterproofed them and not subjected them to repeated soakings, you probably don't need another treatment—and, as we noted above, too much waterproofing isn't a good idea. On the other hand, if you notice white deposits, cracks, or stiffened spots, it's time to retreat.

Boots should be warmed thoroughly to help open the pores in the leather before waterproofing. This is especially necessary for older boots, which may have clogged pores. Leave *already dry* boots near, not on, a heat vent, radiator, or woodstove for an hour, turning occasionally, until the leather is warm. Apply the waterproofing paste or oil evenly with your hand or a brush. Don't neglect the welt area. Use special welt sealer (not airplane glue) if you've experienced leaking in this vulnerable area. Let the waterproofing soak in. That's it.

Another point of contention among experts is whether or not to apply waterproofing to the inside of the tongue. We vote against that for the same reason we advise against putting oil inside the boots during breaking in: it inhibits the movement of moisture and tends to saturate and rot cotton thread (especially oil-based waterproofing).

For basket cases—boots that have been abused, repeatedly soaked, allowed to dry with mud caked on them, used in or near salt water, or dried with heat—you should saddle soap them before applying any coating. Even if you are able to remove all visible dirt and stains with just water, you won't get the deep dirt out. Saddlesoap will not only get that dirt out, it will soften and massage the leather, making it more pliable and less likely to crack.

Saddlesoap is often misunderstood. It is real soap, capable of emulsifying grease and dirt and allowing water to float it away. It is also oil-based, so, unlike detergent, it need not be rinsed out of leather. Saddlesoap is, in fact, a one-step conditioner—if used correctly.

For those basket-case boots, first brush them with a stiff brush to remove as much caked-on crud as possible. Then wash them in clear water, which should get rid of the rest of the surface dirt.

Now, use the saddlesoap. The proper way to use this product is sparingly. It isn't "new and improved," so it requires a bit of elbow grease to work up a lather. And that's exactly what you want: a good, rich lather. The best way to get this is to take a wet sponge that has been rung out and collect a small amount of saddlesoap on it. Then rub the sponge inside a bowl until it is lathered. Use water sparingly. Go back to the can and pick up more soap as needed, but do not just scoop it out—you want leather, not paste.

When you've got a good bowlful of lather, add a little water, and begin to work the soap into the boots with a circular motion. You can use the sponge for this, or a soft-bristled brush.

If the boots were particularly dirty, you'll notice the lather turning brown. Wipe it off and keep wiping off any excess that shows dirt. You may have to go over the entire boot two or three times until the soap stops picking up dirt. Once you've gotten a clear lather, wipe it off and put the boots aside to dry. The boots can then be treated with waterproofing as described above.

REPAIR AND REFURBISHMENT

A good pair of leather boots should last for years. Such minor damage as broken or missing eyelets, pulled stitches, and cracked soles aren't reason enough to buy new boots. You can fix some damage yourself—particularly easy is resewing loose or rotted seams with an awl or two needles.

If you sew your shoes, sew all the seams (or at least as many as you feel comfortable doing). Seams on the uppers, particularly the heels, collars, and moccassin toes, can be easily restitched. Use waxed linen or cotton/-poly thread—the heavy stuff, which you can get at leather stores. Don't mess with broken or torn welts, though; they're a job for a good shoemaker. Ditto for cracked soles.

Broken eyelets can be punched out and replaced with a leatherworker's eyelet tool, although a shoemaker can do this a lot easier than you can. Check eyelets carefully. They can pull and develop sharp edges which will increase your shoelace failure rate beyond endurance.

Sad to say, rotted or torn linings are nearly impossible to repair or replace at reasonable cost. If the lining is coming out in pieces, the boots are about done for and not worth wasting time and money on. That's why you should take care to dry the insides of your boots as thoroughly as you can.

Deteriorating linings are usually accompanied by unpleasant odors, as fungi and bacteria feed on the dirt- and body-oil-soaked leather. You can prevent this social evil by sprinkling a little baking soda, borax, or cornstarch into the boots and letting them sit overnight. This will also help draw moisture out of the leather. Before putting boots on, a good commercial footpowder or baking soda can be used.

Never try to deal with odoriferous boots by spraying disinfectant or other microbe killers inside them. The moisture will do much more harm than good, and the medicinal odor will be just as obnoxious as anything your feet produce.

Mildew spots can be treated with a 50 percent solution of denatured alcohol. Wipe the solution on with a clean cloth and let it dry thoroughly before using the boots.

Hard, lugged, synthetic Vibram soles are extremely popular these days because of their gripping ability on rough terrain. The only problem with them is that they are hard to repair. You can't have a new sole or heel slapped on as you can with other kinds.

Most people tend to walk down one part of the heels more than others.

Take a look at your shoes—you're probably walking toward the outside. In time, your gait will be affected, and that will affect the performance and longevity of your boots. The stress you put on the outside of the shoe can in time break down the welt on that side, as well as pulling the insole away from the welt on the other.

The solution is simple: put plastic or nylon cleats on your new boots, *before* you begin wearing them down. You can figure out where to put them by looking at a worn pair. Cleats are cheap and easy to install. Use ribbed or threaded nails and epoxy cement.

Walkover is one cause of premature boot failure. Another is walking around with unlaced boots. If your boots are so hot you have to unlace them to feel comfortable, you have more boot than you need. Sloppy, floppy, unlaced boots are stressed and strained unnaturally.

Another bad habit is carelessness in putting on and taking off boots. A lot of people jam their feet into the boot, then struggle and wiggle their heels down inside, all the while trying to tug the tongue into place. The counters—the back of the uppers—take a lot of beating from this.

The right way is to unlace the first four or five eyelets (many boots have "speed laces" here; if yours don't you can have them put on at a shoe-maker's shop) and loosen the rest. Pull the tongue forward and put your toe inside. Grasp the top of the collar at the rear (perhaps there's a loop there; if not, you can have one put on or do it yourself), and pull the boot onto your foot. Leave the lower laces loose, but tighten the top ones snug; your foot will probably swell and you'll end up loosening the bottom laces anyway.

Remove your boots just as carefully. Loosen all the laces, pull the tongue forward, and pull the boot off by grasping the heel. A boot jack is a marvelous invention you can make yourself.

"Creeping tongue" is a problem nearly as pernicious as "creeping laces." Both can be fixed with a minimum of effort. Cut two parallel slices lengthwise through the tongue, even with the third eyelet down. When lacing your boots, pass the laces through these slits. The tongue will be kept still. Tie a knot in the exact center of each shoelace before inserting it in the shoe. The knot will ride in the center of the tongue between the bottom eyelets, keeping laces in their places.

Maps

TRAIL AND TOPOGRAPHICAL maps are invaluable in the bush, but they tend to get wet, dirty, and stained with depressing rapidity—usually when you need them most.

Perhaps the best thing you can do with a map is to duplicate it. Cheap photocopying is available everywhere, so take your topo map to the copier and run off a few. You can custom-make maps this way, too: copy maps of adjacent areas, cut away the margins and any parts you won't need, tape them together, and copy the resulting product. For a buck or so, you can have a season's supply of maps custom-made to your specifications.

In the field, it's best to keep maps rolled rather than folded, as they will wear out at the folds, and keep them in plastic if possible.

Canoe and kayak voyageurs will be happy to know that someone has finally figured out a way to keep maps dry. A product called Stormproof, made by the Martenson Co. of Williamsburg, Virginia, is a clear, tough, water-and-mildew-repellent coating which can be applied directly to a paper map with a cloth or brush. It dries invisibly, can be written on with marking pens or pencils, will not peel or crack from folding, and will not stiffen the paper. A pint of it will coat 100 square feet of paper. Sure beats trying to read a map through a plastic baggie.

Mountaineering Gear

MOUNTAINEERING BY ITS very nature is a rough and tumble sport. And if you have ever returned from a climb with sore muscles and bruised shins you can be sure that some of your equipment felt much the same way. A few extra moments spent in organized packing while on a climb can yield years of extra life to much of your gear. A single sharp point or rough edge can, after a few miles of jiggling about in a pack, virtually destroy anything it comes in contract with. The common cork can be used on many of the sharp points in your ice-climbing gear. And unlike specially produced point protectors, your selection can quickly be expanded upon with the consumption of a few more bottles of wine.

Small, lightweight stuff sacks are very useful and can be used to keep an item clean and dry while protecting it in transit. Metal items should be kept dry as much as possible to prevent rust and corrosion. If they are to be stored for a long period, a light spray of oil or lubricant will give added protection.

Continued ongoing care and storage is the most important aspect of keeping your mountaineering equipment in top shape for the longest time. Packing it properly while in use and then cleaning, drying, and checking for problems before storing are the basics that should always be attended to in order to insure the longest life and use from your mountaineering equipment.

ROPES AND HARNESSES

Rope and webbing should be kept out of the sun whenever possible as ultraviolet light speeds deterioration of the fibers. Store ropes and webbing in a dark corner, loosely coiled or folded, and make sure they are dry to the core if placed in a waterproof stuff sack so they do not become moldy. A good washing will normally remedy that problem if it does occur. Modern kernmantle climbing ropes are easily washed in a washing machine with light soap and cold water, and should be rinsed well to assure that all the soap is out.

Never step on the rope as this might cause internal cuts to its core. There have been no failures of modern climbing ropes in many years, but they will cut surprisingly easy over sharp edges when loaded.

When choosing a rope, strength is important, but thickness and sheath strength should be carefully checked. Europeans have long used two 9-millimeter ropes which reduces rope drag substantially and always provides them with a backup in case the rope does cut. And while this would mean purchasing two ropes, their lifespan can be much longer than a traditional single rope due to peace of mind from the double security. Falling on two old ropes is better than falling on just one.

Check the sheath of the rope occasionally for areas of wear or cuts. If they are close to an end, the rope can be cut and the end melted with no significant loss. The ends of the rope itself may need occasional fusing to keep them from fraying. Melting the end over a flame and then shaping with a hot knife will solve the problem and keep the ends neat. Middle and ends can be marked with tape. Do not use paint or dyes as this may weaken the rope. (See *Rope* entry for more on construction and care of ropes.)

Climbing harnesses are most commonly constructed of varying widths of nylon webbing and metal buckles. Stitching is done on special industrial sewing machines that make the stitching as strong as the webbing itself. Check the stitches for excessive wear occasionally. As with common nylon clothing, harnesses can be washed. Cold water and no soap or a weak suds mixture should prove adequate. This gets the dirt and dust from between the fibers, an area of potential wear. As with all nylon webbing keep it out of the sun when not in use.

Higher-grade harnesses often come with a collection of loops and attachment points. As these are not structurally important you can install your own with a few lengths of nylon thread and a couple of feet of web or cord. Holsters may be added by sewing two-inch webbing in half (lengthways) to make it more rigid and keep the holster open, then sewing it in a loop to fit the tool. This can either be permanently attached to the harness or sewn to an additional piece of two-inch webbing and slots cut in it so it can be taken on or off the harness.

CARABINERS, CHOCKS, AND SIMILAR HARDWARE

Carabiner gates should be oiled occasionally with a small amount of light oil or lubricant to keep the gate action smooth. Never throw them (or any gear), as they are brittle and can develop cracks and weak points. It is a good idea to throw out any carabiners you take a substantial fall on. The rapid stress of a single fall can significantly weaken a carabiner and it is best removed from the climbing system.

Belay plates, figure of eights, chocks, and other solid metal items need only be checked for rough edges or burrs. These can all be filed smooth with a standard file. Ascending devices (jumars) and mechanical camming devices (friends) should be checked frequently for proper adjustment of the springs and cams. Light oil on the moving parts will prolong wear and keep the parts working smoothly. Also, if a part breaks, it is possible (with friends, in particular) to order spare parts and fix them quite easily yourself without having to buy an entire new unit. For the more innovative, many items can be fashioned to work well as chocks. Their actual strength may be unknown, but steel nuts and metal fittings with slings attached can provide very good placements for a fraction of the cost of commercially produced products.

SNOW GEAR

Points and teeth of ice tools should always be kept sharp by filing. Do not use a grinding wheel as it can quickly overheat the metal and change its temper. A light linseed oil coating on wooden handles will keep them sealed and the wood from warping. Metal shafts can be wrapped with bicycle or adhesive tape for a better grip. Slings attached to the ends and then to your harness will protect against loss. Wooden handles are aesthetic, but metal is stronger and more resilient over the years. Cap the end points with hollowed out corks or sheaths. Interchangeable pick tools will give you flexibility to use the same tool in a variety of conditions or provide easy replacement if a pick should ever break.

Bent tools can often be reshaped though their strength at that point will be reduced. Place them in a vise and bend slowly back to their original angle. Sharp pick points are essential in ice, but slightly rounded rear teeth will make extraction easier. A small file will serve to do the job.

Ice screws and snow anchors should be checked occasionally for cracks or fractures in their joints or cables. Long falls severely stress any piece of equipment and they should be retired if you have any doubts as to their reliability. Most snow anchors are little more than a length of aluminum with a hole or two in them. A metal drill and an old aluminum window or door frame can quickly provide you with a good supply of anchors. Ice screw points can be kept sharp with a small file. Clogged ice will be less likely to form in ice screws if a good coat of lubricant is sprayed down the tube of the screw.

CRAMPONS

For best results, crampon points should be kept sharp by occasional filings. Rigid crampons can only be used with rigid (full-length shank) boots. Flexible crampons may be used on just about any shoe or boot, as they are flexible in the center. Rigid crampons that have several sections screwed together give you the advantage of being able to replace only the front points when they wear thin. Points can be protected by a supply of corks, or by being carried in a strong stuff sack. Crampons themselves are usually plated to resist rust, but screws will often be uncoated, so a light lubricant spray will make the crampon screws last longer. Again, cleaning them and making sure they are completely dry before storing them is very important.

Neoprene straps are the most commonly used crampon strap. They fray at the edges but a flame run along the edge will quickly seal them. If they break or need to be modified in the field, a length of half-inch webbing will suffice. Several small buckles and ten feet of the half-inch webbing will also provide a spare pair of crampon straps for emergencies. Crampons should always be adjusted to fit tightly around the edge of the boot for best control and to eliminate any extra stress.

HAMMOCKS

Nylon hammocks for hanging bivouacs should be completely seam-sealed to keep the water out. Small scrapes and holes can easily be repaired with nylon patch kits or with a small piece of nylon and some thread (see *Hammocks* and *Nylon* entries).

Pitching the hammock is best under an overhang, as it will be more comfortable and keep the fabric from rubbing against the rock all night. Short lengths of plastic pipe can be used to keep the top of the hammock away from the rock on vertical sections. Pipe is also useful between the supports of the hammock to keep the sides from pressing against you all night.

HELMETS AND GOGGLES

Standard rock-climbing helmets have internal strap suspensions and fiberglass shells. Cracks or dents in the shell can be repaired with fiberglass or plastic glues. Several good alternatives to the standard helmet include hockey or baseball helmets fitted with chin straps. These are lighter, less expensive, and often quite adequate. Standard helmets can be made more comfortable by slipping a tube of soft cloth or leather over the chin strap.

Glacier goggles should be protected in a solid case and an elastic neck strap will keep them readily available. Normal sunglasses with adequate dark lenses can be fitted with makeshift side flaps to keep excess refracted light out by forming adhesive tape around the edges and across the bows. A simple elastic cord will keep them comfortably around your neck. Ski goggles can also be utilized very effectively for snow and ice climbs. They give improved side vision and are less prone to fogging than glacier goggles.

SHOES AND BOOTS

Rock shoe soles are soft, flexible rubber which a few coats of rubber sole repair will make last much longer. Uppers can be covered with an extra layer of nylon or leather. This should be both glued and sewn on so it does not slip or tear off. Nylon cord shoelaces will last much longer than cotton, especially when being continually scraped agaisnt the rock. Resoling is possible with these shoes, and anything from inner tubes and rubber cement to running shoe soles have been glued on the standard rock shoe with success.

Traditional leather mountain boots should always be treated with a silicone wax preparation to keep the leather in good shape. Oils should be avoided, as they break down the leather, causing you to lose support in the ankle area. If the boot and wax are warmed slightly before application the wax will be absorbed better and last longer. Never get boots too close to a fire or heater as the leather will quickly scorch and lose many of its desirable qualities. (See *Leather Boots and Shoes* entry for more on care and repair of boots.)

Sole life can be extended by use of sole rubber glues, and eventually by resoling. Properly cared for boots can often be used through several resolings before the uppers wear out.

Nylon

NYLON FABRIC IS found in many kinds of outdoor gear—tents, shoes, rainwear, sleeping bags, parkas—where its lightness and durability are complemented by its relative low cost. Nylon can be woven into a variety of cloths that are nearly watertight, windproof, downproof, breathable, nonabsorbent, quick-drying, and nonallergenic. Nylon can be made into clothing soft enough to wear next to the body or into cloth strong enough to withstand abrasion and repeated blows from sharp objects. If not the ideal outdoor fabric, it comes close.

On the negative side, nylon is vulnerable to deterioration from exposure to ultraviolet light (sunlight) and is difficult to waterproof (at least without sacrificing its breathability). It is also vulnerable to heat damage and cannot be patched with adhesives. Nylon tends to fray, also, unless the edges are sealed ("fused") with heat. This complicates repair.

TYPES OF WEAVE

The most common weaves of nylon are taffeta, ripstop, and Cordura. Taffeta is a plain, smooth, tightly woven cloth used most often in bags and linings where softness and water repellency are desired. Ripstop might be thought of as taffeta with a reinforcing grid of fibers, which serves to increase the strength and tear resistance of the cloth. Ripstop finds its way into outerwear, bags, backpacks, and tents. Cordura is a heavier, abrasive-resistant cloth with the nylon fibers "bulked"—sort of fluffed up—to make them strong and less likely to puncture. Cordura has shown up in outerwear, packs, and lightweight hiking shoes.

Cotton and nylon go together well. A blend of 60 percent cotton and 40 percent nylon makes a soft, lightweight, breathable, attractive fabric for dressier clothing and light outerwear that is water resistant. This fabric is often coated with one of several materials to make raingear (see *Raingear* entry).

In addition, nylon can be combined with newer hightech laminates such as Goretex to make raingear that breathes and insulates. Nylon fabrics are sometimes rated by weight, with the higher numbers denoting thicker, and therefore stronger (but less flexible), material. Two-ounce taffeta is a common fabric for lightweight bag linings; 3.5-ounce for outer shells of parkas; and 11-ounce Cordura for backpacks.

Outdoor gear manufacturers are constantly developing new blends, weaves, and coatings to try to achieve the perfect outdoor fabric for every application. Any notation of new developments would, of course, become dated rapidly, and the reader must investigate these as they are introduced. Recent innovations as of this writing are Taslan, a weave that looks and feels very much like a cotton-nylon blend but is in fact all nylon, and Tasmania Jr., a similar, but more open fabric. Other names you are likely to encounter are tricot, a smooth, slippery, very lightweight fabric seldom found in outerwear unless as part of a sandwich of several fabrics; oxford, an open-weaved fabric similar in appearance to the cotton fabric of the same name, which is usually found in coated raingear; and twill, a diagonally woven oxford.

COATINGS

Coatings used on nylon are designed to either enhance its water resistance or reduce its susceptibility to ultraviolet damage, or both. By far the most common coating, found on nearly all outerwear, backpacks, and tents, is urethane, a plastic sometimes referred to as polyurethane.

Polyurethane coatings vary in their thickness, and it's worth your while to find out how much polyurethane is on the fabric. The lightest coating is ¼ ounce. It is applied to nylon fabric chiefly to help keep the fabric from fraying during the cutting, handling, sewing, etc., of the manufacturing process, and therefore has little, if any, value to the user. Quarter-ounce urethane coatings make nylon "marginally waterproof" in the words of one outfitter. Heavier coatings in the ½-, 1-, and 1½-ounce range are more effective waterproofers.

You pay a penalty for coating nylon, however. The coating tends to make nylon stiff and inflexible, and that makes nylon weaker. The "slide" or "give" factor is reduced by heavy coatings, and tear strength is reduced in direct proportion to the stiffness of the fabric. The nylon fibers are locked together by the coating, making them vulnerable to abrasion and puncture.

Urethane coating is heat-sensitive, too, and will peel if exposed to high temperatures. It can also trap detergent residue. (See washing instructions below.)

Other coatings commonly applied to nylon are neoprene, the synthetic rubber found on divers' wetsuits; polyvinyl chloride (PVC), a heavy, tough plastic; and acrylonitrile, an extremely durable but heavy synthetic rubber. These coatings are found on rainwear and specialty garments, and so will be discussed in the Raingear entry. A new polymer-based coating called WaterLock is said to make Cordura totally waterproof yet breathable.

WASHING AND STAIN REMOVAL

Nylon, both coated and plain, may be washed by machine in warm water with common detergents. The keys to cleaning nylon well are solubility and temperature. The problem is that detergents operate best at temperatures above those considered safe for nylon. Keep wash and rinse temperatures below 120° F, especially for coated nylon. The barbic profile begins to change above this temperature, and taffeta can in fact lose its water resistance from exposure to high temperatures. Do not bleach. Dry nylon at low heat or air-only settings, and make sure the dryer is large enough to allow the garment to tumble freely, as hot spots can develop quickly, running sections of the cloth.

Fortunately, nylon is stain-resistant, and quick action with a damp cloth will remove most substances before they can penetrate the fibers. Both uncoated and urethane-coated nylon will tolerate solvents, but you should try them only after all else fails to remove a stain. And, of course, you should remain mindful of the fill, linings, seam sealers, etc., which might react to strong chemicals.

Specific stains that might give you trouble are cat urine, citric acid, blood, and mildew.

Cat urine will yield to repeated washings with a detergent to which borax has been added. Take care not to use water that is too warm in either the wash or rinse, as that will set the stain.

Citric acid from fruit juices (and sugar from soft drinks, syrups, etc.) will dry invisibly. When you wash the cloth in warm water, it will produce an ugly brown stain. The solution is to rinse sugar-laden liquids or citrus juice from the fabric with cold water as soon as possible—preferably before they dry—and to wash the item in cold water.

Bloodstains should not be washed. Usually, the blood will sit on top of the fabric, where it can be scraped with a dull metal edge, such as the back of a knife blade. This will remove much of the blood, and that which remains can be removed by daubing hydrogen peroxide onto it and scraping the foam off. Several applications/scrapings will be necessary if the nylon is uncoated or if the blood has soaked through the garment.

Mildew "stains" are really damaged fibers. Mildew will not grow on nylon itself, but will feed on organic material left in the fabric—a good reason for frequent washing of nylon gear. It produces acids that play havoc with nylon, actually eating it away. There's little you can do to repair the damage once it becomes visible, but an alkaline wash (such as a milk solution of lime or baking soda in water) will retard the mildew growth.

Some stains are really trapped detergent or soap residue. If your nylon gear reveals a whitish "cloud" after it has been washed, rinsed, and dried, it probably has a urethane coating that has trapped soap film, which results from washing in top-loaders or from insufficient rinsing. A second or third rinse should remove the film.

Greasy food stains and petroleum stains are harder to remove the longer they are allowed to remain on the fabric. Try rubbing a bit of liquid detergent into the stain before laundering. Cleaning solvents won't harm nylon, but beware of other fabrics and materials present in the garment. If it will not harm the other fabrics, dry cleaning will take most grease stains out of nylon.

Adhesive stains—as from the ever-present duct tape—are tough. Try scraping as much off as you can. Apply hydrogen peroxide and scrape again.

Nylon's care-free attributes are so great that it is a shock to discover something that really harms it. We've mentioned heat and ultraviolet rays, and to those we must add insecticides. Whatever they put into most commercial insecticides—whether stick, lotion oil, or spray—can make nylon weak and vulnerable to abrasion, puncture, and tearing. This happens rapidly, too, so if you spill some on your tent or pack, move quickly. Flood the area with water and get the garment into a washer or pan of water as soon as possible. If the garment is a single layer of nylon without any fill or backing, pour warm water through the stained areas over and over. You can't counteract the chemical reaction, but you can dilute and wash away as much of the offending substance as possible in as short a time as possible.

Nylon fades, period. There is nothing as tough as trying to match the color of a faded nylon garment. Reds and oranges are most notorious for this.

SEAMS AND THEIR CARE

Seams on nylon gear can be problem areas, and it is here that nylon's critics have a field day. The edge of a piece of nylon is vulnerable to fraying, no matter what its weave. Since the fibers themselves are slippery, it is almost impossible to secure an edge any other way than fusing the fibers with heat. The best nylon gear is "hot cut" (cut and fused at the same time), and these seams can be sewn in a variety of ways. The worst gear is simply cut and sewn, often in such a way as to hide the edge from view. Such halfway measures as applying seam sealants or sewing binding tape to seams are also found with depressing regularity.

Too, the type of seam affects the durability, as does the kind of thread used. Nylon thread is softer and less prone to damage from abrasion, but it is harder to sew with and more expensive than cotton/dacron or all-dacron thread. These latter two are often used on nylon gear, despite the fact that their stiffness and lack of stretch makes a weak seam which will not give with the fabric.

Typical seams found on nylon gear are flat, flat lap, flat felled, tuck, rolled, and serged.

A flat seam is made by stitching through two pieces of fabric, as when sewing the edge of one piece to the center of another. It is, or should be, used only for seams that are not subject to stress, as a flat seam is only about three-fourths as strong as the material itself. You can easily repair a flat seam, however, and seam-sealing compounds readily penetrate when applied to one side only. Double-stitching (adding a second row of stitches) can improve security but not strength. As always, the edges of the fabric should be fused, and this is easy to accomplish since both edges are visible.

Flat lap seams are used where two pieces of material are joined at their edges. It is, in effect, a double flat seam with two rows of stitching. The seam is nearly as strong as the material itself and, when combined with an adhesive seam sealant (which should be applied from both sides, if possible), may be even stronger and more resistant to tearing. Sometimes a zig-zag stitch is used on flat lap seams, especially on sails, although that is actually a weaker stitch. Zig-zag stitches are easier to rip out and replace, however.

If the edges are tucked under—"linked" together, as it were—and

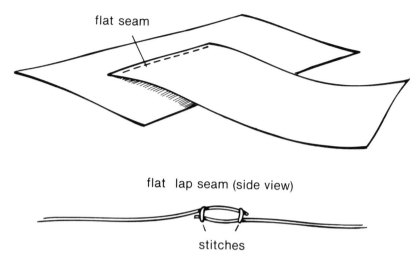

flat seam

flat lap seam (side view)

stitches

Two kinds of seams usually found on nylon gear are flat and flat lap.

double-stitched, the seam, is called a flat-felled seam. This is by far the most common seam found on outdoor gear, for one bad reason: it hides the edges from view, so you cannot see whether they have been fused (they haven't, likely as not). Most mass-produced tents have flat-felled seams, and that is why seam sealants are so popular. It is hard to seal a seam of this type and even harder to repair it once it's frayed enough to pull apart (you have to rip out enough to refold the seam, and you'll still have puckers in the seam area).

Flat-felled seams are touted as the ultimate method of joining two pieces of nylon. Don't believe it. A simple flat lap seam is at least as strong and, with fused edges and adhesive sealant incorporated into the seam, sure to be more waterproof and fray-resistant than a flat-felled seam.

The tuck seam is popular for sewing interior baffles into sleeping bags, as it makes a nice-looking seam with little thread showing on the outside. If you pinch a piece of fabric into a fold and sew the edge of another piece to it with the thread passing through the loop, you've made a tuck seam. (If you merely sew the edges of the piece through the other piece, you've made an insert seam, which doesn't look as nice.)

This seam is not as much of an improvement as might be supposed, for several reasons. For one, the thread now becomes the most stressed part of the exterior; if you pull from either end, the thread will take the force and the seam will tend to open. This is the reason many people lose their baffles when handling wet sleeping bags. The tuck seam is simply not strong enough to withstand the extra weight. Tuck seams are tough to repair, too, because you have to get inside to resew, and that means opening another seam somewhere. Manufacturers sometimes use inferior, coarse threads like polyester on seams of this type, because you cannot see them well enough to complain.

Other than flat seams, several variations are sometimes seen at edges where flatness is not a requirement. Simply folding two edges together—in effect, sewing a flat seam inside out through all four thicknesses of fabric —is a good, strong, simple seam that's easy to seal. A variation involves rolling the edges together, but, of course, you can't see the edges, so suspect a seam of this type is hiding unfused edges. A serged seam is a flat seam with the edges bound with a zig-zag stitch forming a raised edge. It is sometimes called a bound seam since the thread is wrapped around the edges. This type of seam is quick and easy to make, but is vulnerable to abrasion wear since the thread takes the brunt of the abuse.

PATCHING

It is usually better to patch nylon garments or gear by sewing a patch through an existing seam, since adding seams merely detracts from the overall strength and makes waterproofing more difficult to maintain. Flat and flat lap seams are very easy to sew through. Flat-felled and the other seams are more difficult.

When patching nylon, trim all frayed edges from the hole or tear and fuse the edges with a candle flame. In a triangle tear, sew a few stitches across the ends of each leg to stop ripping. Always cut a patch at least one inch larger in all directions than the hole, and coat the area underneath the patch with seam sealant before sewing.

If you can gain access to both sides of the material, make a flat lap seam on the edges where you don't sew through an existing seam. On filled or multi-layer cloth, sew the free edges with a tuck stitch—that is, pinch a small amount of the garment up and sew through it and the patch edge. Always use nylon thread for such raised seams, as the coarser threads will not resist abrasion as well.

To reattach snaps, sew a large patch beneath the area. Chances are, the fibers are weakened around the snap, so you want to insert the new snap on the patch rather than the original fabric.

Optical Instruments

OPTICAL INSTRUMENTS—BINOCULARS, monoculars, and scopes —greatly increase your enjoyment of the outdoors, but can also prove troublesome unless cared for and protected properly. They must be cleaned, protected against temperature and humidity variations, and kept safe from damage due to shock. In many cases, professional care is needed to correct malfunctions, but precautions and simple preventive maintenance minimize the need for service.

PROFESSIONAL CARE

Conditions that require the attention of a professional include misalignment of internal prisms and lenses; fogging or staining of prisms or lenses; stiffening of center-focus knobs, eyepiece adjustments, and hinges; cracks in the body or hinges; mildew or corrosion inside the barrel; and loose, broken, or scratched lenses. Collimation—the adjustment of a binocular to reconcile the separate images—must be performed by a professional technician. Even a carefully handled binocular can become misaligned, often so slightly that the user is unaware of it. A good rule of thumb is this: if you become aware of eyestrain, a "pulling" sensation, while using a binocular, it is out of alignment. There is no easy way for the layperson to determine how badly aligned a binocular is, nor to correct the misalignment. If it feels bad take it to the shop.

A binocular, scope, or monocular that will not focus has internal damage, which probably is due to moisture, shock, or contamination by dirt, chemicals, or lubricants. If the focus wheel or eyepiece adjustment knobs function freely and easily but the instrument will not focus, it needs professional attention. If the instrument has lost brightness, or if the image appears foggy and hazy, internal contamination has occurred and should be dealt with promptly.

Often, letting such a condition go will worsen it; mildew and corrosion can form on internal surfaces, or staining of lenses and prisms can occur, which will ruin the instrument. Most people have trouble differentiating between an "out of focus" binocular or scope and one that has become fogged or stained. Inspect your instrument by looking into the light from the objective side (that is, reversing the instrument). Moisture, mildew, staining, and contamination will be readily apparent. You can also spot cracks, chipped lenses, or separated lenses. Prompt attention will prevent permanent damage.

Internal lens separation, usually due to severe impact or extreme moisture contamination, causes bubbles or patterns to appear around the edges of the image. This condition will gradually worsen and mandates prompt professional attention.

Many owners try to lubricate stiff wheels, knobs, and hinges; this often turns a simple problem into a complex one. Lubricants used on optical instruments are carefully chosen to provide a precise amount of "drag." Oil, graphite, or silicone lubricants that are "too slippery" can penetrate into the internal mechanisms and cause serious damage, often so quickly that the user doesn't realize anything is wrong until it's too late. Even if the lubricant doesn't get inside the optical tube, it may dilute the remaining lubricant on the moving parts, causing accelerated wear of these parts. The temptation to oil or grease the mechanical parts of optical instruments must be resisted. A temporary freeing of stiff or frozen parts may be accomplished at the expense of ruining the instrument. Factory lubricant should last many years (if the instrument is kept clean), but stiffening is a sign that it is breaking down and needs to be replaced, not diluted.

Cracks in hinges or barrels similarly should not be repaired at home. "Super" adhesives have proliferated to the degree that tinkerers are tempted to daub a little glue on anything that's broken, in the belief that it might work and can do no harm. In the case of optical instruments, unfortunately, the potential for damage is greater than the potential for successful repair. High-tech glues and fillers can penetrate exterior surfaces, soften many plastics, corrode or damage metal, and generally play havoc with internal optics. You may get away with repairing a cracked hinge or barrel, but you may also ruin your binoculars forever. Attempts to repair worn eyepiece assemblies are particularly dangerous, as the adhesive can easily flow into gear assemblies and lens mounts.

Loose, broken, scratched, or separated lenses should be promptly repaired by an expert. There is little you can do to improve the situation and a lot you can do to worsen it. Remember, anything that destroys the moisture- and dust-proof quality of the instrument has the potential to cause more serious damage due to internal contamination and resulting deterioration.

Some problems are not worth fixing, even by an expert. If you have broken the center hinge or extensively damaged the prisms or lenses of an inexpensive instrument, for example, the cost of repairing the damage may well exceed the price of replacement.

There is one repair you can safely make. If mounting screws continually work loose, remove them and put a drop of Loc-tite on the threads, then reinsert and tighten.

PROTECTING OPTICAL INSTRUMENTS

With all this bad news, there is some good: as with most equipment, preventive maintenance will greatly prolong your optical instrument's useful life.

As stated earlier, most damage comes from contamination by dirt, chemicals, or moisture, or from severe impact. The remedy is simple: keep the instrument in a protective case. Even if you're trying to keep weight to a minimum, carry a good case for your binoculars, and use it. (There are lightweight cases for cameras and optical instruments on the market.)

A case will protect against shock, but even more important, it will protect against sudden temperature changes that cause moisture condensation and fogging inside the instrument. Never subject your binocular or scope to sudden changes of temperature—either warm to cold or vice versa—without placing it in its case or, if that's not possible, wrapping it in a chamois or large towel. Similarly, you should never store your instrument, even inside its case, in an extremely hot, cold, or damp area. In cold weather, you can keep your instrument inside your shirt or jacket; in hot weather, try to keep it shaded or, in extreme heat, inside a cooler or refrigerator. (One word of caution, however: if you keep a binocular in an area extremely cooler than the environment, store it in its case with a couple of dehydrating packets of silica gel thrown in. Remove it well before you plan to use it, so it has time to warm up in the case. Keeping a binocular or scope in a cooler is only advisable if there is no other way to keep it from extreme heat—for instance, if you are boating in an aluminum craft on a lake during the middle of a summer day.)

Lens caps are usually more trouble than they're worth, unfortunately. If you're using your instrument in foul weather, keep a soft cotton cloth handy and wipe the lenses frequently. That's usually more practical than trying to fumble four lens caps on and off as you use the instrument. Although lens caps are valuable and should be used whenever you store the instrument or when extreme contamination is possible (in a dust storm, for instance), you will still need to wipe moisture off the lenses as you use it. The "fumble factor" is complicated by the "loss factor": lens caps are notorious for falling into inaccessible places, bouncing under cars or rocks, and generally "walking away" if not watched closely. Keep them with the case. Lens caps are valuable for one thing, however: they'll keep the sun from shining directly into the objective lens. Damage to coated optical parts can happen quickly in direct sunlight.

A neck strap is indispensable. Keep it adjusted so that the instrument doesn't get in your way, and if you're traversing rough terrain or climbing, tuck the instrument inside your shirt or jacket to keep it from swinging against rocks or trees.

WATERPROOFING

A word about waterproofing and anti-fogging treatments: they don't work. There is no such thing as a totally waterproof binocular or scope, and trying to coat your instrument with a waterproofing compound will more likely than not result in damage to internal parts by infiltration. Anti-fogging sticks are merely wax which keeps water vapor from condensing on the surface of the lens, but which also attracts and holds dust and grit, making these much harder to remove without scratching the lens.

If you use your instrument in extremely foul conditions or where you may drop it into water, carry it in a large, zip-type plastic food bag. This will seal well enough to keep out most of the water, and if you should drop the instrument into a stream or pool, may provide enough flotation to allow you to retrieve it quickly. The air trapped inside the bag will at least provide some cushion against impact with the bottom.

If you do drop an optical instrument into water, get it to a qualified repairman promptly. Don't try to heat the instrument to evaporate the moisture quickly; that will only result in separated lenses, melted plastic parts, and deteriorated (and possibly corrosive) lubricants.

CHECKING FOR DAMAGE

A binocular or scope that has been dropped or otherwise handled roughly should be inspected carefully for damage. First, check for chipped, separated, or dislodged optics. Look carefully at each ocular (eyepiece) lens for cracks or chips. A separation can show as a "rainbow discoloration" or newly formed bubbles. Also note very closely if the optics seem to be properly set in their mounts, and not fallen out of place or cocked off in a slanted position. Repeat the same procedure with each objective lens. Then hold the binocular up to the light and view through the reverse (objective lens) opening. Note the interior prisms, checking for chips. At this same time, you can also see if there are any loose metal parts or lens diaphragms rattling around inside. Deep in the interior you should be able to detect any injury to the other lens components in the ocular system (eyepiece assembly).

Check eyepieces and/or center focus controls for smooth and proper function. This is the time to look for jammed parts, cracked eyecups, broken center focus bridges (and center hinges). A broken bridge or a cracked center hinge means the instrument has taken a pretty serious fall and the binocular is more than likely useless (until repaired). Also carefully scrutinize the ocular mounts (at the body) and objective lens mounts (also at the body base). There are many instances in which such components are knocked out of position and yet hold their place. This is a cross-threaded condition that will impair both the optical and mechanical function of the instrument. Any of these points noted should alert you that professional help is needed.

Look through the instrument after your careful outside inspection. You have owned the instrument for some time and should know what to expect when viewing through it. Be aware of any double image condition, eyestrain, or loss of definition. A prism or a lens knocked out of position (even slightly) will give you a pulling on the eyes or an actual double image. Chipped or separated optics will produce a blurriness or loss of sharpness, either overall or at some particular place in the field of view. Distortion, image inequality (as related to image size), or complete loss of an image can be caused by misplaced optics, chipped optics, or a combination of both. The point is that any change in what you are accustomed to expect from your binocular indicates damage requiring expert attention to correct.

CLEANING

Clean the exterior of your instrument as needed, but do not use copious amounts of water. Never use detergents or soaps because these increase the likelihood of moisture infiltrating the instrument. Brush the instrument with a soft, natural-bristle brush, paying careful attention to hinges, then wipe with a moistened chamois or cotton cloth.

Clean lenses with lens-cleaning solution and cloth, available at camera supply stores. A lens brush, available at camera stores, is a good investment. A soft, natural-bristle paintbrush is also effective and a good bit cheaper. It's bad to use any solvent on a lens; acetone in particular will destroy the lens coating. There is no harm in breathing on a lens to clean it if you have no lens-cleaning solution available. It is preferable to leaving stains and smudges on the lens.

Fingerprints are especially bad for lenses. Acids present in skin oils can etch the print permanently onto the glass. Remove fingerprints promptly and avoid handling lenses.

Plastic Canoes

HEAT-FORMED PLASTICS HAVE changed the face of the canoe industry within the past few years. Strong, light, inexpensive canoes and kayaks of molded ABS, ABS laminate, and polyethylene have done more to popularize whitewater sports than all the "gusto" beer commercials ever made. For still-water use, plastics are quiet and they don't heat up in the sun, two big drawbacks of aluminum.

ABS CANOES—HULL REPAIRS

ABS (acrylonitrile/butadiene/styrene) is used to make telephones, and you know how tough they are. It makes a tough yet flexible canoe or kayak when used in a single layer, and a tough, flexible, *buoyant* canoe or kayak when used in its most common form, a five-layer sandwich of two ABS layers over an ABS foam core, covered with inside and outside layers of cross-linked vinyl to protect against ultraviolet damage and provide a cosmetic outer and inner shell (ABS itself isn't very pretty.) Uniroyal's Royalex is the most familiar name for ABS laminates, with some canoe manufacturers using their own trade names for the same material, such as Sawyerlex and Oltonar.

ABS laminate canoes have two features that have endeared them to whitewater fans: they will "remember" the shape they were formed in and will pop back after a severe dent; and they are extremely resistant to puncture wounds. On the minus side, ABS doesn't stand up to abrasion very well, even when coated with tough vinyl. If you remove the gunwales for some reason, an ABS laminate hull can tear very easily, too, although we can't think of any way you would do this unless you purposely set out to ruin your canoe. At bottom, then, the repairs you'll need to make most often are removing dents and patching abrasion, particularly in the stem area.

Removing Dents. A moderately dented ABS hull will return to its original shape if left in the sun, or you can *carefully* apply a bit of heat with an electric hair dryer or light bulb to speed up the process, pushing gently on the inside of the hull and holding the area in place until it cools. Your hand is a good temperature guide: if you feel the inside warming up, you've got the outside too hot. Those high-powered hair dryers can make the vinyl coating bubble if left on too long.

Patching. If the dent is deep enough and severe enough to crack the vinyl or ABS layer, a fiberglass or Kevlar cloth patch can be applied. You've got to remove the vinyl layer and rough up the ABS layer with a *slow, very coarse* grinder to make it ready for the patch. Don't try to use a home electric drill with a disk sander attached—they rotate too fast. The ideal tool is a hand buffer that rotates at about 1000 rpm with a #24 grit disk attached. Too fine a grit at too high a speed will melt the ABS, smearing it and leaving it unfit for patching. You can't get away with hand-rasping it, either—it's too tough.

With the area to be patched roughed up, apply layers of fiberglass cloth saturated with *epoxy* resin. Polyester and vinylester resins will not stick. Finish this functional patch by sanding and touching up with epoxy-based paint or polyurethane enamel. (Note: all epoxy resins are not the same. Before attempting to patch an ABS canoe, make sure the resin you've got is compatible. Uniroyal makes a compatible epoxy resin, and there are sure to be several more on the market. Check your canoe shop.)

You can also fill cracks or small holes in ABS laminate canoes with epoxy putty or epoxy resin to which you've added shredded fiberglass cloth. For this kind of patch, you should cut some of the ABS foam core away to provide good seating for the putty. Wipe the putty smooth with a wet rag before it sets, and finish with polyurethane or acrylic-based enamel.

Fiberglass and epoxy patches of these types will be as strong or stronger than the original hull, but they will not be as flexible. Therefore, they are likely to loosen in time from the canoe's flexing. If the damage has occurred in a severely curved area, you can fill the crack with a putty made from dissolving ABS plastic in methyl-ethyl-ketone (MEK), an extremely toxic solvent which must be handled with care. (Note: this is *not* the same as the MEKP component used to harden polyester resins used with fiberglass.)

MEK is not only toxic, it is volatile and extremely violent in its action on ABS. If you drop a blob of it on the canoe, you'll have a hole! Therefore it should be handled with extreme care. Make a thick putty and apply it thinly—*very* thinly—to prevent it from eating its way into the foam core. Practice on a scrap piece if you can.

MEK is also found in the hardware store in ABS pipe cement. This jet black goo is ideal for strengthening abraded areas of an ABS canoe, but, again, you must proceed with caution. Apply it in thin layers, let it dry for several hours before applying a second layer; repeat this procedure several times. This material is not suitable for filling deep gouges or for use under ABS or fiberglass patches because it needs exposure to oxygen to set up. MEK pipe cement will not add structural strength either. Nor is it any good if the foam core is exposed. Its best application is preventive: you can mask the abraded area and apply several thin layers to build up a protective coat over the ABS.

You can apply a strong patch to ABS hulls with an industrial acrylic adhesive called Versalock. This product is not available in retail outlets for two very good reasons: it is poisonous and it is extremely expensive. If you can locate some through a canoe repair shop or industrial source, handle with extreme caution and practice on scrap pieces first.

The procedure for patching ABS hulls is simple if you have the adhesive and a piece of ABS stock (single layer, not laminate). All you need to do is soften the ABS plastic in a 400°F oven, and, wearing gloves, place it over the area to be patched and hold it until it cools. Once it has cooled, grind off the vinyl layer of the hull, apply a thin layer of adhesive and lay the patch in place. Hold it until it sets up and paint it with urethane-based paint to finish. Simple, but because of the adhesive, dangerous and costly. Nevertheless, if you're talking to a canoe repair shop and they've never used this method to repair ABS canoes, suggest it—it works!

It is possible to install a major patch (or skid plate, see below) with bolts and washers, but the results are mediocre to say the least. The flexing hull will surely loosen the patch or plate in time. If you do try this method, follow the instructions given for aluminum patching in the *Aluminum Canoes* entry, with the exception that you'll use ABS stock instead of aluminum, and bolts and nuts instead of rivets. Use plenty of silicone sealant under the patch, and place large flat washers under the bolts and nuts. You could call this a "temporary/permanent patch," one that will stand up to hard use for a season at least. The only real advantage to this patch is that it leaves the hull intact (except for the bolt holes), so that when induction welding repair systems become commonplace (see below), you won't have a messed up hull to work with. We can't recommend them, however.

Installing a Skid Plate. Since most whitewater canoes suffer from abrasion damage in two areas—the bow and stern—manufacturers try to put as much material in those areas as they can. You can add strength there, too, by putting on a skid plate. We've already described how you can build up layers of MEK pipe cement, and that's a good way to start. For more protection, or if the foam core has been exposed, you should cover the entire area with an ABS skid plate to add flexible strength.

The procedure described above for patching major damage with ABS stock and acrylic adhesive should be followed, if you can get the adhesive. There are "skid plate kits" on the market, which contain a piece of Kevlar felt cloth and a resin/adhesive, and these are much easier to use than the ABS/acrylic system simply because it is easier to form the felt cloth over the sharply curved hull at this point. You'll find, though, that this skid plate won't stand up to hard knocks, and it is therefore not recommended for use on severely damaged hulls or on hulls that will see prolonged hard use. (A kit of this kind can be applied easily and quickly to polyethylene canoes and kayaks, however, and is probably the simplest and most effective way to reinforce the bow and stern of these craft. More about repairing poly canoes below.)

Maintenance. Little or no maintenance is required for ABS canoes. You don't need to wash, wax, polish or paint them. In fact, although paints that will adhere to vinyl are available, fading due to ultraviolet light exposure makes it hard to match existing hull colors and the cost and preparation necessary for a complete repainting makes such a job prohibitively expensive. If the vinyl layer has been abraded or gouged to expose the ABS layer, sunlight will, in time, degrade the plastic. This is so slow a process, however, that it is nearly inconsequential. You can fill cracks and gouges as described above, but don't worry too much about scratches through the vinyl layer.

POLYETHYLENE CANOES—HULL REPAIRS

Polyethylene canoes and kayaks have made their appearance in the past half decade and have quickly moved to dominate the low-priced canoe market. The reasons are simple: they don't cost as much as ABS or fiberglass craft; they're nearly as strong and flexible; they're quiet and light. Coleman has led the field with various canoes made of RAM-X, its trademark for linear polyethylene.

A more expensive kind of polyethylene is used in kayaks and some canoes. Called "cross-linked" poly because of the molecular structure, this material is most often seen on kayaks made by Perception and Hydra, two well-known companies at the forefront of kayak design. Cross-linked poly can be patched with fiberglass resins and cloth as we've already described.

Linear poly is another story. To put it charitably, it's a bear to repair. Coleman has sold repair kits for its RAM-X canoes which contain pieces of poly and a two-part adhesive. The repair procedure is complicated and requires "flame-treating" (with a propane or butane torch) of the poly before applying the adhesive. In other words, it's tricky—*very* tricky, we're told—and very tough to apply a patch to a curved surface (of which there are many on a canoe). If you're contemplating patching a poly canoe with one of these kits, get help from someone who has done it.

For field repairs to poly canoes, your best bet is duct tape. If you somehow get a small, round hole in your hull, insert a stainless steel bolt, nut, and washer coated with silicone sealant.

Linear poly *can* be mended by welding polyethylene into cracks, tears, etc., with a nitrogen-welding system. These outfits are rare, expensive, and not available to the home handyman. Coleman has set up many of its dealers with nitrogen-welding outfits specifically to allow them to work on RAM-X canoes. As with all thermoplastics, heat sources pose a grave risk to poly, so don't try to use a torch to weld your boat or you might not have a boat to weld.

One suggestion that seems to hold merit is to melt polyethylene into a crack or hole with a medium-hot clothes iron. This sounds like a viable alternative because you don't heat the hull or have a flame near it. Sounds messy, though, and we've not encountered anyone who has actually used the system with repeated success. As always, practice on scrap before touching your craft.

You can bolt or rivet an ABS patch to poly canoes, using the procedure described for aluminum patches. Be sure to use plenty of silicone sealant and use stainless steel washers inside the hull on either bolts or rivets.

If we've sounded negative about most of the repair methods for linear poly, it's because we are: the stuff has proven tough to work on, and until or unless someone develops an easy-to-use adhesive that will bond well to poly, it always will be difficult to repair. There's hope on the horizon, however, in the form of induction welding.

INDUCTION WELDING

Though it sounds complicated, induction welding is simple, safe, and quick. For that reason alone, it will undoubtedly come to dominate thermoplastic repair in the near future. Developed by NASA-contracted scientists for use in pressurized and oxygen-less environments, induction welding uses a magnetic field to bond two pieces of thermoplastic so firmly that they actually fuse into one.

Although you won't be able to buy an induction-welding system for some time to come—and probably won't have enough call to use one to purchase one anyway—we'll describe the procedure. You'll undoubtedly see induction welding at canoe and boat repair shops, and you can use the following description of the process to help you understand what the repairman is doing.

To patch a thermoplastic surface, all that's needed is a piece of the same material that the hull is made of, a piece of steel screen (window screen) the same size, and an induction-welding gun. After the vinyl layer (on an ABS laminate hull), has been removed, the repairman places the screen on the hull and lays the patch over it. He then places the welding gun on the patch and, in minutes, a firm weld is achieved.

How? Simple. The gun, a powerful electromagnet, produces an extremely strong, yet limited in area, alternating magnetic field that is turned on and off so rapidly that it makes the steel screen vibrate intensely enough to become red hot. The hot screen melts the thermoplastic, which flows through the screen openings and fuses. The screen stays in the patch and serves as reinforcement, making the patch stronger than the original hull!

The advantages of this system are apparent. No heat is applied to the outside of the hull or patch, there are no messy solvents to mix, no waiting for set-up. Canoe repairmen and manufacturers are working out the bugs at this writing, including how to apply a large, curved patch with one shot.

With the perfection of induction welding, thermoplastic canoes and kayaks will undoubtedly become even more common, and new plastics will surely be developed to take advantage of this technology.

REPAIRS TO UPPER STRUCTURES

If all the caveats about hull repair on thermoplastic craft have distressed you, you'll be glad to know that upper structure repairs on thermoplastic canoes are easier than on aluminum canoes. Most makers of flexible ABS and poly canoes use lightly tempered aluminum for gunwales, reinforcing members, deck plates, etc., and these can be bent into shape easily.

Seat frames and thwarts, however, are tempered hard and should be replaced rather than rebent. Most companies have made the bolts or rivets holding the thwarts in place extremely accessible, so replacement is easy.

Replacing an entire gunwale isn't recommended unless the existing gunwale is beyond hope. You can splice U-channel or L-channel aluminum stock over and against the gunwales easily (The procedure is described in the Aluminum Canoes entry.) Remember that once you've taken a gunwale off a thermoplastic canoe, the hull is without support and can very easily be torn from the exposed edge. Straightening a bent gunwale allows the deformed hull to return to its original shape, so a few minutes spent whacking a gunwale with a piece of two-by-four can turn a drastic-looking injury into no more than a memory.

Raingear

KEEPING DRY IN the woods is one of the most difficult things campers face, next to keeping warm. A variety of outerwear designed solely to repel water is on the market in a number of fabrics and coatings. Most are effective, durable, and easy to care for. Outerwear styles include ponchos, anoraks, cagoules, parkas, rainpants, and chaps. Fabrics include nylon with several kinds of coatings, vinyl, cotton with coatings, nylon/PTFE laminates, polyester/cotton blends with coatings, and Dacron/polyurethane laminate.

The goal of all raingear is to keep moisture from entering while allowing sweat to evaporate and pass through. This seeming contradiction has caused the great variety in fabrics and designs, with further developments sure to come.

Of the various kinds of tops, ponchos are cheapest and, to some outdoorspeople, superior. Simple in design, a poncho is merely a square of material with a hole in the center covered by a hood. Some are slightly elongated in shape to accommodate arms or packs. Their beauty is that they can do double duty as emergency shelter (with a few grommets added), equipment covers, or ground cloths. Indeed, ponchos are often the only raingear found in a backpacker's pack. On the negative side, ponchos are clumsy, billowy drapes which will dump water onto your legs or boots in a wind. For complete protection, ponchos need to be worn with rainpants.

Coated fabrics work well in the poncho style, since the drape fit allows ample air to circulate beneath the garment, and some ponchos are made of ultra-cheap (and nonbreathing) vinyl.

Anoraks are pullovers with sleeves and hoods, with a short zipper to provide an opening at the neck. They're form-fitting and cut rather short, which maximizes mobility but mandates rainpants for complete protection. Anoraks are made in a variety of fabrics including coated nylon, coated cotton/polyester, and nylon/PTFE laminates.

The biggest problem with anoraks is their proclivity to leak at the front opening. The half-zipper configuration invites water to run down the gusset and collect at the bottom, where it seeps through unsealed seams.

Cagoules might be described as ponchos with pretensions to high fashion. Basically large bags with an opening for your head, cagoules are closed at the bottom with a drawstring closure, which eliminates the billowing problem but adds a condensation problem since most cagoules are made of coated, nonbreathing fabrics.

Parkas are included here because they're the only outerwear most people have, rain or shine. With full-front opening, often with two-way zippers, parkas provide ventilation alternatives not available to anorak, poncho, or cagoule wearers. Parkas come in a variety of fabrics and weights.

Rainpants are a necessary addition to the raingear equipment of a serious backpacker or boater, since the various tops cover only the upper body and, often, merely channel rainwater to the legs and feet. Rainpants usually don't have enough ventilation, although some models have zippered or Velcro-fastened openings at the lower legs, waist, or, more rarely, at the groin. Overalls, which extend up to the chest, and chaps, which have no lower trunk covering, are also available in a variety of fabrics.

Of the fabrics commonly used in raingear, vinyl is cheapest and PTFE laminates (Goretex and Klimate are the two most popular brand names) are the most expensive, with the other fabrics somewhere in between. The price of the garment only loosely reflects the price of the fabric, of course, since fit, finish, type of seams, and extras like pockets and Velcro influence the retail price. In general, though, vinyl ponchos are cheapest; Goretex and similar anoraks and ponchos, the most expensive.

As befits an inexpensive fabric, vinyl is short-lived. It is completely waterproof both ways—it doesn't breathe at all. Because it is vulnerable to cracking in cold weather and melting from high temperatures, it must be handled with care and kept away from direct sources of heat. Vinyl is mildew proof and easily cleaned by hand washing in warm, soapy water. No solvents should be used on vinyl, and abrasive cleansers of all kinds will hasten its demise. Keep insect sprays, gasoline, and stove fuel away.

Vinyl ponchos should be considered one-season gear. You may get a couple of years use out of them, though, if you take care not to leave them folded or rolled any more than absolutely necessary. Store by hanging in a dark, cool place.

You can patch vinyl with any sort of tape that will stick. Electrician's plastic tape is ideal. Tiny pinholes can be sealed with fingernail polish, or household glue.

A useful addition to a vinyl poncho is a series of grommets to make the garment do double-duty as a shelter or tent fly. To install grommets, use a grommet kit available at hardware stores and marine supply stores. Before installing the grommet, glue patches to both sides of the poncho to provide adequate support for the grommet. A square piece of vinyl at least one inch larger than the grommet on each side is ideal.

Vinyl gear should not be confused with vinyl-*coated* gear, which is how cotton and nylon barbics coated with polyvinyl chloride (PVC) plastic is sometimes described. PVC-coated cotton is extremely rugged and extremely heavy. It is commonly used on full rainsuits worn by seagoing folk.

PVC-coated fabric is ultraviolet resistant, tear resistant, abrasion resistant, crack resistant, chemical and oil resistant, and resistant to cracking at low temperatures. It can be washed in warm water with mild detergents, but not dry-cleaned. Stains seldom set, and a sponging with alcohol will remove those that threaten to. PVC-coated cotton and nylon fabric can be sewn by hand or machine, although the most common way to patch it is to tape it. You can patch it with a piece of vinyl glued to the surface, too.

PVC-coated garments should be allowed to dry thoroughly before being stored, and should not be left wet in tightly closed containers, since cotton is vulnerable to mildew. Antifungal sprays available at marine houses are effective.

Condensation is a problem with PVC-coated cloth since it is absolutely waterproof. Most PVC garments are loose fitting, though, or have ventilation at strategic points. You can add ventilation by installing eyelets of the sort commonly found in fabric stores; be cautious about where you put them however, as you could be creating a leak. The best spots are under the arms and along the sides of the garment.

Urethane-coated nylon is by far the most common outdoor fabric, turning up in garments, backpacks, tents, bags, etc. There's a reason for this: it works. Urethane-coated nylon is available in various coating weights, and it's worthwhile to find out how much coating is on the fabric before buying. Any weight above ½ ounce is okay, but the thicker coatings may peel off. Peeling often takes place first at the seams, just where leakage is a problem anyway. If a seam shows evidence of peeling, wash the garment in warm water with mild detergent, wipe the area down with denatured alcohol, and apply a coating of seam sealant or a product called Recoat. Urethane coating weakens nylon fabric somewhat, and this is another negative feature. On the plus side, it's breathable, reasonably inexpensive and waterproof. Patching large tears is easy (see the *Nylon* and *Down and Synthetic-Fill Clothing* entries) and, with Recoat and seam sealers, doesn't affect the watertight capability of the fabric.

Neoprene and acrylonitrile are two common "synthetic rubbers" often used to coat cotton or nylon fabric. Neoprene is most often found in skin divers' wetsuits, which should give you some idea of its durability. Neoprene resists abrasion, solvents, ultraviolet rays, punctures, and cracking at low temperatures. It is very heavy, however, and for that reason is rarely found in outdoor gear other than wetsuits. Garments coated with neoprene can be washed in lukewarm water with mild detergent or soap. It should be hand-washed and allowed to dry thoroughly before storage.

Acrylonitrile is a heavy-duty coating with unusual durability at low weight. It is usually applied to heavy twills, canvas, or oxford-weave nylon fabrics. Pound for pound it is probably the best all-around waterproof coating, since it is resistant to most chemical, temperature, and ultraviolet hazards. Its expense makes it rare on any but the most expensive outdoor gear, though. Hand washing in warm water with soap is recommended for acrylonitrile-coated fabrics. This coating can be stored wet without risk, a plus in changeable weather.

Leaks in garments made of neoprene or acrylonitrile can be patched with adhesive available at scuba diving shops. Large patches can be sewn by hand or machine.

A cotton/polyester fabric known as Storm Shed is probably the best all-around raingear fabric, from the standpoint of price, durability, breathability, and ease of maintenance. It has a water-repellent chemical applied to the inside, and is remarkably breathable. The tight weave makes Storm Shed as waterproof and nearly as breathable as its chief competition, Goretex. Storm Shed garments may be washed by hand or machine or dry-cleaned without loosing their water resistance. Garments of Storm Shed should be dried thoroughly before being stored, as all cottons should, and may be sewn by hand or machine for patching. Small iron-on patches can also be applied.

The Goretex revolution hit outerwear several years back, and it is still going on, with competitors like Klimate improving the formula of maximum waterproofing and breathability at minimum weight. For more information on PTFE laminates, see the *Goretex* entry.

The seams are the crucial parts of all outerwear designed for wet-weather use. Most manufacturers have thought out location and sealing combinations that minimize infiltration, but you still need to check the sealing and replenish the liquid sealant from time to time. Even taped seams can deteriorate, as they are sometimes coated with sealant. Coarser fabrics like Storm Shed are at a disadvantage here, as the liquid sealant resists penetration. About all you can do is keep slapping it on.

Reels

BAIT CASTING, FLY, and spinning reels suffer most from dirt and sand, which gets into gears, bearings, and bushings and wears them down. Cleaning and lubricating reels is an essential maintenance chore.

Reels of all types can be cleaned with warm, soapy water or gun solvent. They should always be cleaned at the end of the fishing season or before storing them for any length of time.

If you've dropped your reel into mud or sand, dismantle it as soon as you can, degrease everything with solvent (use a spray solvent to reach nooks and crannies), and relubricate, using whatever lubricant the manufacturer recommends. Most will recommend silicone-based reel grease.

Saltwater gear should be completely dismantled and washed with fresh water and detergent, or solvent, and relubricated after *every* fishing trip. Salt is very corrosive and even the best reels need to be flushed. If impossible to clean the reel, at least run the line through fresh water before transporting.

When taking a reel apart, pay attention to the screws. Be sure to use the right size screwdriver, and don't force the threads. Although screws on fishing reels don't take as much of a beating as gun screws, they still need proper handling. Use Lock-tite.

Always cover your reel when transporting it. If nothing else is handy, a large zip-lock bag can help. Since rods are the most awkward tackle, remove reels from rods before transporting. More reel seats and handles are broken from blows to reels than anything else. Pack reels with silica gel packets to prevent condensation from forming inside.

BAIT CASTING REELS

Bait casting reels, whether simple storage reels or more sophisticated geared "multiplying" reels, should be cleaned and lubricated at least once a year, more if abused. Since there are so many different models of this type, with individual gear and handle configurations, you'll have to consult an expert or proceed on logic alone. Make sure you get all the old lubricant out of the gears and bearings, and allow the reel to dry completely before regreasing. Remove the handle and get sand out of the threads. Work the line-winding gears while soaking them in solvent to remove grit and old grease. Remove any metal burrs, rust spots, or grooves from the line guide with 00 or finer steel wool and solvent.

Bait casting reels have small-diameter spools, designed to hold as much line as possible. Keep the line spool as full as possible, both to give you a reserve and to increase your cranking leverage. (It's much easier to crank a full spool because each turn of the handle yields or retrieves more line than when the spool is nearly empty.) Either use a backing line or cut a piece of cork rod handle to fit on the spool shaft.

FLY REELS

Manual fly reels are similar to bait casting reels—simple, in other words. Periodic dismantling and cleaning are all that you really need, as there are few moving parts that you can replace.

Automatic fly reels with spring-loaded retrieve get out of adjustment quite easily. There's little to do but keep adjusting the tension screws until you get it where you like it. Be careful when dismantling a spring-loaded reel for cleaning, as the spring can pop out with surprising force.

SPINNING REELS

Spinning reels are quite complicated. Both the open-face and closed-face models have as many as 100 moving parts. Because they're so complex, they need more frequent cleaning and lubrication than other types of reels.

To clean and lubricate an open-faced reel, remove the handle and the screws attaching the side plate, then remove the gears and clean with solvent. Lubricate the gear surfaces with silicone-based reel grease and apply oil to the center shaft where it comes out in front of the reel body.

If your reel has a rear-mounted drag, it is not necessary to disassemble and lubricate it. If it is a front-mounted drag, remove the drag retention knob, spring, and drag washers. Clean off all the existing lubrication and lubricate them. It is not necessary to dab a large amount of grease on these washers. A small amount will do, and rotating them between your fingers will apply a sufficient amount of lubrication.

Closed-face spinning reels are similar in construction. To clean and lubricate them, first remove the front cover, spool, and rear cover. Clean the reel covers with a mild detergent solution or solvent. Use a toothbrush or paintbrush. Scrub and rinse all the visible gunk from the inside of your reel.

Dry with a cloth or small can of compressed air, then apply a light coating of silicone-based reel grease to the gears, turning the handle as you do.

Oil the center shaft where it comes out in front of the reel body and the crank handle where it contacts the bushing or bearing.

Wipe all lubrication from the front of the reel where the spool has been removed, the drag washers, and the bottom of the spool where the drag washer comes in contact with it. Put a small amount of grease between your thumb and index finger and rotate and lubricate the drag washers.

Dealing with Fouled Line. One of the most vexing problems with spinning reels is having a loop of line come off the spool, get behind it, and wrap around the shaft. If this happens often, you probably have overfilled the spool and/or not kept enough tension on the line when you loaded the spool. New line sometimes tends to loop until it "sets" on the spool. See the section on coils, twists, and balloons in the *Fishing Line* entry for tips on loading and removing curl.

To remove fouled line from the shaft of an open-face spinning reel, remove the drag assembly, which consists of a knob, a bent washer and several flat washers, and a spring, then remove the spool. The fouled line should be easy to untwist from the shaft, but you'll have to strip the spool and rewind the line to get it back on the spool.

For closed-face reels, the procedure is similar. First, with a screwdriver or coin loosen the screw that holds the front cover and remove the cover by turning it counterclockwise, at the same time pulling it forward. Hold the reel so the handle will not turn and remove the "spinner" head by turning it counterclockwise. If it's too tight, rap it with the screwdriver handle, but do not bend it.

Once this head is removed, you'll be able to see where the line begins to wrap around the main shaft. Unwind it and pull it off, then either cut it off (if kinked or abraded) or replace it (if not damaged). To rewind it, pull about twelve inches of line off the spool and replace the spinner head carefully so the threads don't cross. Run the line through the front cover and reattach the front cover, making sure the drain hole is toward the bottom. Tighten the cover lock screw.

Setting the Drag. In addition to not overfilling spools, you can prevent line problems by making sure the drag is correctly set. Spinning reels either have front or rear drag adjustments, and their adjustment is similar. Consult your owner's manual for specifics. To adjust the drag on any kind of reel, attach your reel to the rod. Run the line through the guides and tie it to something sturdy. Set the drag adjustment very lightly.

Gradually lift the rod until it bends, tightening the drag as you increase the tension on the line. Now jerk the rod as if setting the hook on a fish. The drag should slip lightly at this point. If it does not, gradually loosen the drag until it does.

To be on the super-safe side, set your drag at no more than 30 percent of your line's breaking test. If, for example, you are using 12-pound line, the drag pressure should be set at approximately 4 pounds.

Regardless of fishing conditions or size of line, however, it's better to have a drag too loose than too tight. You can always tighten it. As more line goes out, the friction in the water against the line actually increases the drag on the spool.

Rope

ROPE IS PERHAPS the most widely used and widely misused outdoor gear. The misuse of rope isn't cheap and your life can depend on it. A little care will keep ropes in service for years.

Knowing the ropes means knowing how ropes are made, how to take care of them, and how to use them. Certain fibers are more durable than others. Hemp rope can appear perfectly strong and actually be rotten clear through. Nylon is super strong, but stretches so much that it may not be suitable for all jobs. Coarse rope is hard to work with, and heavy rope is hard to tie. Before you buy rope, match the rope to the job by comparing strength, elongation, resistance to abrasion, weight, resistance to weather, and cost.

NATURAL FIBER ROPE

Natural vegetable fibers were the major material used for making rope until after World War II. Natural ropes are generally coarser, heavier, and harder to handle than nylon or polyester ropes, and will decay in situations where nylon or other synthetics do not. In a British test, a piece of hemp and a piece of nylon were buried side by side. After nine weeks, the hemp had disintegrated completely while the nylon was unaffected.

Some natural fibers are more rot resistant than others especially if waterproofed. Hemp rope can be tarred to keep out the moisture, though this reduces strength somewhat.

Other natural fibers include abaca (Manila), sisal or henequen, jute, flax, and cotton. Abaca, like hemp, is a hard fiber and is twisted into the strongest of all the natural fiber ropes. The strongest abaca rope has about half the tesile strength of nylon.

Sisal is more resistant to moisture. Jute, cotton, and flax, the most commonly used soft fibers, are usually woven into twine and small cords, and sometimes blended with hemp or abaca to make inexpensive combination rope.

SYNTHETIC FIBERS

Synthetic rope is something of a miracle. Twice as strong as the strongest natural fiber, it lasts four or five times longer. Synthetic rope is made from continuous filaments of long molecular-chain polymers which will not harbor destructive bacteria as natural fibers do. These filaments are stronger than the short molecular structure of natural fiber rope. The most common synthetic ropes are made of nylon, polyester, polypropylene, and polyethylene.

Nylon is the standard against which synthetic ropes are judged. Everything we've said about synthetic fibers is true about nylon: it is strong, durable, rot resistant. It is also stretchy and will elongate as much as much as 8 percent of its length and then return to its original size when released. Stretching does not reduce its strength, unless sustained and repeated many times.

Nylon can also be soaked thoroughly—even stored wet—and it will regain full strength when dry. This is another advantage over vegetable fiber rope which does not always recover full strength and is often swollen, distorted, and stiff after drying. Wet nylon rope retains 85 to 90 percent of its strength while vegetable fiber retains only 70 to 75 percent.

Nylon will, however, deteriorate when exposed to sunlight for long periods, especially when the sunlight comes through a glass window.

Some of the trade names for polyester are Dacron, Fortrel, Kodel, and Terylene. Rope made of polyester is less likely to deteriorate in the sun, it resists abrasion, and is almost as strong as nylon. Polyester can replace nylon in applications where nylon's greater elasticity is a drawback. Like nylon it resists decay from water or bacteria; in fact, it is practically impervious to water and does not lose strength at all when wet.

Polypropylene is the lightest synthetic, very smooth to handle, and 75 percent as strong as nylon. It is usually less expensive than polyester or nylon.

On the negative side, polypropylene rope, like nylon, breaks down with exposure to the sun. Twine made from this synthetic is still useful outdoors, however, if it is used in the shade. It has the added benefit of being rotproof.

Polyethylene is similar to polypropylene but with more stretch and 5 percent less strength. Neither polyethylene nor polypropylene rope are recommended for heavy loads because they tend to "creep" under heavy weight and will break rather than absorbing shock.

CONSTRUCTION OF ROPE

How a rope is made is as important as what it's made of. The simplest method of constructing rope is the three-strand plain lay. Plant fibers or synthetic chemical filaments are twisted into yarns, the first twist usually being to the left. If the process was stopped at this point, the result would be twine, similar to bailer's twine.

To make a rope, however, the yarn must be twisted into strands, this time to the right to counteract the previous left-hand twist.

Next, three strands are twisted together in the opposite direction; the result is two twists to the left and only one to the right. The rope will tend to unravel unless it is given an extra twist at the end of the last right-hand twist to counteract it. The degree of the twist is the "amount of lay."

Lay affects rope strength. If a rope has a soft lay (a shallow angle to the final twist), it will be stronger but more susceptible to abrasion; if the lay is tight, the rope will be less strong.

Nylon and msot vegetable fiber ropes are plain laid, but many synthetic ropes are braided. The most popular braiding is double-braiding which uses an outer covering of tightly braided fibers to enclose a closely braided inner core. Double-braided rope is 20 to 30 percent stronger and less elastic than plain-laid rope; it does not kink and is smooth and easy to handle, but difficult to splice. Polyester ropes are often braided.

FINDING A SAFE WORK LOAD

The chart shown here gives the tensile strengths and working loads of common types of rope. Since new ropes were tested, the figures in the chart represent the highest strength possible.

Tensile strength is the maximum weight the rope can bear; the working-load limits indicate the most weight a rope in good condition can carry. The weight limits in the chart are for handling loads slowly and smoothly;

TENSILE STRENGTH AND WORKING LOADS OF VARIOUS ROPES

	MANILA		NYLON		POLYESTER		POLYPROPYLENE	
	New Rope Tensile Strength (lbs.)	Working Load (lbs)	New Rope Tensile Strength (lbs)	Working Load (lbs)	New Rope Tensile Strength (lbs)	Working Load (lbs)	New Rope Tensile Strength (lbs)	Working Load (lbs)
	406	41	1490	124	1490	149	1130	113
	1220	122	3340	278	3340	334	2440	244
	2380	264	5750	525	5750	640	3780	420
	4860	695	12800	1420	11,300	1610	7650	1090
	8100	1160	22600	2520	19,800	2820	12,600	1800

Source: Cordage Institute, May 1979

[1]Working loads are for rope in good condition with appropriate splices, in noncritical applications, and under normal service conditions. Loads must be handled slowly and smoothly to minimize dynamic effects. Working-load values do not apply where there is a rapidly increased force due to dynamic loading (i.e., picking up a tow on a slack line or using a rope to stop a falling object).

sudden jerking increases the dynamic load on a line equal to two or three times the actual weight.

Always allow a large working margin. For a 200-pound work load, it would be best to buy ½-inch manila or ⅜-inch polyester. Although 200 pounds is under the limit for ⅜-inch nylon and polypropylene, ½-inch rope would be safer.

CARE OF ROPES

To keep a rope functioning at the correct working loads, you must maintain it. Store it in a dry, well-ventilated place to avoid the weakening effects of humidity, especially if using vegetable fiber ropes. Heat, moisture, and direct sunlight will weaken rope, especially nylon. Never store rope wet or cover rope so that moisture is trapped inside. If a rope becomes wet, allow it to dry away from direct sunlight.

Kinks will weaken a rope. The best way to prevent them is to uncoil a new rope by pulling from the opening in the center of the coil, called the eye. Turn the coil over so that the inside end is pointing down, reach into the eye, then pull the end through the top. The rope should uncoil counterclockwise, without kinking.

To coil a rope, lay a loop on the ground, then lay additional loops of the same size and shape on top of the first loop, watching for kinks in the line and smoothing them out as they occur.

Once the line is coiled, turn it over so that it is in the correct position for uncoiling. Rope with a right-hand lay should always be coiled in a clockwise direction; left-hand rope, in a counterclockwise direction.

Most rope, especially that made of natural fiber, shrinks when wet. If it is taut during dry weather or exposure to the sun, it will be strained when it becomes wet. Because of this, the rope should not be tied taut or it should be slacked off during wet periods.

A rope under tension should never be stepped on or dragged along the ground or over sharp rocks. Nylon, though it is impervious to mildew, will pick up dirt and organic debris which *will* harbor fungal growths. Often, the waste products these microbes produce while digesting the matter will deteriorate the rope.

Never use a frozen rope—thaw it beforehand. Never store a rope by hanging it over a nail.

A worn rope is perhaps the most dangerous of all. Natural fibers may deteriorate so slowly that you'll not notice the loss of strength until it's too late. One telltale sign is the presence of puffs of fiber along the rope. If you see *one* such area, discard the entire rope because there is without doubt extensive internal damage and wear which is not yet apparent.

If your rope has been subjected to unusual strain—holding a heavy weight aloft for a long time or breaking a climber's fall, for instance—go over every inch of it before using it in such situations again. Any time you subject a rope to forces at or near its breaking point, you cause wear and strain inside the rope.

Nylon ropes should be kept clean. You can wash them in mild detergent, but be sure to rinse them thoroughly, as organic matter left in the rope invites microbial growth.

Keep all volatile chemicals away from ropes of any kind. Gasoline,

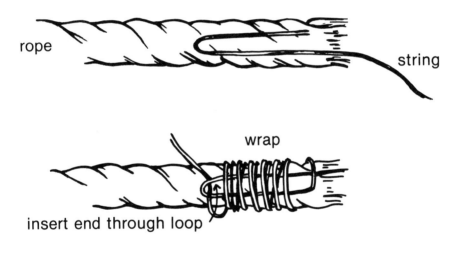

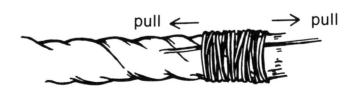

Rope ends that have been whipped won't unravel. Remember to tuck the end of the whipping string through the loop still protruding from the coils before you pull.

solvents, paints, thinners, glues, etc., will weaken natural fibers and destroy synthetics.

Know your knots. Part of keeping rope and string in service is tying it so that the rope is uniformly stressed and not kinked. And any cleat, eye, pulley, hook or other piece of tackle through which the rope will pass should be inspected for rust, rough edges, and chemical contamination.

Whipping Rope Ends. To keep ropes from unraveling, "whip" the ends.

To whip a plain-laid vegetable fiber rope you'll need a piece of fiber string about six inches long to make a 1½-inch whip at the end of the rope. First, make a loop with the string about two inches long, and place it against the rope so that the open end is toward the end of the rope, the closed loop is toward the center of the rope, and the shorter of the two strands is even with the end of the rope. Take the longer end of the string and begin wrapping the rope and both strands of the string, laying even, tight coils back toward the center of the rope. When you've used up all the free string in the longer end, insert the end of it through the part of the loop still protruding from the coils.

Now pull the other end of the string, pulling the loop underneath the coils until it is tight. Snip off the free ends and dip the whipped end in enamel, lacquer, or polyurethane varnish. This coating will weaken the rope somewhat, but there will be little stress on this part of the rope anyway, and the waterproofing and stiffening such a coating provides is valuable, especially when you need to thread the rope through tight areas.

Braided ropes can be satisfactorily whipped with tape. Either electrician's tape or fiber tape will do, but duct tape tends to pull off, leaving a messy, gooey end to contend with.

You can keep nylon rope from unraveling by passing the end through a flame until it flows, then carefully molding the softened material into a stiff knob.

Rubber Boots

"RUBBER" BOOTS MAY in fact be genuine rubber, but more likely a clever synthetic substitute. As with all synthetics, find out just what you've got before you start applying adhesive or other materials.

The rubber footware most often used in the outdoors are waders and "pacs" (rubber-bottomed leather boots which have become very popular in recent years for general foul-weather use).

Waders may be either rubber (or a synthetic analogue), rubber-coated canvas, or canvas with a rubber liner inside. (Chest waders are often made this way.) Care of the rubber parts of these outfits is simple.

Rubber, in fact, needs little care and no maintenance to give long service. About the only things that will destroy it are heat and solvents designed to melt it. Store rubber items far from those two and you're halfway home.

Leather-and-rubber pacs require little care beyond treatment of the leather parts (see *Leather Boots and Shoes* entry). You should keep any leather dressing, oils, waterproofers, etc., away from the rubber.

Waders are another matter. Because of their length, waders are inherently hard to store well. If you hand them up by the uppers, the weight will stretch the rubber and weaken it; if you stash them in a closet, they'll flop over, weakening the rubber where it creases. Hanging waders by their straps is nearly as bad, as the straps will stretch and weaken.

The solution is to hang waders upside down with both the heels and toes supported. You'll probably have to make a rack yourself, as there doesn't seem to be any on the market. Use wood, and finish the edges well so that they don't dig into the rubber. Avoid metal for the same reason.

One of the most vexing problems with waders is keeping them up. They always sag. Try cutting a couple of rubber bands from old bicycle inner tubes and wrapping them around your pants legs at the ankles. The friction between the two surfaces will keep the waders up—we hope.

FINDING AND FIXING LEAKS

Large tears and holes are nearly impossible to fix well enough to be watertight. Small holes, though, can be patched—providing, of course, that you can find them. Nothing is as frustrating as patching the wrong hole—or a "non-hole"—and finding out you're still getting the icy foot treatment from another pinhole.

Find that leak by filling the boot with water and hanging it foot down, outside. Eventually, the water will find its way through the hole, leaving you a nice big stain or puddle to locate it. You can also trap some air in the boot and put it into a bathtub full of water. Look for bubbles.

Mark the leak well, and let the boots dry completely.

Use an automobile or bicycle tube patching kit to patch the boot. Don't use the metal rasp usually supplied with the kit to roughen the area to be patched, however; it is much too abrasive for the coating of the boot. Instead, rough up the damaged area slightly with sandpaper.

Patching kits have their own directions, so we won't go into how to use them here. Remember, though, that you won't have the benefit of air pressure pushing against the patch to help keep it firmly in place, so be sure to rub it well to set it.

There are also patching kits available from the makers of air rafts, inflatable boats, and waterbeds. Again, make sure you know what you're patching—the wrong adhesive can ruin your boots. For real rubber and most synthetics, Shoe Goo, designed for repairing running shoes, is recommended.

If your chest waders have canvas on the outside, patch with a piece of canvas stock secured with a rubberized canvas patch secured with canvas cement (see *Canvas* entry).

Sleeping Bags

PROBABLY NO ITEM of outdoor gear is as important as a sleeping bag to the backpacker and tent camper. Sleeping bags, like all outdoor gear, have become incredibly complicated in recent years, as the manufacturers seek the ideal compromise between warmth, weight, durability, versatility, and cost. An adequate compromise is one that suits you, and that of course depends upon your intended use.

Sleeping bags *per se* have given way to "bag systems," where a number of bags, liners, and outer shells are offered for purchase together or separately. These systems are a distinct improvement on the "three-season bag" which was touted as warm enough for spring and fall but cool enough for summer. Bag systems are truly four-season systems.

CONSTRUCTION OF BAGS

There has been a lot of talk (and writing) about various construction methods employed in sleeping bags, and less about materials, although the down/synthetic-fill battle still rages (see *Down and Synthetic-Fill Clothing* entry). Most bags are made of closely woven nylon, usually taffeta, on the inside for softness, and ripstop on the outside for strength. For care and maintenance of nylon fabric, see the *Nylon* entry.

Although the kind of outside material and fill is pretty much agreed upon, there is still a lot of discussion and misinformation about construction methods—chiefly, how and why the fill should be controlled inside the bag. Jack Stephenson, maker of Warmlite bag systems, offers the following overview of the various construction techniques.

Baffles. There has been a baffling amount of misinformation spread around concerning baffle design in down sleeping bags. All down baffles are constructed with soft, nonconductive fabric which the down clings to. The two functions of a baffle are to constrain the inner and outer covers from moving apart more than the down can expand and to prevent lateral shift of the down. If the baffles allow more volume between the covers than the volume of down fill, then the down can easily fall off to the lower areas (along sides), leaving a thin, cold top.

Down is an expandable insulator, but like a spring, it will only expand to a certain volume. If the covers of a sleeping bag were perfectly rigid, and thus could not spread apart more than the down could expand, then the down could not shift in any direction. But, sleeping bags are made of soft fabric, which can easily spread apart. With no baffles (or with oversize baffles which do not limit fabric spread), the down will simply fall to the lowest areas, spreading fabric apart to make room, leaving the top thin and cold. If baffles are sewn in such a way that the fabric can't spread more than the fill thickness, then there will be no room for the down to fall into, so it must stay in place.

Presently, there are three baffle systems which meet this requirement: quilt, V baffles, and vertical baffles. Quilt construction leaves lines of no insulation, and thus is only used on very crude, cheap bags, or with two quilt layers with sewn-through lines offset. The double quilt requires two extra fabric layers and thus is excessively heavy.

A simplification of the double quilt is the V baffle system. This is often referred to as overlap tube construction. Each section or "tube" of down formed by baffles has a thick center and thin edges. The thin edges would be cold (like quilt construction), but it overlaps the thick section of an adjacent tube, thus curing the *mythical* problem. Actually, the down is just a uniformly thick layer, and putting a baffle through it on an angle does not change the thickness.

It is possible that the small angle a V baffle makes with the cover could keep down out of the corner, thus leaving a void. It is more likely that down will be pushed into the corner, will stick there, then be overcompressed when the bag is stretched out, thus decreasing loft. The main disadvantage of V baffle is excessive fabric weight.

A vertical baffle does the required job most directly, with minimum fabric weight, and without acute angles between baffle and cover, thus avoiding overcompression of down caught in the corner or voids caused by down kept out of the corner.

Obviously, the space between baffles can expand. Thus, the maximum space will be greater than the rectangular space indicated by flat surfaces. The ratio of fully expanded volume to flat surface volume depends on the ratio of designed baffle depth to baffle spacing. To achieve a given average thickness, with no down shift, the baffles must hold covers slightly closer together where sewn, and down fill must be adequate to expand covers to the fully expanded condition. Slant baffle bags are notorious for large down shifts, due to expansion ratio of 2.15 for the typical 6-inch spacing and 4-inch thickness. A vertical box baffle could be spaced 12.8 inches apart with down shift no worse than the slant baffle with 6 inches spacing!

You must wonder then why so many manufacturers use slant baffles. The reasons are varied, but the most common is simple "so and so does it, and has so much advertising for it, that we simply must do the same."

It appears that the real reason slant baffles got started was overselling of the "overlapping tube" idea of V baffles. When manufacturers wanted to make a cheaper, lighter bag, they simply eliminated one-half of the V, so they could still show "overlapping tubes," totally ignoring the fact that they lost the required cover restraint when they removed half the baffling.

A major reason for continuing with slant baffles, despite all the complaints about down shift, is ease of selling underfilled bags in the typical hanging rack. When hung from the foot, vertically, the underfill is not so obvious with slant baffles as with vertical baffles. You can easily see light through the unfilled areas of an underfilled vertical baffle bag, while the overlapping sections of slant or V baffles make the underfill less obvious, although all would have similar heat loss.

To detect such underfilled bags, hold the bag horizontally by one side and *gently* shake it; then lay it flat on the floor and observe down shift by loft difference between sides. (Violent shaking can pack the down, compressing it, and thus mislead you. In use you will not shake the bag violently, but you will gently shake it.)

Slant baffles, being grossly underfilled by design, have very large down shift. Even considerably underfilled vertical or V baffle bags will have less shift than slant baffle bags, and probably will be quite useful as long as you carefully distribute the down evenly before each use, and avoid active tossing and turning.

There is one exception. North Face calls its bags slant baffle, when in fact, they approximate vertical baffles. These bags have undersize baffles, only slightly offset, filled to almost full expansion, resulting in vertical baffles with twisted ends.

Various materials are used for baffles, for various reasons. Porous, non-downproof fabrics are generally preferred, since some of the down can stick to the baffle. This is especially important in underfilled bags, and you'll notice an emphasis on net, or loose-knit, baffling in bags that have had problems with down shift. We have heard of net baffles tearing loose, but that was generally due to mistreatment.

It is possible to have down restricted too much. When you pack a bag you must compress the down, and in so doing you are likely to shift the down. When the bag is unrolled, light shaking and patting will normally distribute the down properly if the tubes are not too small, or restricted by down stuck to baffles (as often is the case with close V baffles).

By now you may be wondering why everyone uses cross baffles instead of lengthwise baffles, since there would be less tendency for shift with lengthwise baffles. The problems with lengthwise tubes is a much greater tendency to shift while packing, difficulty in redistributing over a longer tube, difficulty in thinning uniformly in warm weather, and problems with layout and marking on tapered bags. With properly baffled and filled bags there is no problem with down shift with cross tubes, and the makers of improperly baffled and filled bags obviously don't know enough, or care enough, to make lengthwise baffled bags. There is also a bad image problem: some very poor down bags were made in the past with lengthwise baffles, so considerable advertising effort was put into convincing people to identify quality with cross tubes, junk with lengthwise tubes.

Seams and Zippers. Other things to look at in a bag are zippers and seams. Avoid the the tuck seam method of securing baffles to shells (see the description of this seam in the *Nylon* entry. Metal zippers prove problematic in cold weather and may overheat when your bag is dried in a clothes dryer.

Pads, Liners, and Coatings. Since down and synthetic fill won't insulate when compressed, manufacturers have long grappled with the problem of how to keep your bottom warm. A foam pad helps, an air mattress less so. Keeping the pad under you all night is a problem however. One manufacturer offers a detachable foam pad which can be snapped to the bag. Stephenson's system includes a provision to insert a sleeping mat, either foam, air-filled, or down-and-air.

If you're not fortunate enough to have one of these systems, you can sew Velcro strips to your bag and glue corresponding strips to a foam pad, thus creating your own system. Velcro strips can also be sewn to parkas and bags to allow you to use the parka as an added outside insulation layer, which eliminates the bulk and space problem associated with wearing outerwear inside the bag.

Another way to make your one-season bag into a versatile system is to use liners. These can be made as fancy or as simple as you desire, and can be anything from a folded-and-sewn flannel sheet with a drawstring to a vapor barrier liner, now all the rage. Wool, though heavy, is an excellent material for a bag liner. It keeps you warm even if you sweat, is sturdy and easily cleaned, and is inexpensive. Its weight is its only drawback. Liners can be designed with drawstrings to keep them on you or with Velcro fasteners to keep them secured to the bag.

A lot of attention has been given to condensation and evaporation lately, due mainly to the development of fabrics and coatings that make it possible for the first time to have truly waterproof cloth that breathes. Studies on heat loss have shown that evaporative heat loss during the night may be the greatest single factor in discomfort. No matter how much air your bag traps against you, if it breathes, you're losing heat by evaporation.

This has led to the development of vapor barrier fabrics for use *inside* bags, where it keeps the moisture next to your skin rather than allowing it to pass into the insulation. The seeming contradiction here is that evaporation will take place at a controlled rate—you control it by opening or closing the bag—rather than continually, as is the case when moisture gets into the fill (and eventually out the other side). And, of course, the fill stays dry, preserving its insulating qualities.

Keeping the interior of a bag dry keeps you warmer, in other words, although you'll be wetter than in a porous-lined bag.

With down or fiberfill taking care of convective heat loss and a vapor barrier liner taking care of evaporative heat loss, all you really need for a full winterproof bag system is a way to take care of radiant heat loss. The best solution is to cover the bag with a reflective coating. "Space blankets" have been around for years and, despite their fragility, can add many degrees of comfort when placed over a bag, reflective side in. Again, Velcro or snaps can be arranged to keep the blanket and bag together. Another solution is to aluminize the interior surfaces of the shell to provide a reflective covering without adding another layer. This is expensive but worthwhile for severe conditions, and some manufacturers do it on their top-of-the-line bags.

KEEPING YOUR BAG CLEAN

You may have read that sleeping nude is best for you and your bag. It may do a lot for your head, but you'll get the inside of your bag much dirtier that way. Of course, if you're climbing into a bag with muddy clothes on, you won't do it any good either. Best is to sleep in long underwear or clean, absorbent clothing.

The dirtier your bag, the more it will need washing. The more it's washed, the quicker it wears out. In the *Down and Synthetic-Fill Clothing* entry, we warned against handling wet clothing carelessly. The same goes double for sleeping bags; they are at their most vulnerable when wet and heavy, and should be handled from beneath, with your hands supporting the weight of the soaked fill.

You've probably read, too, that you can break up clumps of down fill by pummeling the bag—either with a stick, or by adding a tennis shoe to the dryer while drying your bag. This is a sure way to damage your bag, both shell and baffle, and it doesn't do the down fill much good, either. Down is continually breaking up on its own, and the tiny particles that detach themselves are worthless as insulation because they do not contribute to the air-holding capacity of the fill. Beating it up, then, accelerates this process. Separate matted fill with your hands, gently shaking and pulling it apart. If you dry it correctly, you won't need to break up clumps.

It's much better to wash your bag too much than leave it dirty. Mildew loves dirt. Bags lined with vapor barrier material are easy to wipe off with a damp rag or sponge, and that will minimize the need to wash the entire bag, which will pay off in longer service. Of course, you must keep the outside clean, too, but a ground cloth will take care of that.

Down-filled bags may be dry-cleaned, although careful washing is just as good and a lot cheaper. If you have your bag dry-cleaned, make sure you hang it up to let it air thoroughly before using. There actually have been cases of campers being overcome by dry-cleaning fluid fumes while snuggled in their mummy bags. If you can still smell the fluid, you need more airing time.

STUFFING AND STORING

Stuffing your bag into a sack is sure to shorten its life. Manufacturers like to tout the compressibility of their products, bragging about how small a sack you can get by with. The problem with stuffing is that you crease and fold the fabric and compress the part you put into the bag first much more than the part you put in last. As most people start stuffing foot-first, you'll break down the fill at the critical bottom of the bag sooner than at the less-critical head! Plus you'll almost inevitably strain some baffles more than others and perhaps pinch some fabric in the zipper.

All in all, stuffing isn't a good idea. Instead, roll up your bag, beginning with the narrow foot, taking care not to fold or crease it too much. Of course, this will mean you'll need a somewhat bigger sack—and will have a somewhat bigger package to tote around—but the benefits in longevity are worth it.

Storing a bag is pretty much a matter of keeping it away from excessive heat and sunlight, and not compressing it. Why not use your bag as a comforter during the winter? Oh, and keep mice away—they love to nest in down!

Snowshoes

AS WITH MANY kinds of outdoor gear, there has been a technological revolution in snowshoe design and construction in the past few years, with plastics and metals taking their place alongside traditional materials in the ranks of satisfactory construction material. Traditional snowshoes are made of wood—usually split ash—with rawhide lacings. Like wooden skis, wooden snowshoes work well but need extra care. One-piece plastic (polypropylene) and aluminum-tubing-and-plastic (neoprene) snowshoes are virtually maintenance free, but may perform less well under certain conditions. Their durability and repairability is also open to question, though for the casual user this may not be a concern.

There are a wide variety of snowshoe shapes and styles, with the wooden models offering the greatest choice. A discussion of the merits and liabilities of each shape is beyond the scope of this book; however, from the standpoint of getting the most snowshoe for the money and getting the most use out of the snowshoe for the longest time, a beginner is well advised to buy a shorter, wider, tail-less shoe, whatever the chosen material.

The reason for this recommendation is simple: a longer, tailed shoe is harder to handle in brush, and will become snagged more often, opening the possibility of damage to bindings or frame. Also, a longer shoe tempts the user to "bridge" ditches and small streams, which increases the possibility of breaking or bending the frame, or tearing the binding. Shorter shoes are simply easier to handle and, unless you're planning to travel through deep powder, will probably perform just as well.

The question of durability raised earlier should be explained. Polypropylene and aluminum-framed snowshoes are probably as strong as wooden ones, but they may be subject to breakage and deterioration that will not affect traditional materials, and repairs to aluminum and plastic can be more difficult, and sometimes impossible. Since the purpose of this book is to enable you to get more mileage out of your gear, you should consider the long-term positive and negative characteristics of these materials and think about what kind of damage you're likely to do to your snowshoes.

For instance, if you choose aluminum-framed shoes, are you prepared to straighten bends or kinks or splice over breaks? This can be done (see section on tent poles in *Tents* entry) without a great deal of trouble, but if you usually traverse rough country with a lot of rocky stream banks, you may find yourself repairing aluminum frames quite often.

Because plastics are sensitive to ultraviolet rays, sunlight will break them down over time. So, if you are in the habit of leaving your snowshoes in the rear of a hatchback-model auto or standing in the snow outside your winter retreat, perhaps traditional shoes will last longer.

Too, you should consider the temperatures and type of snow you'll encounter. Plastics and aluminum can become quite brittle at extremely low temperatures. On the other hand, rawhide will soak up water from melting snow and will then stretch and become less efficient.

One big advantage of synthetic materials is that there's little variation from shoe to shoe. Since many wooden snowshoes are made by hand, there is always the possibility that inferior materials may have been used. Though most craftsmen are careful about their products, you should check wooden shoes carefully.

Wooden frames should be free of knots, cracks, and discolored areas indicating weakness. Most mass-produced wooden shoes are made of sawn, kiln-dried ash, but handmade shoes may be made of split ash that has been aged slowly, a superior wood. You can recognize split-grain frames by the fact that the grain will be straight—that is, the lines of the grain will be continuous from end to end. Straight-grained ash will resist splitting better than wood sawed on the bias.

Wooden frames should be smooth, the joints should be tight, and the webbing holes countersunk and free of splinters to protect lacings from abrasion damage.

Rawhide lacing should be of even thickness, with no rough spots, stretch or scar marks, or cracks. The "master cord"—the heavy cord that goes across the body of the snowshoe at the front of the webbing, where the foot rests—should be especially strong and free of blemishes.

Having the right size snowshoe is also important. Too small shoes will sink deeper and hit more rocks (not to mention becoming difficult to handle); too large shoes will be hard to handle, increasing the likelihood of a misstep and damage or injury. Use the following chart to find out what size snowshoe you need.

If your weight (with gear) is:	*The length plus width of your snowshoes should be:*		
	Oval shoe	*Medium shoe*	*Narrow shoe*
Under 175 lbs.	45"	62"	66"
175 to 200 lbs.	48"	64"	72"
More than 200 lbs.	50"	66"	77"

The main disadvantage of wooden snowshoes is the tendency of the rawhide bindings to soak up water. This can be prevented by liberally coating the rawhide with marine spar varnish or epoxy resin. Silicone spray waterproofing and oils are generally less efficient because they are easily rubbed off and, in the case of oil, evaporate rather quickly. Neoprene-coated nylon laces can also be substituted for rawhide with satisfactory results.

It's best to keep wooden snowshoes outside during short periods between treks. A cold snowshoe performs better because the snow won't stick to it as readily. Also, snow won't melt and soak into leather or wood. Warm lacings stretch, losing their ability to support.

For long term storage, however, indoors is best. Before putting wooden snowshoes away for the summer, wipe off all dirt. Try to get the dirt out of lacing holes with a Q-tip soaked in oil. Coat the entire shoe liberally with marine spar varnish or epoxy resin. Lacings should be especially well coated to prevent them from soaking up moisture. Work the varnish into the lacing holes with a small paintbrush.

When dry, tie the shoes together bottom to bottom, or make a rectangular frame with bolts and wing nuts similar to a tennis racket press and secure the shoes firmly in it. If the shoes are the kind with an upturned toe, put a block of wood between the toes before tying them together. These precautions are to help prevent warping, a big problem with wooden shoes, especially the bias-sawed, kiln-dried frame kind. Hang the tied or pressed snowshoes by their tails (or by the press), not by the lacing, in a dry area.

Storing aluminum and plastic snowshoes is easier. Again, keep them cold by storing them outside for short periods. For summer storage, just wipe them off and hang them up in a cool, dry area, away from sunlight.

BINDINGS

There are many types of snowshoe bindings, with proponents of each type swearing by their own and at the others. No lengthy discussion of binding

styles is possible here, but snowshoe owners should know how to rig temporary bindings and crampons in case their bindings break or they find themselves on sheer ice or crust.

A simple binding that can be prepared in advance and taken along on
the trail uses two pieces of inner tube. Cut two straps, each 1½–2 inches
wide. Loop them around the master cord and over the boot toe, sliding the
end up as far as necessary to keep the boot securely on the shoe.

A piece of aluminum angle stock as long as the snowshoe is wide will
make an effective crampon. Rivet it to a piece of leather long enough to lash
to the webbing behind the master cord. The "arm" of the angle should be
pointing down to dig in to ice and crust. This is particularly effective for
hilly terrain in icy weather. The crampons can be easily taken off the shoes
and carried in a pocket or pack.

A length of manila or hemp rope will also serve as an effective crampon
if lashed across the bottom of the shoe. Some snowshoers put long wood
screws through the crossbar, letting the point protrude a half inch or so,
to serve as cleats.

Tents

MOST MODERN TENTS are made of coated nylon, but plenty of older canvas tents are still around. General care of canvas tents is discussed in the Canvas chapter.

PITCHING A TENT

Damage often occurs because tents have been pitched improperly. Never pitch a floored tent on rough, rocky, or uneven ground; sweep the area thoroughly and cut off roots and stumps before laying a thick ground cloth. Cots, stoves, coolers, etc., should be set on a double-thick cardboard or folded plastic padding. In wet weather, use two ground cloths—one inside, one beneath the floor—to prevent water from wicking through the tent.

It's a good idea to require campers to remove their boots before entering a tent, if for no other reason than to keep loose dirt from accumulating on the floor at the entrance. A piece of carpeting placed strategically at the doorway can help minimize cleaning chores.

Stretching the fabric too tight places stress on seams and sockets for internal poles, and allows no give for sudden winds, heavy rains, or falling objects.

Build in "shock absorbers" by looping the tent lines and securing each loop with a metal spring clip like those used to secure papers. This will provide an adjustable, easily released safety loop in each line which will give under stress on the tent or line itself.

Another way to provide some give in the line is to cut loops of old inner tubes and incorporate them into the line at the peg end. Trial and error will produce acceptably tight yet springy lines that will take a good jolt before breaking, pulling the peg, or transferring the stress to the tent fabric. Rubber loops will also allow the tent to billow without slacking the lines.

A similar though less effective way to build safety into tent lines is to tie a stick into the knot and twist it to tighten or slacken the line.

Never pitch a tent beneath a large tree. No matter how inviting the spot may seem, more bad things than good can happen there. Pine trees drop pitch-filled cones and "seat" on hot summer nights; deciduous trees are prone to splitting or breaking off limbs in high winds. Leaf stains are almost impossible to remove from canvas, so if leaves blow or drop onto your tent, remove them as soon as possible. Remove sap by scraping, but don't use solvents.

No matter how well you pitch your tent, water can pool on it, creating stress and possible leakage. Never try to empty the puddle by poking from below. The pressure will cause the water to wick through to the inside, and your tent will leak there evermore. Instead, start at the peak or ridge of the tent and lift with a canoe paddle or fishing rod case held along the ridge pole. Push toward the bottom, letting the water flow over the edge. Even better, dump collected water by slacking the line or lines securing that part of the tent to lower the edge.

MODIFICATIONS TO YOUR TENT

Adding a loop to the peak of a pyramid or cabin tent is a worthwhile project. Begin with a piece of canvas six inches wide by one foot long. Fold each side in to meet in the middle and sew a seam securing them, turning the cloth so that the seam is continuous and ends about one inch from each end. Saturate the seam with seam sealer.

Open the seams on either side of the peak by cutting individual stitches with a razor blade and pulling them out. Insert the prepared loop, seam side in, and resew, using a locking stitch such as the backstitch described in the patching and sewing section in the *Canvas* entry. Apply seam sealer and/or waterproofing compound to the entire area. A similar loop is handy to have inside a tent for hanging lanterns.

Another sewing project that will help keep your tent alive is a fireproof, protective pad sewn onto the inside ground cloth to protect it from the heat of stoves, lanterns, etc. For small stoves, a potholder will do the trick. Larger stoves can be accommodated with a piece of a welder's fireproof apron or several potholders stitched together. Sew from the outside with large, loose stitches so the pad can be removed and replaced when it wears out. You can also use snaps or Velcro fasteners.

CLEANING AND STORING

The worst enemy of cotton canvas is mildew, and mildew can be prevented as detailed in the *Canvas* entry. Keeping your tent clean is a good place to start. Take the time to set up and clean your tent after returning from a camping trip.

Your home vacuum cleaner will do a good job of getting loose dirt off the sidewalls, both inside and out, and will help suck moisture out of double seams, where mildew often starts. Use the cleaner's upholstery brush attachment to loosen ground in dirt.

Hose the tent and use a soft brush and detergent to work on any stubborn spots, rinse thoroughly to remove soap residue. Pine pitch, tar, and similar spots can be removed by scraping with a dull blade or plastic scraper, but take care not to abrade the fabric.

Allow the tent to dry thoroughly before packing. Make sure that the interior seams have dried. Use the reverse flow of your vacuum cleaner or a hand-held hair dryer set on cool or warm (not hot) to dry seams.

Ropes and poles can soak up a lot of water during washing or merely from dew and condensation. Lay them in the sun to dry thoroughly, and pack them separately from the tent itself.

After drying, canvas tents should be rolled up loosely for storage. Store in a cool, dry location away from sunlight. Unroll the tent a few times during the off season and inspect for mildew, mouse damage, etc.

Most backpacking or mountaineering tents are made of nylon, and the care and repair information in the *Nylon* entry applies. Be aware of what coatings the manufacturer has added to the nylon, though, because some urethane coatings will tend to peel if washed in too warm water.

Other than following the manufacturer's guidance for cleaning and repair, there's not much to do to prolong the life of a modern tent. Seam sealing is simple, either with tape or liquids, and should be done as a matter of course.

Lines should be washed and dried before storage, and screens should be removed if possible and washed. Store nylon ropes and screens out of direct heat and sunlight. (See *Rope* entry for detailed information on care and storage of ropes.)

KEEPING DRY IN A TENT

Most lightweight tents aren't truly waterproof and so some tent systems include an outer "fly," which is really a second tent. Naturally, this complicates things—you have two tents to pitch instead of one.

Some manufacturers are now offering integrated double-layer tents with a porous inner layer and a repellent outer layer fused into one, in another attempt to solve the problem of keeping rain and dew out while letting condensation from perspiration through to the outside.

Despite these attempts, the moisture problem has yet to be solved to everyone's satisfaction. Like raingear, tents tend to be "either-or"; they either keep moisture from passing both ways or let it through both ways.

Until the perfect material is found, or the perfect system developed, you'll have most success by keeping as many sources of condensation under control as you can.

Don't bring wet gear inside a closed tent, and avoid cooking or boiling water inside when the outside temperature is low. The temperature difference can bring about your own internal rainstorm. Use a ground cloth inside the tent in rainy weather or when camping on snow.

Many campers are puzzled to find condensation underneath their sleeping pads even though the surrounding floor is dry. Sometimes this is actually perspiration that has soaked *through* the foam pad and condensed on the floor.

TENT POLES

Wooden tent poles should be marked and stored separate from the tent. Multi-section aluminum tent poles can be kept together by running a cord through the pole sections and tying them together. That will simplify sorting out the various sections when it comes time to rig the tent.

Nylon backpacking tents usually have a rigid frame system made of flexible aluminum, fiberglass, or graphite poles that are joined to form an arch or A-frame. In an effort to make the entire package as light as possible, manufacturers have made these poles as thin as possible, which can cause problems.

Multi-section poles connected with lengths of shock cord are prone to breakage from letting them snap together, especially when they're cold. For the same reason, don't step on them.

Sometimes a high wind will break external support frames by pushing against the tent which decreases the radius of the frame. You can prevent this by attaching lines to the frame and tying them to trees, stakes, or other braces.

Larger-diameter aluminum poles often found on cabin tents can be repaired if they bend or break. The instructions for bending aluminum back into shape found in the *Aluminum Canoes* and *Backpacks* entries apply.

You can also straighten a shallow bend in a long aluminum pole by filling the pole with sand and bending it back into shape by lightly hitting it with a rubber mallet as you apply pressure in the proper direction. The sand will keep the pole from kinking.

If the pole has buckled, a length of dowel can be used as a splice. Cut the pole in two pieces at the break, insert a length of dowel, and with the pole and dowel secured in a vise, drill several small holes through each section of pole into the dowel. Small sheet metal screws will hold the pole together. Use plastic aluminum or duct tape to make a smooth joint.

Fiberglass poles are subject to breaking if bent too far when cold. There's little you can do to fix a broken pole, so pack an extra or two when winter camping. If the outer layer becomes nicked or scratched, a touch-up with clear resin will restore it.

Terminal Tackle

MOST FISHERFOLK, EVEN those who are otherwise conscientious about cleaning and caring for their gear, neglect lures and other terminal tackle. Time was, these items were inexpensive—at least compared to rods and reels. Today, however, all tackle is pricey, and repair, refurbishment, cleaning, and storage of terminal tackle should be a part of every angler's skill box.

Foremost among ways to keep your terminal tackle alive is having the right storage. A tackle box with individual compartments for plugs, flies, spinners, spoons, and the like is basic. Nothing kills plugs faster than tossing them into a box, where they nick and scratch each other, get caught in hinges, tangle and twist. For your better lures, individual plastic boxes are ideal. Line tackle boxes with cork.

If you're a fly fisherman, or just have a lot of plugs, flies, etc., you simplify nighttime lure changes by slipping a loop of nylon monofilament line or leader through each lure's eye before you begin fishing. Just a couple inches will do, and you'll have a handy "lure threader" available for each one.

Where you put plugs is important, and so is the condition you store them in. After a day on the water, wash your plugs in soap and water to remove oil, scum, bits of weed, and fish scales. None of these will do your plug any drastic harm, but over the long haul, finishes will dull, molds form, hooks corrode. Lures used in salt water should be washed in fresh water.

The problem of rusty hooks is a vexing one. You can't oil them with petroleum oils, as you'll create a mini-oil slick everytime you cast. Besides, fish hate the smell of oil. Fish love the smell of fish, however, so why not use fish oil? It won't stay on as long and will make your tackle box most popular with the local tomcats, but it can help prevent rusty hooks. Coating hooks with a durable, clear coating is also worthwhile. Try clear nail polish, or a similar clear lacquer.

If a hook's been around long enough to get really rusty, you're probably better off replacing it—especially if it's been snagged and recovered a few times. Weakened hooks are responsible for some of the best "one that got away" stories you'll ever hear. When replacing hooks, make sure you use the same size and weight, otherwise you'll change your plug's action and increase the chances of fouling and missed strikes.

Treble hooks should be placed "odd hook down"—that is, the base of the triangle formed by the three hooks, when attached to the plug, should be against the plug's body. This will prevent unusual and possibly counterproductive agitation and wobble, and will make the lure easier to store in its box.

Mildly rusted or corroded hooks can be cleaned with steel wool or similar abrasive, and sharpened on a whetstone. It's usually futile to try to repaint or replate hooks, but you can, if you can roughen the existing finish sufficiently, paint them flat black.

Tarnished spoons and spinners respond well to silver polish. You can also use wet sand or wet pipe tobacco to put a shine on your spoons. If they're badly corroded try the compound used to grind automobile engine valves. Spoons can be replated, but you're better off painting them. Use flat white as a base coat, paint spots, stripes, or whatever's your fancy, and finish with a clear spray lacquer or enamel compatible with the type of paint you used.

When cleaning plugs and/or hooks, check the screw eye used to attach the hook to the plug body. If it's begun to separate, corrode, or pull out of the plug, replace it. Replacement eyes are available at most good tackle shops, and all you need to do is turn them in with a pair of pliers. If the hole has been stripped and the eye is wobbly, a drop of epoxy or cyanoacrylate glue will keep it tight—permanently.

Cyanoacrylate (super glue) is one of the handiest chemicals in your tool box. You can easily patch tiny dents and gouges by sifting some bicarbonate of soda (common baking soda) onto fresh liquid cyanoacrylate glue. The chemical reaction between them causes the glue to set up immediately into a hard, waterproof, permanent—yet easily sanded—filler. It is much more effective, lighter, and faster than plastic or epoxy fillers and it's a nice, basic white color.

Painting wooden lures is easy and quick. Be sure to sand down all the shiny surfaces and remove screw eyes, "lips," etc., before painting. Use model airplane enamel or lacquer, beginning with a base coat of flat white. You can paint "scales" on the back or belly of a plug by using nylon netting as a stencil.

Hang the plug in a protected place—a large cardboard box makes an excellent paint booth—and suspend a piece of nylon screen securely before it. (Nylon screening with an octagonal pattern can be purchased at fabric and notions stores.) Spray very rapidly and lightly with silver, gold, or grey paint, depending on your plug color. You may have to experiment with this a few times before you get it right, but you'll be able to paint realistic scales on plugs eventually.

After painting and scaling, spray the lure with a protective coat of clear lacquer or enamel.

Everybody loves plastic worms. Nobody likes to store them, untangle them, separate them when they've melted together, or replace them when they've become deteriorated from oil, gasoline, or insect repellent, all of which will melt plastic worms quickly.

The best way to keep the wigglers clean and ready for use is to store them in a jar of plain water. This will keep them soft and yet prevent them from becoming *too* soft, as they often do when left in a tackle box in the sun for long periods. After using a plastic worm, wash it with soap and water, rinse thoroughly and dry it, then sprinkle with talcum powder if you plan to store it dry. Otherwise, just keep it in the water jar all the time. Never refrigerate plastic worms because they can become brittle and vulnerable to cracking.

To rejuvenate a dried out, flattened plastic worm, place it in warm water. It may soften.

Rubber or synthetic skirts and "hair" on poppers is vulnerable to drying out, cracking, and deterioration from exposure to solvents, oils, and sunlight. Unfortunately, there's not much you can do to protect it. Replacing these items is easy, however, as they're usually either secured with a plastic band around the plug body or inserted into the body.

Cut the band and replace with a new skirt, band and all, securing the band to the plug with epoxy or super glue. You can make a skirt easily enough from a couple of rubber bands and the band from plastic tape. Get the color you want from a hardware or interior decorating supply store.

Rinsing these hairy monsters in fresh water and sprinkling them with a little talc after use will help keep the rubber supple and soft.

Natural hair on flies, bucktails, and poppers gets limp with use, particularly if constantly exposed to scummy water and oil. You can sometimes rejuvenate flies and plugs of this kind by holding them above a boiling teakettle, in the steam but not so close to the kettle that the heat causes the hair to wilt further. Feathers will also respond to this treatment, shape them with your fingers after steaming. There are several good spray and dry-granule fly cleaners on the market, and pastes to make dry flies float are also available.

How you use your lures is as important as how you clean, repair, and store them. Always use swivels, especially when spin casting or trolling. Swivels prevent twist in the line and prevent monofilament line from cutting into the attachment eye. Swivels should be black rather than shiny, as fish will hit a shiny swivel, sometimes breaking the line at that point, losing your lure or foul-hooking themselves.

Everybody snags lures, and everybody loses some and gets some free. The worst thing you can do is to heave and haul and flail away at the water with your rod—you'll just snag your lure worse.

If you can, maneuver around the snagged lure, keeping gentle pressure on the line. Take up slack and feed line, working the rod from side to side, up and down—but *gently.*

If that doesn't work, try knocking the lure loose by attaching a heavy sinker to the line with a clip and short length of line and letting the weight slide down the line to the fouled lure. Surprisingly, this simple tactic often works.

Folks who fish swamps and marshes are used to getting snagged, and many of them have rigged poles with old rod tips as probes. Take any pole of convenient length and secure a length of fiberglass or metal rod to it with the guide tip extending past the end of the pole. Use the probe by securing it to the line with a clip and work the pole and the rod together, letting the probe follow the line to the snagged lure, working the probe to dislodge the lure.

Wooden Boats

THE BEAUTY AND strength of wooden boats are apparent, but you pay a high maintenance penalty for these qualities. Yearly refinishing of exterior surfaces, periodic sealing and caulking chores, and constant vigilance against rot—both wet and dry—are the lot of the wooden boat owner, and most wouldn't have it any other way.

PREVENTING ROT

Rot, the big culprit, occurs in any hard-to-get-at area of the boat that is allowed to trap and hold moisture from splashing, condensation, or leakage. Obviously, then, getting rid of the moisture will forestall rot.

Ventilation and drainage are the keys. Decked-in craft—especially if they're used with gasoline or diesel engines or routinely transport such fuels —should have ventilator scoops built in. If your motorized craft is capable of planing speed, you might consider a removable drain plug kit. These kits include a threaded metal socket and plug which is installed through the bottom planking at the stern. While at planing speed, bilge water will flow to the stern, and will be siphoned out by the rushing water flowing past the opened drain. Once the water has drained, you screw the plug back in. Automatic and manual bilge pumps are good investments, and an assortment of sponges, cans, cut-off bleach bottles, and other bailers are familiar equipment to most boaters.

A hot linseed oil application can help prevent rot. Always heat the oil over water in a double-boiler-type system to prevent it scorching or catching fire. Apply it liberally, let it soak in, and reapply. The oil will repel moisture without coating the wood, which will interfere with the boat's ability to breathe.

Dry rot is another kind of beast. It is a fungus that actually feeds on wood. Again, damp, unventilated, dark corners are the trouble spots, and dry rot will spread if not checked. To prevent dry rot, wash out the bilge, under-deck areas, and the inside of the hull with salt water, which kills the fungus.

CAULKING

Old-timers left their wooden boats in the water constantly between thaw and freeze-up. The reasoning behind this was simple: as wood dries, it shrinks. Wooden boats constantly hauled in and out of the water, therefore, would always leak upon launching. Too, the oakum caulking—a loosely-twisted jute treated with tar—would shrink when dry and swell when wet, making a boat with water in it actually more resistant to leaking than one perfectly dry. Those old-timers did a lot of bailing.

Modern caulking compounds are flexible enough to maintain a constant seal, so you should endeavor to keep the inside of the boat dry whether you leave it in the water or not. To caulk properly, make sure you fill the entire seam, as the caulk will not expand, and any tiny openings will admit water.

PAINTING AND VARNISHING

Painting and varnishing wood protects it from rot, algae, and other marine critters, and beautifies the craft. To paint a new boat, you must first seal the wood with sanding sealer and fill all nail and screw holes with plastic wood or the equivalent. After sealing, a primer compatible with the paint you intend to use should be applied and allowed to set for at least two or three days (in moderate humidity and temperature). This is best done indoors.

After a thorough drying period, sand this primer down to the bare wood and apply several undercoats, letting them dry completely and sanding them with medium-grit sandpaper between coats, gradually building up a base of paint without runs, thick areas, or thin spots.

The finish coats should be of high-quality, high-gloss marine paint with anti-fouling characteristics. The more coats the better. Sand between coats with fine wet/dry sandpaper used wet before the final two coats. Be sure to follow instructions for thinning the paint and, most important, allow adequate drying time between coats. Spray painting gives a nice finish, but make sure you don't let the paint run or "orange peel." Finish the paint job with several coats of paste wax.

Varnish is applied the same way as paint, but you must be doubly careful to keep sand and dirt away from the fresh varnish.

COMBATTING ALGAE

You should inspect your hull frequently and repair any damage caused by contact with flotsam, piers, etc. Fight algae growth with whatever weapon you can devise. Actually, the only thing that keeps plants from growing on your boat is making it too smooth for them to adhere—that's the reason for waxing the hull. In time, though, the grass will grow, and you have to scrape, scrub, and curse it off. The problem is, these little floral goblins actually grow into the paint, so you'll be removing paint, too. Like we said, high maintenance . . . It's things like this that drive wooden boat owners to fiberglass.

Actually, fiberglass craft have as much trouble with growth as do wooden craft. They're just easier to clean and don't suffer from seeping moisture if their outer skins are damaged. For that reason, many wooden boat owners apply fiberglass to the outside of their boats.

FIBERGLASS COATINGS

Fiberglass-coated wooden boats have breathing problems, so you'll have to provide adequate ventilation for under-deck and bilge areas. Don't fiberglass inside the hull, as the wood must be able to dispel moisture in one direction at least. Too, once you've fiberglassed a hull, you cannot let gouges, cracks, etc., go unrepaired, as water will enter the crack, soak into the wood, and be trapped in a perfect environment for rot.

Fiberglassing is a simple, albeit messy, process with pitfalls for the unwary. The biggest mistake you can make is not removing all the old finish, dirt, scum, sanding dust, etc. Work that hull with a belt sander, stripper, scraper, or whatever you can. But don't burn the paint off with a blowtorch, as that will melt the previous finish and allow it to soak into the wood. That will make the fiberglass reluctant to stick. Leave the hull rough for better adhesion.

Get all the filler and caulking out of screw holes, seams, cracks, and other places. And don't use any petroleum product or solvent to clean the wood—fiberglass will not stick to it. Fill cracks, holes, and seams with chopped glass and resin mixed into a paste.

Follow directions supplied by the manufacturer for mixing resin, preparing cloth, etc., to the letter. Be especially conscious of mixing, set-up, and drying times. When applying the resin, look for areas where it soaks in—they'll appear dark—and apply more.

Work the cloth over one area at a time, and overlap several inches at the seams. You'll have to smooth the cloth as you go with your hands. After the cloth is applied, apply a resin coat, and work the rough edges down with a knife, belt sander, or hand sanding. Finish with a thin, even resin coat and fine sand to a smooth finish. When worn or patched, fiberglass can and should be painted.

Fiberglass is an excellent reinforcing material for areas where cleats, lights, and other apparatus have been installed. Roughen the wood underneath the deck or hull, apply resin, cloth and resin. When hard, drill out holes as needed and apply resin to the inside of the hole to keep moisture from seeping into the wood at those points.

STORAGE

Wooden boats should be stored upside down in a well-ventilated area, away from any potential hazard such as tree limbs. Indoors is best. Before storing, wash down the inside with salt water to prevent dry rot, and remove algae, scum, and debris from the hull with a brush and detergent.

Wood/Canvas Canoes

WOOD-AND-CANVAS canoes are quiet and smooth in the water. Aside from their beauty, these are their main advantages, though you pay a high maintenance premium for them. Wooden-hulled canoes float, eliminating the need for added flotation material (which takes up space), and though they're vulnerable to abrasion and small tears in the canvas covering, streamside repairs are easy. On a long fishing trip through outback lakes and rivers, they really shine; on fast water, or where frequent portages are necessary, their vulnerability and weight speak against them.

Wood-and-canvas canoes are still with us, thanks to the dedicated efforts of a few individuals, companies, and organizations. The classic plank-sided, canvas-covered still-water canoe is still manufactured by Old Town Canoe, Co., of Old Town, Maine, and that company has an extensive line of wooden and metal parts available for restoration and repair. In fact, you could probably construct a canoe from scratch by buying the parts from Old Town.

The Wooden Canoe Heritage Association is another good source for information on repair, restoration, and maintenance of these canoes. Anyone contemplating tackling a repair or restoration job is well advised to contact the WCHA, Box 5634, Madison, WI 53705.

The following information on restoration was written by John McGreivey and published in *Canoe* Magazine in 1978. We are indebted to the author and to that fine publication for permission to reprint excerpts here.

In common with anything possessing more than utilitarian value, the monetary value of an old canoe is difficult to determine. Both sellers and buyers often feel the value of a canoe increases with age. To a certain extent,

287

this assumption is true, but not always. Individual manufacturers built their most popular models for many years. Consequently, to buy an old canoe rather than its younger double may only buy unnecessary headaches. At the same time, a 60- or 70-year-old canoe need not be avoided. Properly restored, a very old canoe will last as long as a younger one. As a rule, plan to spend no more for a canoe and its restoration than the cost of a new metal or plastic canoe of good quality. Of course, a very old and rare canoe, such as a Rushton "American Beauty," is an exception to this rule.

Certain maladies are normal in any old canoe. Rot in and around the decks, missing or broken thwarts and seats, cracked ribs, and ruptured planking are not causes for alarm. But look closely at the inner rails. If one or both are cracked across the grain, replacement may involve more effort and expense than the canoe deserves, particularly if it needs other major repairs.

Usually, an old canoe will need a new canvas. Often, however, a sound canvas lies under many layers of cracked paint. A salvageable canvas represents a savings of between $75 and $100.

Once a canoe has been obtained, the following procedure should cover most problems encountered during restoration. Individual canoes will present special problems, but solving these special problems is part of the fun.

DISMANTLING

Canvas. Before removing the canvas, remove the outer gunwales, keel, and stem bands. On some canoes the ends of the gunwales are fastened to the inner rails with sunken finishing nails. Try to drive these nails through the gunwales. If this fails, the nails must be drilled out.

If the canoe is of closed gunwale construction, save the irreplaceable brass nails which fasten the finishing strips to the inner gunwales. Also, save broken brass stem bands: they will be useful for making hold-downs for floor racks. For a long-lasting restoration, remove the canvas even if it will be used again. Avoid folding a salvageable canvas.

Decks. Inevitably, some of the eight or ten screws holding the decks to the inner rails are hidden beneath ribs. Try slipping a hacksaw blade between the deck and inner rail. If there is no room for the blade, locate the positions of the hidden screws and blind-drill them through the ribs. Solid decks may be left in place, but their removal will make working in the narrow ends of the canoe considerably easier. Do not neglect to mark the position of the decks before removing them.

Ribs. Ribs passing under the stem can be removed by pulling the nails holding the stem to the planking. Loosen the stem only enough to withdraw the ribs.

PREPARATION

Old Canvas. Every method of paint removal has its advantages and disadvantages. Sanding allows the paint removal to stop at the original primer, but the process is slow and dusty. Softening the paint with heat from an old flat iron or a propane torch fitted with a flame spreader is very effective, but requires considerable sanding afterwards. Paint remover, in addition to being messy and expensive, may require the application of a new coat of filler. The great advantage of paint remover is that is softens the old filler just enough so that the canvas can be stretched tightly over the hull. Removal of the paint by sanding or heating should be done with the canvas on the hull. If paint remover is used, remove the paint before tacking the canvas.

Interior. After removing the old finish with paint and varnish remover, sand the ribs and planking, but do not try to remove every imperfection. As in antique furniture, "distress marks" enhance the beauty of an old wood canoe. Follow the sanding with the application of a mixture of five parts turpentine (*not* paint thinner) and one part boiled linseed oil. This mixture will restore the color of the wood and will replace evaporated natural oils. Do not, however, apply the mixture to new wood that will be visible when the restoration is complete.

Stems. If a stem is rotted or broken near the deck, cut back to sound wood and shape a new piece from ash. Scarf-cut each piece and join them with waterproof glue. Finish the job by pressing wood dough into the old tack holes.

If, for one or another reason, there is not enough of the stem or contiguous planking to serve as pattern for the new piece, the original curve will have to be reconstructed. The easiest way to do this is to refer to another canoe of the same model. If another canoe is unavailable, install the deck and, if necessary, replace the missing ends of the inner rails. Hold a heavy sheet of paper against the hull and draw a gently curved line from the tips of the inner rails to the remnant of the original stem. The paper can then be made into a template.

Planking. Repair small areas of damaged planking by cutting patches with a sharp knife from straight-grained red cedar. Using the patches as templates, outline the areas to be replaced, then cut out the sections to be removed. To avoid splitting small patches, use glue rather than tacks.

Because new wood will differ in color and grain from old wood, large or very visible patches may be cut from a section of planking under the decks. New wood in these areas will be almost invisible.

Sanding the interior loosens many tacks. Do not attempt to re-clinch these loose tacks; instead, pry them out and drive in new ones. Tacks with raised heads also should be replaced.

Nail down any buckled planking, sand the hull lightly, then brush on two coats of turpentine and boiled linseed oil mixed in equal proportions.

If the decks have not been installed already, install them at this time. Some work with a rasp may be necessary for new decks to follow the curve of the gunwales.

Rib Installation. For bending ribs, a steam cabinet is a necessity. Do not immerse ribs in boiling water because it extracts the protective oils from the wood. A serviceable steamer operable on the kitchen stove or backyard barbecue can be constructed from scrap materials such as plywood, aluminum flashing, and a discarded refrigerator drawer.

Using the old rib as a pattern, plane the new rib to the correct thickness and shape, but leave it two to four inches longer than the original. In removing the old rib, it may have been necessary to cut away narrow strips of planking to pull the nails holding the rib to the inner rail. If not, remove the strips at this time. Their removal will facilitate the insertion of the new rib.

Holding the rib inside the hull, bend the rib enough to insert the near end between the planking and the inner rail. While moving the rib toward its position at the opposite rail, pull the already inserted end upward far enough to allow the far end to slip into place. Press the rib into the hull. Once the wood fibers have been stretched, the rib will return to its proper curvature if pressure must be momentarily released.

With a small C-clamp, attach one end of the rib to the inner rail. Press the rib back into the hull, then clinch-nail the rib to the planking with three or four tacks at the place where the hull bends most radically. Repeat the process with the other end of the rib. Clinch the remaining tacks, then remove the clamps and fasten each rib end to the inner rails with aluminum nails. On open gunwale canoes, trim the ends of the ribs after the outer gunwales have been mounted.

Ribs may be bent by pressing them over the hull rather than into it. However, this method risks inexact curvature and makes the installation of the ribs quite difficult.

Seats and Thwarts. Split seat rails may be tied together with glue and countersunk brass screws, but replacement of defective wood is preferable. For aesthetic reasons, it is best to replace all seats and thwarts if any new wood is needed. Caning is simple, inexpensive, and boring, so plan to watch some television while doing it. New thwarts may be fashioned in a few hours with a saber saw, rasp, and sandpaper.

FINISHING

Old Canvas. A large pair of pliers and a lexicon of appropriate oaths are helpful in mounting an old canvas. Aligning holes in the canvas with the screw holes in the hull may be difficult. To prevent leaks, lay a strip of canvas along the keel line before placing the canvas on the hull. After the canvas has been tacked to the hull, fill any spots where the weave in the canvas is invisible with canvas filler or canvas cement. If paint remover has been used, dampening the canvas with remover allows the canvas to be pulled tightly over the hull.

New Canvas. Important to remember in applying a new canvas is that the canvas must be pulled across its bias as well as vertically toward the gunwales and horizontally toward the bow and stern. The bias and horizontal pulls become increasingly critical where the canoe begins to narrow. Flat-jawed, locking pliers are invaluable in stretching the canvas.

With the canoe resting on its gunwales on saw horses, locate the center rib, then drape the canvas evenly over the hull. For tacking to the first three or four ribs in each direction from the center rib, the canvas needs only to be stretched vertically (fore-and-aft). After the canvas has been tacked through or near about eight ribs, begin pulling downward and across the

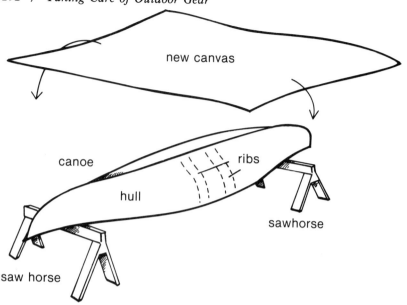

Important to remember in applying new canvas is that the canvas must be pulled across the bias as well as vertically toward the gunwales and horizontally toward the bow and stern.

bias simultaneously. When wrinkles appear, go to the ends of the canoe and give the canvas a firm horizontal tug. Secure the canvas temporarily with a tack driven into each stem piece. Repeat the horizontal pull frequently. Be sure to alternate the tacking from one side to the other and to work from center towards the ends.

When wrinkles refuse to disappear, return to the center rib and begin the process over again. After two or three complete retackings, the canvas will be tight and free of wrinkles.

Because the canvas must be stretched and tacked two or three times, do not waste expensive brass tacks on the temporary tackings. Use ordinary half-inch steel tacks instead. To avoid splitting the planking, place the temporary tacks into the ribs above the planking. Angle the tacks toward the keel of the canoe to prevent splitting the ribs. On closed gunwale models, tack directly into the tops of the gunwales. Once the gunwale finishing strips are on, the tack holes will be hidden. A single tack in or near each rib suffices for the temporary tacking.

At the ends, slit the canvas enough to allow the canvas to lie smoothly. Pull one flap around the stem and secure it with $\frac{3}{16}$-inch brass tacks spaced about one half inch apart. With a razor, trim the excess canvas as closely as possible to the tack heads. Spread marine bedding compound over the tack heads and into the space between the planking and the tacked edge of the flap. Pull the second flap around the stem, tack it down, and trim it in the same way as the first.

Permanent tacks may be driven at this time. A better procedure, however, is to delay the final tacking until the filler has been applied and allowed to dry for a few days. With the filler on, the canvas can be given a final smoothing. In either case, do not trim the excess canvas from the gunwales until after the final tacking. For the final tacking, use $^{11}/_{16}$-inch brass tacks. Two tacks should pass through the planking and ribs and into the gunwales at each rib end.

Apply the canvas filler according to the directions on the container. After three weeks of optimum drying conditions, sand and prime the filled canvas. Prime the keel and spread a thin layer of bedding compound along its length before attaching it to the hull. Smooth the primed hull and keel with fine sandpaper and brass wool, then paint the hull with a good marine enamel.

Factory canvasing methods may be adapted for home use. Details are explained in Atwood Manley's *Rushton and His Times in American Canoeing* (Syracuse, 1968), which may be obtained through the American Canoe Association's book service.

Varnishing. By deferring the interior hull varnishing until near the end of the restoration, the amount of water that can seep between planking and canvas will be substantially reduced. The varnish fills the spaces between the planks.

Full authenticity suggests the use of orange shellac rather than varnish on some canoes. In deciding between shellac and varnish, consider that shellac diminishes the contrast between the red and white cedar and was probably used many years ago only because it was more durable than existing varnish.

MINOR REPAIRS

Wood-and-canvas canoes are perhaps the easiest of all to patch, whether you're working in the field or at home. Such structural damage as broken ribs and thwarts can be repaired temporarily with little difficulty. Ease of repair is one of the great benefits of owning a traditional canoe, and is doubtless one of the reasons so many old-timers are still in service.

Patching. The most typical injury to wood-and-canvas canoes is a small triangular cut in the canvas, often the result of an unscheduled encounter with a snag, rock, or "sweeper" tree.

To repair a small triangular cut, carefully lift the two "flaps" away from the hull and remove any foreign material that may have become lodged between the canvas and wood. Cut a piece of canvas at least 1 inch larger in each direction than the longest leg of the triangle. (That is, if the triangular cut is 2 inches by 1 inch long, cut a rectangular patch 3 by 2 inches.) Coat the patch liberally with canvas cement or household glue and carefully insert it between the canvas and wood, being careful not to extend the tear by handling it roughly. Smooth the patch on the wooden hull and press the canvas against it, taking care to remove wrinkles and avoid rolled edges and corners.

Cut a second patch somewhat larger; another half inch on each side should do it. Round the corners. Hold the patch against the hull and mark the edges, then spread a thin coat of adhesive within the marks. Coat one side of the patch with adhesive and press it into place. Hold it firmly until it has dried thoroughly; the time will vary depending upon temperature, humidity, and the particular adhesive.

Once dry, the patch can be filled and painted as described above.

Larger tears can be patched this way, too, but it is advisable to try to secure the inner patch to the canvas. Depending upon where on the canoe the damage is located, you may be able to pull the canvas away from the hull far enough to do a neat sewing job with a needle and thread. If not, perhaps an awl designed for sewing leather and heavy canvas will do. As noted above, take care not to tear the canvas further. If you can't sew completely around the inner patch, at least try to secure it to the hull canvas at the end of each leg of the tear.

Repairing Ribs, Thwarts, and Gunwales. Streamside repair of a broken rib or thwart is easy. Your chief concern is strength, not beauty, and you want to make sure you don't create further damage which would make permanent repair difficult.

A broken rib can be replaced with a split green sapling cut from the bank. Peel the bark of a 2-inch diameter tree trunk, cut it to fit, and wedge it into position over the top of the broken rib. Lash it to the gunwales. The sapling should fit as close to the rib as possible so keep cutting saplings until you have one that matches the curve of the existing rib and fits within 2 inches along the entire length of the rib. Next, cut a series of blocks from hard wood—wedge-shaped chips from a camp-clearing operation will do—and force them into the space between the sapling and the broken rib.

The idea is to use the sapling's spring to force the blocks against the broken rib in such a way that the rib is pushed into the hull, maintaining the tension and giving support to the planking. Take your time and get this splint in securely. A weak spot on the hull due to a missing or improperly splinted rib is very vulnerable to serious damage to the planking and/or canvas, which will almost always mean a tedious and difficult repair job.

If the rib can be pulled away from the inside of the hull, try lashing it back together with copper wire, wet rawhide, or, in a pinch, roots from a spruce tree that have been boiled in water until soft.

Gunwales and thwarts can and should be splinted or spliced with whatever material is handy. Lashing with wire, rawhide, string, nylon webbing, or whatever else is available can preserve the structural integrity of the canoe and prevent further and more serious damage from flexing or lack of support.

GENERAL CARE

Properly cared for, a wood-and-canvas canoe requires only a few hours' work each year. To prevent alligatoring, do not apply "hard" paint over "soft" paint. In other words, stick to the same *type* of paint, even when changing colors. Paint the entire hull only when spot painting proves unsatisfactory. The fewer layers of paint, the lighter the canoe will be.

Pull the canoe from the water at the end of the day, and avoid leaving it upturned on wet grass for long periods. In winter, store it upside down and well above dampness. For everyday use and for trips without difficult portages, use a floor rack to minimize wear on the varnish and strain on the ribs.

Wood-Strip Canoes

MADE OF LONG strips of wood—often cedar or other colorful, full-grained wood—covered with a clear fiberglass resin, "strippers" are light, flexible, responsive, strong—and beautiful. Unfortunately, anything more than a minor repair is quite a task.

Minor dings and gouges in the fiberglass coat are no problem. You can sand and fill with poly or epoxy resin, then sand and buff until the hull looks like new.

Big breaks are another story, one well beyond the scope of this book. It is very hard for even an experienced boat builder to cut into an edge-laminated hull and insert an inlay to match the original structure. Other than putting on a "functional"—but terrible-looking—fiberglass patch (see section on permanent patches in the *Fiberglass Canoes* entry), about the best you can do is try to inlay a solid piece of some attractive wood and replenish the resin coat. Even this will need a reinforcing patch of fiberglass cloth on the inside, and considerable wood putty and elbow grease to make the outside look half good. No job for an amateur, in other words.

The Mansfield canoes from the Stowe Canoe Company in Vermont are another matter entirely. With mahogany ribs running gunwale-to-gunwale, other wood parts of tough ash and spruce, woven nylon seats, aluminum strips at strategic spots, and an outside skin of fiberglass cloth, these canoes are strong yet easy to repair. The following information on repairing Mansfield canoes was furnished by the manufacturer, who encourages home repair by making keels, gunwales, seats, thwarts, stems, and decks available.

MAINTENANCE

A Mansfield canoe is very easy to maintain and will last a lifetime with a little care.

The light wood (gunwales, decks, stems, seat frames, thwart, and keel) should be lightly sanded and varnished about once a year with a high-quality spar varnish. Most of the new polypropylene varnishes will also work but first check to make sure they are compatible with the existing finish.

The ribs will probably need no attention for at least five years but if they appear to be drying out, rough sand and paint them with a clean coat of polyester resin.

The hull itself needs no attention. It will lose some of its gloss in time, but can be waxed with a good car wax to restore the shine.

Most scratches in the fiberglass can be removed by sand and polishing. Deep scratches will have to be filled with a fiberglass paste.

To remove minor scratches first try compounding them out, using a coarse grade rubbing compound. If the scratches persist use some 600A grit wet/dry sandpaper to sand the scratch out. Use the paper wet. After the scratch is gone, soap your sandpaper and, still using plenty of water, sand the area to remove any minor sanding marks. Now using your rubbing compound buff the sanded area back to a shine. Most scratches can be removed in this manner.

Very deep scratches can be filled with fiberglass paste. First rough sand or file the scratch, then mix the paste per instructions supplied with it, and fill the scratch. Place some wax paper over the patch and, using a straight-edge, smooth the area. After the paste has dried remove the wax paper, sand the patch, and buff back to a shine.

PATCHING

Most repairs on Mansfield canoes can be readily effected with a stock fiberglass repair kit, available at marine and automotive stores. Instructions are usually included for preparing the resin and if they are followed you will have no problems. Also refer to the sections on fiberglass repair.

Usual damage is a tear, not a hole. A piece of fiberglass cloth at least two inches larger in all directions than the tear and resins is needed.

First, push the sides of the tear back to their original position, then get some sticks to use as braces to hold the hull in its original shape. Brace against the opposite gunwale, a seat frame, or the thwart; tie a board lengthwise to the seats and thwart and brace against it; or tie a board across the gunwales (side to side) by passing a cord around the canoe.

Once you have the tear in its original position, and have some braces prepared, you're ready to patch.

Remove any splinters of fractured rib that may prevent the repair cloth from coming in contact with as much surface as possible, then sand the area that will be covered with the cloth. The sanding is just to remove bumps and scuff up the surface. If the tear is large enough to permit liquid to pass through, tape the outside area over the hole.

Mix a little resin according to instructions, wet the surface you have sanded, then place the fiberglass cloth in position and saturate it, using a tongue depressor or popsicle stick. Make sure the cloth is fully saturated, and remove air bubbles by working them out to the sides with the stick. Put in the braces to hold the ribs in place, and check to see that there are no air pockets. Let it set. This "functional" patch will keep you on the water and will last indefinitely.

For a "cosmetic" job on the outside of your canoe, repair as just described, then clean the tear on the outside with a file. Don't be too fussy, but you're going to use a paste of thickened resin and you need some place for it to lodge. Mix resin with thickening agent until it's like soft putty, then add hardener and fill the crack slightly higher than the surface of the canoe. When it dries, file until flush.

Then get out the wet/dry sandpaper, and go to work. Use wet 300-grit paper until you have things well smoothed out, then switch to 600 grit. Take out all the little scratches, then use rubbing compound on a cloth or your electric drill buffer. (This is also the method for removing scratches.)

REPAIRING RIBS, BANG IRONS, STEMS, AND KEEL

Cracked ribs need not be replaced. A strip of fiberglass cloth soaked in resin and laid along the rib will be as strong as the original.

If you have a badly broken rib you need only replace about four inches on either side of the break. Cut straight across and evenly through the rib with a sharp saw. Pry off as much as you can and chisel out the rest. Hold the new rib in place and cut it exactly to length, forcing it into position to be sure it fits. Remove it, mix up some resin, wet the canoe, wet the rib, and force it back into position. Hold it with some braces. If you think you need more strength cover the whole area with cloth. Otherwise, just cover the new rib with resin and you're back in business.

The bang irons are the next most common fatality. They are ⅛-inch by ⅜-inch half oval aluminum or brass, 48 inches long, secured with annular-threaded nails. Both strips and nails are available from Stowe.

Rip off the old strip and cut off the nails—you can't pull them. File the stem smooth. Place the new strips in position starting at the keel but don't line up the holes with the old ones. Mark and drill a $\frac{1}{16}$-inch hole and hammer in the first nail. Continue drilling and hammering till you come to the end of the stem at the deck. Bend the bang iron over onto the deck and nail.

Stems and the keel come next. If it's a stem you'll have to replace the whole piece; if it's the keel replace the broken section plus a foot or so on each end.

Stems are fastened from the outside, so after the bang iron is removed it is easy to remove the old one and replace it. Start where the stem meets the keel. Mark the angle of the keel and cut off the stem, noting where the first screw was on the old stem. Replace it. (Screws will come with the replacement stem.) Using about the same spacing as on the original, attach the stem to the canoe. Pre-drill and countersink each hole in turn, using a ⅛-inch drill. Draw the screws in very tight. It really doesn't matter if the stem isn't perfectly tight to the hull, but do your best to make it so.

To replace a section of keel, first cut the new section to match the old. To do this, clamp and brace the new section to the broken keel, and cut both on an angle 8 to 12 inches past both sides of the break. Saw off the old screws and file the stubs flush to the hull. Tape the new section in place, turn the boat over and brace so the hull is flat. Drill screw holes with a ⅛-inch drill and countersink. Insert the screws and fill the holes with resin or paste.

To repair the inside stem, first remove the bang irons from the outside stem, the main deck, and the under deck. If these parts are in good condition they can be reused, so remove them carefully. Chisel out the inside stem, thus opening the entire end of the canoe. The manufacturer uses a special end mold to install the inside stem, but you'll have to strap the end together and hold it in place with braces and tape. Take your time because proper positioning now will prevent later problems. Hold the inside stem in place with fiberglass paste, and screw from the outside, through the hull, into the stem. Keep the screws as flush as possible so a strip of cloth on the outside hides them and makes it look like new. Screw from both sides at about 4-inch intervals, starting from the bottom of the canoe near the keel.

After completely securing the stem, trim it even with the gunwales, and, using resin mixed with a thickening agent, completely fill the space between the sides of the hull and the stem. Also cover the screws and fill inside along the stem. Allow this to dry and sand the outside smooth. Now replace the piece of cloth on the outside. First rough-sand the old piece so it's flush with the hull. Be careful when sanding so as to retain the outline of the original cloth. Tape with masking tape around the outline, remove the deck, and mix up resin to cover the taped-in area. Now lay the cloth over the area with one end in the V at the canoe bottom, work the cloth so it is flat, and soak resin through it. Wait about an hour or until the resin has begun to harden and trim off the excess cloth along the tape line.

REPLACING DECKS, GUNWALES, AND TRIM

Replacing decks requires care when removing the old decks so as to notice where to place the new screws. The under deck is screwed four times, two on each side, to the main gunwale. In order to position this deck, clamp one side to the gunwale so the edges are flush with each other, then pull in the sides of the canoe so both edges of the deck are flush with the outside edges of the gunwales. Clamp in place. Now place a piece of scrap wood, about 1 inch by 1 inch by 12 inches, under the front portion of the deck and another running along the inside stem. Pound on the horizontal piece to push on the vertical piece, thus bringing the deck up to the gunwale where it can be clamped in place. Drill, countersink, and screw tight.

Next, place the finish deck on top of the lower deck and push toward the end of the canoe until it is snug. Pull in the sides of the canoe with a strap or rope and drill through the gunwale into the deck about an inch from the bottom edge. The placement of this screw can be determined by one of two ways. If the outside trim has not been removed or will not be removed, drill through the trim and countersink the screw. Otherwise merely drill through the hull and gunwale and into the deck. Repeat on both sides using 1½-inch screws (which are supplied). There are three 1¼-inch-long screws holding the deck down. These are placed in the same position as on the old decks and countersunk.

Replacing a gunwale requires much care. If it's broken or rotted on only one end, a piece may be used instead of an entire gunwale. Remove the decks, and clamp the replacement piece next to the broken gunwale. Cut both at the same angle, using a fine-toothed saw. Screw the new piece to the original gunwale, and nail through the trim into the new gunwale after drilling. Replace decks, varnish, and be on your way.

To replace the entire gunwale, remove both decks on the bow and stern. Remove the trim. (This can be sawed or split off; you'll need new trim anyway.) Now carefully separate the gunwale from the ribs with a knife or chisel. You'll find two inside gunwales, and must replace the main gunwale first. Find and mark the center points of the gunwale and the canoe. Spread glue on the gunwale and clamp in position. (Epoxy glue will hold the gunwale in place.) Now replace the decks using the procedures mentioned above.

Next, find the center point of your inner gunwale, line it up with the center of the main gunwale, spread glue on the inside and clamp in position. Starting at the bow end, drill $\frac{1}{16}$-inch holes through the inner gunwale and into the main gunwale. Drill opposite the first four ribs, then at every other rib, until you reach the stern end. Drill opposite the last three ribs. Nail the gunwales, placing a block of wood opposite each nail as you pound it in.

To replace the outside trim, which comes in two sections, start by drilling and nailing at one end of the canoe, placing the tapered end of the trim at the bow or stern. Do this for both pieces. They will overlap considerably; clamp this overlap in position and saw both off, being careful not to cut the hull. Drill and nail in position through to the inside gunwale.

Wool

WOOL GARMENTS HAVE distinct advantages for the outdoorsperson. Chief among them is wool's ability to insulate even when soaking wet, a distinct advantage over down garments (but not over synthetic-fill bags or garments). Wool may be woven into a number of different finishes, spun into yarns and knitted, left "natural" (that is, with much of the lanolin and oils left in), or treated with a thin chemical coating to make it machine washable. As always, find out what you have before you try to clean or repair it.

"Machine washable" woolens are often coated with chemicals that react badly to extreme temperatures. Always consult the manufacturer's instructions before washing any wool or wool-blend garment.

Untreated woolens can be washed with care or dry-cleaned. Careless treatment of woolens will cause them to roughen, shrink, mat, or pill—and once ruined, they can never be restored. Adverse treatment includes exposure to strong alkaline detergents and water softeners, chlorine bleach, hot water, and sunlight, all of which can ruin wool. Additionally, vigorous scrubbing, rubbing, twisting, agitation, or even excessive handling of wet woolens can roughen, stretch, or ruin the finish of wool garments.

Always use a mild soap designed for use on wool, of which there are several on the market. Since hot water shrinks wool fabric, use cool to lukewarm (under 95° F) water, and make sure the soap is completely dissolved in it.

Spots and minor stains should be treated before washing with some of the detergent you're using. Moisten the fabric, apply a little detergent solution, and brush gently with a soft brush, or you can let the garment soak for 15 minutes. Rinse by soaking. Don't agitate, dunk, twist or squeeze wet wool.

Wash by letting the garment soak. Do not scrub, rub, or twist.

After washing, rinse by soaking and draining. Repeat several times to make sure you get all the soap out, since soap or detergent residue in wool will weaken it and make it less waterproof. Squeeze the garment gently, roll it in a towel, and either hang it to dry in a warm place (not in direct sunlight) or lay it flat on a towel.

Wool should be pressed only with steam. Use a steam iron or dry iron with a heavy cotton cloth soaked in water and wrung out to protect the wool from scorching. Do not press down heavily, as you will mark the cloth permanently if you do.

Sweaters can be blocked to shape and left to dry that way. Before washing, lay the sweater flat on a towel which you've placed on a flat surface. With straight pins, outline the sweater—sleeves and all—and let the pins stay while you wash the sweater. Use the pins to guide you in laying the sweater out to dry.

Sweaters often "pill," that is, develop little dangly balls of fuzz which are tough to remove and always seem to come back. Minimize pilling by washing sweaters inside out. Remove pills by stretching the garment gently over a surface and carefully trimming off the protruding pills with a scissors or razor blade. Depilling gadgets on the market will also do a creditable job.

Wool is so versatile and strong that it is used in a number of different weaves and knits, so we'll not attempt to tell you how to patch them here. A talented tailor can make nearly invisible repairs to most garments. Don't try to patch woolens with tape, as the adhesive will be tough to remove later.

Moths love wool. Always store woolens in an airtight container to which you've added moth flakes, balls, or crystals, either naphthalene or paradichlorabenzene. Herbal preparations such as patchouly oil will chase moths, but be careful not to let the oil stain the garment; soak cotton with the oil, and place it inside a plastic bag to protect the clothing. Storing woolens in a cedar-lined chest or closet will also keep them safe from bugs.

Appendix

Ski Equipment
Ski Industries America
8377B Greensboro Dr.
McLean, VA 22102

Inflatable Boats
Northwest River Supplies
Box 9186
Moscow, ID 83843

Hammocks
Hatteras Hammocks Inc.
Box 1602
Greenville, NC 27834

Blue Mountain Industries
Blue Mountain, AL 36201

Insect Repellents
Johnson Wax Co.
Racine, WI 53403

Cookware
Metal Cookware Mfg Assn.
Box D
Fontana, WI 53125

Mirro Corp.
Box 409
Manitowoc, WI 54220

Mountain Gear
Robbins Mountain Gear
Box 4536
Modesto, CA 95352

Forrest Mountaineering Ltd.
1517 Platte St.
Denver, CO 80202

Ropes
The Cordage Institute
1625 Massachusetts Ave. NW, Suite 505
Washington, DC 20036

Binoculars, Scopes, Cameras
Tele-Optics Binocular Repair Service
5514 Lawrence Ave.
Chicago, IL 60630

Chamois
Sponge and Chamois Institute
60 E. 42nd St.
New York, NY 10017

Canteens
M. E. Shaw & Sons, Inc.
Box 31428
Los Angeles, CA 90031

Lanterns, Flashlights
The Coleman Co. Inc.
Wichita, KS 67201

Bright Star Ind.
Subsidiary of Kidde Inc.
600 Getty Ave.
Clifton, NJ 07015

Teledyne Big Beam
Crystal Lake, IL 60014

Wonder Corp. of America
Box 5070
Norwalk, CT 06856

Knives, Axes

W. R. Case & Sons Cutlery Co.
Bradford, PA 16701

Imperial Knife Co. Inc.
Providence, RI 02903

American Cutlery Mfg. Assn.
1000 Vermont Ave. NW
Washington, DC 20005

Buck Knives Inc.
Box 1267
El Cajon, CA 92020

Stoves

Mountain Safety Research
Box 3978 Terminal Station
Seattle, WA 98124

The Coleman Co. Inc.
Wichita, KS 67201

Optimus-Princess Inc.
12423-T E. Florence Ave.
Santa Fe Springs, CA 90670

Decoys, Calls

P. S. Olt Co.
Box 550
Pekin, IL 61554

Quack Decoy Crop.
4 Mill St.
Cumberland, RI 02864

Archery Equipment
Jennings Compound Bow Inc.
28756 N. Castaic Canyon Rd.
Valencia, CA 91355

Bear Archery
Subsidiary of Kidde Inc.
RR#4 Fred Bear Dr. at Archer Rd.
Gainesville, FL 32601

Canvas, Cotton Chambray, Corduroy, Nylon
Industrial Fabrics Assn. Intl.
350 Endicott Bldg.
St. Paul, MN 55101

Canoes, Kayaks, Boats
Wooden Canoe Heritage Assn. Inc.
Box 5634
Madison, WI 53705

Grumman Boats
12 E. 41st St.
New York, NY 10017

The Blue Hole Canoe Co.
Sunbright, TN 37872

Stone Canoe Co.
Box 207
Stowe, VT 05672

Coleman Marine Products
Wichita, KS 67201

American Canoe Association
Box 248
Lorton, VA 22079

Great Falls Canoe & Kayak Repair
9328 Old Court House Rd.
Vienna, VA 22180

Perception Kayaks
Box 686
Liberty, SC 29657

Hans Klepper Corp.
35 Union Square West
New York, NY 10003

Canoe Magazine
Highland Mill
Camden, ME 04843

Batteries
Union Carbide Corp.
Battery Products Division
Old Ridgebury Rd.
Danbury, CT 06817

Battery Council Intl.
111 Wacker Dr.
Chicago, IL 60601

Snowshoes
Sherpa Outdoor Products
2222 Diversey Parkway
Chicago, IL 60647

Woodstream Corp.
Lititz, PA 17543

Firearms, Ammunition
Sporting Arms and Ammunition Mfg. Inst. Inc.
Box 218
Wallingford, CT 06492

Fishing Tackle
Zebco Division
The Brunswick Corp.
Box 270
Tulsa, OK 74101

Featherweight Products
3456-8 Ocean View Blvd.
Glendale, CA 91208

Shakespeare Company
Drawer S
Columbia, SC 29260

Plas/Steel Products Inc.
Walkerton, IN 46574

Wright and McGill Co.
Denver, CO 80216

Cortland Line Co.
Cortland, NY 13045

DuPont Company
Wilmington, DE 19898

Continental Arms Corp.
697 5th Ave
New York, NY 10022

Tents, Packs, Bags, Down Gear
Marmont Mountain Works Ltd.
827 Bellevue Way NE
Bellevue, WA 98004

Sierra Designs
247 Fourth St.
Oakland, CA 94607

Industrial Fabrics Assn. Int.
350 Endicott Bldg.
St. Paul, MN 55101

Moss Tent Works Inc.
Mt. Battie St.
Camden, ME 04843

Jansport
Paine Field Industrial Park
Bldg. 306
Everett, WA 98204

Wilderness Experience
20675 Nordhoff St.
Chatsworth, CA 91311

Mountain Mend
6595-D Odell Pl.
Boulder, CO 80301

Stephenson (Warmlite)
RFD#4 Box 145
Gilford, NH 03246

Class 5
1480 66th St.
Emeryville, CA 94608

Feather & Down Assn. Inc.
4441 Auburn Blvd. Suite "O"
Sacramento, CA 95841

Down Home
West Fork Rd.
Deadwood, OR 97430

Wildware Ltd.
995 Pieffers Lane
Harrisburg, PA 17109

Shank's Mare Outfitters
46 S. Pershing Ave.
York, PA 17404